D0852747

INTELLECTUAL HISTORY IN AMERICA

Intellectual History
in America

CONTEMPORARY ESSAYS
ON PURITANISM,
THE ENLIGHTENMENT,
AND ROMANTICISM

Volume I

Edited by **CUSHING STROUT**

Cornell University

HARPER & ROW, PUBLISHERS
New York, Evanston, and London

To the memory of Carl L. Becker and Perry Miller,
pioneers of American intellectual history.

INTELLECTUAL HISTORY IN AMERICA: Contemporary Essays on
Puritanism, the Enlightenment, and Romanticism, Volume I

Copyright © 1968 by Cushing Strout

Library of Congress Catalog Card Number: 68–12932

CONTENTS

PREFACE

Intellectual history in this country is as old as 1897 when Moses Coit Tyler of Cornell University wrote, in his introduction to *A History of American Literature: 1607–1765*, "there is but one thing more interesting than the intellectual history of a man and that is the intellectual history of a nation." Courses in intellectual history are now a familiar item in the college catalogue. Yet historians, when pressed, have trouble defining the boundaries of the subject. Does it include the arts or only expository argument? Does it deal at the summit with major thinkers only, or does it also entail the study of the popularization of ideas? Is there a unifying climate of opinion or only a dialectic of controversy? Does it move towards philosophy or social history? Do quasi-rational images and myths count as ideas or only as prejudices?

The actual work of intellectual historians does not warrant clear-cut answers to these alternatives. The historian of intellectual history can be identified only by his use of two strategies. He pays more attention to the social and personal setting of ideas than philosophers or literary critics usually do, and he does more justice to the theoretical aspirations of men than political or social historians ordinarily do. He occupies the terrain which this conventional division of labor creates, putting ideas into contexts and finding ideas in the complex currents of historical change. In practice he makes his contribution by finding a theory where others see only practical policy, by recreating the specific context of debate in which men formulate their ideas, by remarking on subtle or dramatic changes in the outlook of a man or a group, by finding themes in disparate activities of mind, by discovering intellectual styles which link men in movements, by decoding the significance of contradictions and tensions in a mind or a theory, and by seeing in fiction or fantasy an historical pattern of meaning. The selections in this volume illustrate all these modes of studying intellectual history.

Ideas and the men who develop them are, of course, part of the international "republic of letters." Yet there is a legitimate interest in the particular twist that a specific culture has given to the growth of ideas which have no national boundaries. The diversity of life is both the charm and necessity of historical studies. The historian is particularly attracted to those men and movements whose ideas have overflowed particular disciplines, generated controversy outside the academy, and enjoyed (as a physicist might say) a long half-life.

Any anthologist must feel grateful, dizzy, and sad: grateful for the contributions of those who made his volume possible; dizzy from the spectacle of possible materials he might include; sad in the face of the inevitable limitations of space. I have tried to pick material by scholars who have shown how post-war historiography has changed the terrain of the subject. They all contribute to making our sense of the past more sophisticated. Intellectual history before the Civil War can be meaningfully organized around the broad themes of Puritanism, the Enlightenment, and Romanticism as major movements and styles of mind. The essays in this volume show in detail what these terms concretely mean.

No anthology is a substitute for reading books. It can only assist students and teachers in making raids on the library. My own have been gracefully and greatly assisted by the help of Andrea Kisch in the preparation of this text.

CUSHING STROUT

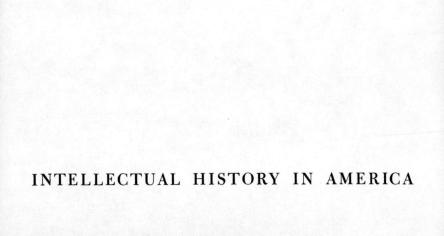

INTELLECTUAL HISTORY IN AMERICA

The Puritans as Revolutionaries

MICHAEL WALZER

The English Puritans who emigrated to New England in the seventeenth century were part of an international movement of Calvinism whose style of mind has left a deep impression on Western civilization. Looking backward, many historians have been tempted to view the Puritans as forerunners of liberalism and capitalism, thereby reading results back into intentions. Congregational church polity has been called democratic; the Puritan doctrine of the calling as a gospel of work has been called capitalistic; and the Puritan emphasis on the individual's saving experience has been called liberal. These themes have been stressed by nineteenth-century Whigs and later by scholars influenced by the economist Marx or the sociologist Max Weber.

In reaction against reading the Puritans out of their context, some scholars have countered by underscoring the traditional Reformation, English, or humanistic elements in the Puritan outlook. If we take Puritan culture as a whole, according to Perry Miller and Thomas H. Johnson in their influential *The Puritans* (1938), "we shall find, let us say, that about ninety per cent of the intellectual life, scientific knowledge, morality, manners and customs, notions and prejudices, was that of all Englishmen." This strategy may miss, however, the peculiar intensity of Puritan zeal. With a modern sensitivity to social psychology, Michael Walzer seeks to focus on the specific meaning and setting of Puritan ideology for the men who needed it. His analysis challenges the image of the Puritans as either traditionalists or liberals.

PURITANISM HAS TWICE BEEN ASSIGNED A UNIQUE AND CREATIVE ROLE in Western history. Neither of these assignments was made by a Marxist historian; it was rather the Whigs and the Weberians who found moder-

Michael Walzer, "Puritanism as a Revolutionary Ideology," *History and Theory*, *3*, no. 1 (1963), pp. 61–88. Copyright © 1963 by Wesleyan University. Reprinted with deletions and renumbered footnotes by permission of Wesleyan University Press.

nity in the mind of the saints. But in a curious fashion, Marxists have been driven to adopt the insights of both these groups of writers, since both have defended and elaborated the historical connection which the Marxists themselves have so persistently sought to establish—that is, the connection of Puritanism with capitalism and liberalism.

Whig historians of the nineteenth centuries saw in Protestantism in general, but more particularly in English Calvinism, the seed-bed of liberal politics. The purely individualistic relationship of the saint to his God, the emphasis upon voluntary association and mutual consent to church government among the saints themselves, the extraordinary reliance upon the printed word, with each man his own interpreter—all this, we have been told, trained and prepared the liberal mind.[1] And then the natural alliance of Puritans and parliamentarians created the liberal society. It is a clear implication of this view, though one not often expressed by Whig writers, that Puritanism *is* liberalism in theological garb, that is, in a primitive and somewhat confused form.[2]

Max Weber credited Puritanism with a rather different character and a different but related contribution to Western development. Writing in a more modern vein and free, up to a point, from Whig prejudices, he suggested that Calvin's ideas—again, especially in England—played a decisive part in the creation of the "spirit of capitalism." His views are so familiar that they need not be described in any detail here. But it should be said that they involve two rather distinct arguments, which will be considered separately below. Weber thought that Puritanism had sponsored a significant rationalization in behavior, especially in work: it had trained men to work in a sustained, systematic fashion, to pay attention to detail, to watch the clock. In this sense, the Calvinist ethic is related to that long-term process which culminates, but does not end, in a rational-legal (bureaucratic) society. Weber argued in addition to this that Puritanism had produced an extraordinary and apparently *irrational* impulse toward acquisition, which is more directly connected with the rise of a capitalist economy. The source of both impulses, toward rationalization and endless gain, lay in the anxiety induced by the theory

---

[1] A classic example of this argument is to be found in A. D. Lindsay, *The Modern Democratic State* (Oxford, 1943), 115–121; also G. P. Gooch, *English Democratic Ideas in the Seventeenth Century* (New York, 1959). The argument appears in a more sophisticated form in the introduction of A. S. P. Woodhouse's edition of the army debates, *Puritanism and Liberty* (London, 1951).

[2] That ideas are merely "clothed" in religious fashion for convenience, out of force of habit, or because other clothing was somehow not available is, of course, a Marxist argument. See Perez Zagorin, *A History of Political Thought in the English Revolution* (London, 1954). It presupposes a very awkward theory of expression according to which content and form have little intrinsic connection.

of predestination—but the two are not the same and it is at least plausible to imagine the first without the second.[3]

A Marxist historian would obviously deny the views of historical causation expressed or implied by both Whigs and Weberians, but he would defend ardently the close connection of Puritanism with the liberal and capitalist worlds. So ardently, indeed, would he do so, that he would probably concede, for the sake of the connection, a kind of "interaction" between economics, politics and religion, and thus open the way for an eclectic amalgamation of the three different points of view. Thus, contemporary Marxist writers tend still to describe Puritanism as the reflection of a rising bourgeoisie, though not necessarily its direct reflection (and this point—suggested, for example, by Tawney's notion of a "magic mirror"—is none too clear). But they then go on to argue that the reflection reacts somehow upon the original subject, reinforcing latent, perhaps underdeveloped class characteristics, meeting psychic needs, and generally accelerating the progressive evolution.[4] This second argument is made in terms with which Whigs and Weberians would hardly disagree —especially since it constitutes a Marxist appropriation of their own insights. Such an eclecticism may incidentally make more sophisticated the history of all who adopt it; but it does not necessarily do so, for it provides no new insights and often involves the suspension of criticism for the sake of coherence. Giving up the hapless debate over whether Puritanism or capitalism came first would be, perhaps, no such loss. However, it would be a great loss indeed if no one called the union itself into question and sought to work out in a new way the historical experience of the saints.

The resemblance between the Calvinist covenant and the capitalist contract—often invoked and elaborated by Marxist writers—will serve to suggest the kind of questions which need to be raised. The voluntarism of both covenant and contract clearly distinguish them from earlier traditionalistic relationships; but they are also distinguished from one another by two facts which the Marxists have surely underrated. First, they are based upon very different, indeed, precisely opposite, views of human nature. The contract assumes trust, a mutual recognition of economic rationality and even of good will. The covenant, as will be argued

---

[3] Max Weber, *The Protestant Ethic and the Spirit of Capitalism,* trans. Talcott Parsons (New York, 1958), esp. 26–27, 53. When Herbert Marcuse analyzes Soviet Marxism, he discovers a "protestant ethic"—but this is clearly a rationalist ethic and not an acquisitive one; *Soviet Marxism: A Critical Analysis* (New York, 1961), 217, 222–23.

[4] This view is most clearly argued by Christopher Hill, *Puritanism and Revolution* (London, 1958), esp. chapters 1 and 7; compare this with Hill's earlier pamphlet, *The English Revolution: 1640* (London, 1940).

below, institutionalizes suspicion and mutual surveillance. If it is true that sober-minded capitalists preferred to do business with members of the Puritan brotherhood, this may well have been because they knew that the brethren were being watched. Secondly, the two forms of association serve very different human purposes. Puritan godliness and capitalist gain have, perhaps, something to do with one another, though they have little enough in common. The suggestion that they are *really the same thing*, or one the mere reflex, in thought or in action, of the other, has long distorted our understanding of the saints and their English enterprise. In order to grasp the precise nature of this distortion it is necessary not only to point out the basic incompatibility of Puritanism with both liberalism and capitalism, but also to discuss the various methods by which their similarity has been discovered and to attack the attitude toward historical experience which these methods imply.

A number of recent writers have gone so far as to describe the Puritan saints as traditionalists in both politics and economics, a description which has the virtue of standing the older theorists neatly on their heads, but which also makes the revolution incomprehensible.[5] This is not the view which will be argued here; it describes at best only the cautious conformity of Puritan preachers in dealing with such conventional topics as monarchy, rebellion, usury and charity. On the other hand, it is not difficult to detect the sharply anti-traditionalist ideology of these same men working itself out in their attacks upon hierarchy, their new views of ecclesiastical organization, their treatises on family government, their almost Manichean warfare against Satan and his worldly allies, their nervous lust for systematic repression and control. The last two of these are obviously not compatible with liberal thinking (or with entrepreneurial activity). They point directly to the revolution, when the struggle against Anti-Christ would be acted out and, for a brief moment, the repressive Holy Commonwealth established. In the years before the actual revolution, the nature of Puritanism was best revealed in the endless discussions of church government and in the practices of such Puritan congregations as already existed. These practices can by no means be called liberal, even though they were founded upon consent. Precisely because of this foundation, however, they cannot be called traditionalist either. The experience of the saints suggests something very different.

. . .

[5] See Perry Miller, *Orthodoxy in Massachusetts, 1630–1650* (Boston, 1959), chapter I; Charles H. and Katherine George, *The Protestant Mind of the English Reformation, 1570–1640* (Princeton, 1961), chapter 6; Richard Schlatter, *Richard Baxter and Puritan Politics* (New Brunswick, 1957), introduction.

It was, perhaps, not without a certain malice that the early Puritans were called "disciplinarians." But malice has its insights and this one is worth pursuing. The association of the brethren was voluntary indeed, but it gave rise to a collectivist discipline marked above all by a tense mutual "watchfulness." Puritan individualism never led to a respect for privacy. Tender conscience had its rights, but it was protected only against the interference of worldlings and not against "brotherly admonition." And the admonitions of the brethren were anxious, insistent, continuous. They felt themselves to be living in an age of chaos and crime and sought to train conscience to be permanently on guard against sin. The extent to which they would have carried the moral discipline can be seen in the following list of offenses which merited excommunication in one seventeenth-century congregation:[6]

—for unfaithfulness in his master's service.
—for admitting cardplaying in his house . . .
—for sloth in business.
—for being overtaken in beer.
—for borrowing a pillion and not returning it.
—for jumping for wagers . . .
—for dancing and other vanities.

Had the saints been successful in establishing their Holy Commonwealth, the enforcement of this discipline would have constituted the Puritan terror. In the congregation there was already a kind of local terrorism, maintained by the godly elders as the national discipline would have been by an elite of the saints. Thus, Richard Baxter reported that in his Kidderminster parish the enforcement of the new moral order was made possible "by the zeal and diligence of the godly people of the place who thirsted after the salvation of their neighbours and were in private my assistants."[7]

It was for this moral discipline that the saints fought most persistently, and it was over this issue that Baxter and his colleagues left the Established Church in 1662. Their failure to win from Charles II's bishops the congregational rights of admonition and excommunication finally forced them—as the political Restoration had not done—to acknowledge the failure of their revolutionary effort to turn "all England into a land of the saints." By that time, however, the effort had had a certain prosaic success—not at all of the sort which Puritan preachers once imagined.

---

[6] Quoted in Horton Davies, *The Worship of the English Puritans* (Westminster, 1948), 235.
[7] Richard Baxter, *Reliquiae Baxterianae,* ed. M. Sylvester (London, 1696), 87.

The crucial feature of the Puritan discipline was its tendency to transform repression into self-control: worldlings might be forced to be godly, but saints voluntarily gave themselves to godliness. Liberalism also required such voluntary subjection and self-control but, in sharp contrast to Puritanism, its political and social theory were marked by an extraordinary confidence in the possibility of both a firm sense of human reasonableness and of the ease with which order might be attained. Liberal confidence made repression and the endless struggle against sin unnecessary; it also tended to make self-control invisible, to forget its painful history and naively assume its existence. The result was that liberalism did not create the self-control it required. The Lockeian state was not a disciplinary institution, as was the Calvinist Holy Commonwealth, but rather rested on the assumed political virtue—the "natural political virtue"[8]—of its citizens. It is one of the central arguments of this essay that Puritan repression has its place in the practical history, so to speak, of that strange assumption.

It is not possible, of course, to judge the effectiveness of this repression or the extent of the social need for it. For the moment it can only be said that Puritans knew about human sinfulness and that Locke did not need to know. This probably reflects not only different temperaments, but also different experiences. The very existence and spread of Puritanism in the years before the Revolution surely argue the presence in English society of an acute fear of disorder and "wickedness." The anxious tone of Tudor legislation—which Puritan leaders like William Perkins often vigorously seconded—is itself a parallel argument. On the other hand, the triumph of Lockeian ideas suggests the overcoming of that anxiety and fear, the appearance of men for whom sin is no longer a problem. In a sense, it might be said that liberalism is dependent upon the existence of "saints"—that is, of men whose good behavior can be relied upon. At the same time, the secular and genteel character of liberalism is determined by the fact that these are men whose goodness (sociability, self-discipline, moral decency, or mere respectability) is self-assured and

---

[8] The term "natural political virtue" is that of Locke's latest editor; see Peter Laslett's edition of the *Two Treatises* (Cambridge, 1960), 108 f. The extraordinary difficulty with which self-control is learned is best described—that is, described with some sensitivity to human pain—by Nietzsche, in *The Genealogy of Morals*. He is writing of a very early period in human history, but his insights have some relevance to the sixteenth and seventeenth centuries. How free Locke was from any sense of the dangers of *uncontrolled* men is evident in his "Letter on Toleration." Compare his description there of voluntary association in religious matters with Jean Bodin's demand a century earlier for a strict moral discipline enforced by elders, *The Six Books of the Republic,* trans. M. J. Tooley (Oxford, n.d.), 184–85. On this point, as on many others, Bodin is very close to the Calvinists.

relaxed, entirely free from the nervousness and fanaticism of Calvinist godliness.

This, then, is the relationship of Puritanism to the liberal world: it is perhaps one of historical preparation, but not at all of theoretical contribution. Indeed, there was much to be forgotten and much to be surrendered before the saint could become a liberal bourgeois. During the great creative period of English Puritanism, the faith of the saints and the tolerant reasonableness of the liberals had very little in common.

Roughly the same things can be said about the putative connection of Calvinism and capitalism. The moral discipline of the saints can be interpreted as the historical conditioning of the capitalist man; but the discipline was not itself capitalist. It can be argued that the faith of the brethren, with its emphasis upon methodical endeavor and self-control, was an admirable preparation for systematic work in shops, offices and factories. It trained men for the minute-to-minute attentiveness required in a modern economic system; it taught them to forego their afternoon naps—as they had but recently foregone their saints' day holidays—and to devote spare hours to bookkeeping and moral introspection. It somehow made the deprivation and repression inevitable in sustained labor bearable and even desirable for the saints. And by teaching self-control, it provided the basis for impersonal, contractual relationships among men, allowing workmanlike cooperation but not involving any exchange of affection or any of the risks of intimacy. All this, Calvinism did or helped to do. Whether it did so in a creative fashion or as the ideological reflection of new economic processes is not immediately relevant. The saints learned, as Weber has suggested, a kind of rational and worldly asceticism, and this was probably something more than the economic routine required. They sought in work itself what mere work can never give: a sense of vocation and discipline which would free them from sinfulness and the fear of disorder.[9]

But Weber has said more than this; he has argued that systematic acquisition as well as asceticism has a Calvinist origin. The psychological tension induced by the theory of predestination, working itself out in worldly activity, presumably drove men to seek success as a sign of salvation. The sheer willfulness of an inscrutable God produced in its turn, if Weber is correct, the willfulness of an anxious man, and set off the entrepreneurial pursuit of better business techniques and more and more profit. At this point his argument breaks down. If there is in fact a peculiar and irrational quality to the capitalists' lust for gain, its

---

[9] Weber's most recent critic, Kurt Samuelsson, hardly discusses the idea of rationalization which is so central to his argument; *Religion and Economic Action,* trans. E. G. French (Stockholm, 1961).

sources must be sought elsewhere than among the saints. For Puritanism was hardly an ideology which encouraged continuous or unrestrained accumulation. Instead, the saints tended to be narrow and conservative in their economic views, urging men to seek no more wealth than they needed for a modest life, or, alternatively, to use up their surplus in charitable giving. The anxiety of the Puritans led to a fearful demand for economic restriction (and political control) rather than to entrepreneurial activity as Weber has described it. Unremitting and relatively unremunerative work was the greatest help toward saintliness and virtue.[10]

The ideas of Puritan writers are here very close to those of such proto-Jacobins as Mably and Morelli in eighteenth-century France, who also watched the development of capitalist enterprise with unfriendly eyes, dreaming of a Spartan republic where bankers and great merchants would be unwelcome.[11] The collective discipline of the Puritans—their Christian Sparta—was equally incompatible with purely acquisitive activity. Virtue would almost certainly require economic regulation. This would be very different from the regulation of medieval corporatism, and perhaps it was the first sense of that difference which received the name *freedom*. It was accompanied by a keen economic realism: thus the Calvinist acknowledgement of the lawfulness of usury. But Calvinist realism was in the service of effective control and not of free activity or self-expression. Who can doubt that, had the Holy Commonwealth ever been firmly established, godly self-discipline and mutual surveillance would have been far more repressive than the corporate system? Once again, in the absence of a Puritan state the discipline was enforced through the congregation. The minutes of a seventeenth-century consistory provide a routine example: "The church was satisfied with Mrs. Carlton," they read, "as to the weight of her butter." Did Mrs. Carlton tremble, awaiting that verdict? Surely if the brethren were unwilling to grant liberty to the local butter-seller, they would hardly have granted it to the new capitalist. The ministerial literature, at least, is full of denunciations of enclosers, usurers, monopolists, and projectors—and oc-

---

[10] For a detailed criticism of Weber on these points, see George, *op. cit.*, chapters 2 and 3; also Samuelsson, *op. cit.*, esp. 27 ff. Samuelsson's first chapter discusses the men who have accepted or been significantly influenced by this aspect of Weber's argument; these are the men who are called "Weberians" in this essay. It should be said that Weber himself—if not always his followers—was very conscious of the savage repression which Calvinism sponsored; the question of why bourgeois men should accept such discipline is central to his book (*op. cit.*, 37). Nevertheless, the particular forms of repression and control described above are not considered in *The Protestant Ethic*.

[11] The restrictionist attitudes of Mably and Morelli are discussed in J. L. Talmon, *The Origins of Totalitarian Democracy*, (New York, 1960), 58 ff.

casionally even of wily merchants. Puritan casuistry, perhaps, left such men sufficient room in which to range, but it hardly offered them what Weber considers so essential—a good conscience. Only a sustained endeavor in hypocrisy, so crude as to astonish even the Marxist epigone, could have earned them that. The final judgment of the saints with regard to the pursuit of money is that of Bunyan's pilgrim, angry and ill-at-ease in the town of Vanity, disdainful of such companions as Mr. Money-love and Mr. Save-all.

The converse is equally true: to the triumphant bourgeois sainthood, with all its attendant enthusiasm and asceticism, would appear atavistic. And this is perhaps the clearest argument of all against the casual acceptance of the Whig or Weberian views of Puritanism. It suggests forcefully that the two views (and the Marxist also, for surprisingly similar reasons) are founded upon anachronism. Even if it is correct to argue that Calvinist faith and discipline played a part in that transformation of character which created the bourgeois—and too little is known about the historical development of character to say this without qualification—the anachronism remains. The historical present is hopelessly distorted unless the tension and repression so essential to the life of the saint are described and accounted for. Even more important, the effort to establish a holy commonwealth (to universalize the tension and repression) is rendered inexplicable once liberalism and capitalism are, so to speak, read into the Puritan experience. For then Puritanism is turned into a grand paradox: its radical voluntarism culminates in a rigid discipline; its saints watch their neighbors with brotherly love and suspicion; its ethic teaches sustained and systematic work but warns men against the lust for acquisition and gain. In fact, of course, these seeming contrasts are not paradoxical. The saints experienced a unity, common enough among men, of willfulness and repression, of fanatical *self-control*. Latter-day historians do the Puritans little honor when they search among the elements of the Puritan faith for something more liberal in its political implications or more economically rational. Indeed, the methods of that search invite in their turn the most searching criticism.

. . .

The study of the Puritans is best begun with the idea of discipline, and all the tension and strain that underlies it, both in their writing and in what can be known of their experience. It is strange that theorists have had so little to say on this topic, especially since the rebellion against Puritan repression, or rather against its ugly remnants—devoid, as Weber's capitalism is, of theological reason—is still a part of our own experience. The persecution of witches, of course, was not a vital aspect of Puritan endeavor, but the active, fearful struggle against wickedness was. And the saints imagined wickedness as a creative and omnipresent demonic force, that is, as a continuous threat. Like Hobbes, they saw disorder and war as the natural state of fallen men, out of which they had been drawn by God's command and by the painful efforts of their own regenerate wills. But they lived always on the very brink of chaos, maintaining their position only through a constant vigilance and, indeed, a constant warfare against their own natural inclinations and against the devil and his worldlings.

The goal of this warfare was repression and its apparent cause was an extraordinary anxiety. It is by no means necessary to argue that these two constitute the "essence" of Puritanism, only that their full significance has not been realized. In Calvin's own work anxiety is presented as central to the experience of fallen man: this is anxiety of a special sort; it is not the fear of death and damnation, but rather the fear of sudden and violent death. Hobbes would recognize it as the dominant passion of man in his natural state. Thus Calvin:[12]

Now, whithersoever you turn, all the objects around you are not only unworthy of your confidence, but almost openly menace you, and seem to threaten immediate death. Embark in a ship; there is but a single step between you and death. Mount a horse; the slipping of one foot endangers your life. Walk through the streets of a city; you are liable to as many dangers as there are tiles on the roofs. If there be a sharp weapon in your hand, or that of your friend, the mischief is manifest. All the ferocious animals you see are armed for your destruction. If you endeavor to shut yourself in a garden surrounded with a good fence, and exhibiting nothing but what is delightful, even there sometimes lurks a serpent. Your house, perpetually liable to fire, menaces you by day with poverty, and by night with falling on your head. Your land, exposed to hail, frost, drought and various tempests, threatens you with sterility, and with its attendant, famine. I omit poison, treachery, robbery and open violence, which partly beset us at home and partly pursue us abroad. . . . You will say that these things happen seldom, or certainly not always, nor to every man, [and] never all at once. I grant it; but we are admonished by the examples of others, that it is possible for them to happen to us. . . .

Among the saints such terrible fearfulness was overcome, and that was the great benefit of sainthood: it did not so much promise future ecstasy as present "tranquillity." "When the light of Divine Providence," wrote Calvin, "has once shined on a pious man, he is relieved and delivered not

[12] *Institutes of the Christian Religion* (Allen translation), Book, I, chapter XVII, x.

only from the extreme anxiety and dread with which he was previously oppressed, but also from all care."[13] But relief was not rest in the Calvinist world; it was rather that security of mind which might well manifest itself as self-righteousness—or as fanaticism.

In Puritan literature this same fearfulness is made specific in social terms. Once again, it is a fear which Hobbes would understand: the fear of disorder in society. It is apparent in the nervous hostility with which Puritan writers regarded carousal, vagabondage, idleness, all forms of individualistic extravagance (especially in clothing), country dances and urban crowds, the theater with its gay (undisciplined) audiences, gossip, witty talk, love-play, dawdling in taverns—the list could be extended.[14] The shrewdest among their contemporaries sensed that this pervasive hostility was a key to Puritanism—though they could hardly help but regard it as hypocritical. Ben Jonson's Zeal-of-the-land Busy is a caricature based, like all good caricatures, on a kernel of truth. Zeal-of-the-land is, for all his comical hypocrisy, insistently and anxiously concerned about the world he lives in—and the aim of his concern is supervision and repression.[15]

At times, Puritan preachers sounded very much like Hobbes: ". . . take sovereignty from the face of the earth," proclaimed Robert Bolton, "and you turn it into a cockpit. Men would become cut-throats and cannibals. . . . Murder, adulteries, incests, rapes, robberies, perjuries, witchcrafts, blasphemies, all kinds of villainies, outrages and savage cruelty would overflow all countries."[16] But secular sovereignty was not their usual appeal. They looked rather to congregational discipline, as has been argued above. Thus Thomas Cartwright promised that the new discipline would restrain stealing, adultery and murder. Even more, it would "correct" sins "which the magistrate doth not commonly punish"— he listed lying, jesting, choleric speeches.[17] It need hardly be said that John Locke, a century later, was not terribly worried about such sins. Walsingham's spies reported in the 1580's and '90's that Puritan agitators were promising "that if discipline were planted, there should be no more vagabonds nor beggars." John Penry foresaw the "amendment"

[13] Ibid., xi.

[14] Alfred Harbage has pointed out that Puritans objected more to the audience at the theaters than to the plays: see his Shakespeare's Audience (New York, 1951).

[15] Jonson, Bartholomew Fair; see also his characterizations of two Puritans in The Alchemist.

[16] Bolton, Two Sermons (London, 1635), I, 10. The passage is a curious one since it opens with a paraphrase of Hooker, Ecclesiastical Polity, I, iii, 2; but Hooker says nothing about the effects of disobedience among men, which is the Puritan writer's chief concern.

[17] John Whitgift, Works, I, 21.

of idleness and hence, he thought, of poverty.[18] Now none of these concerns was unusual in Tudor or early Stuart England, but the intensity and extent of Puritan worry and the novelty of the proposed solution have no parallel among statesmen or traditional moralists. These latter groups also watched with apprehension the growth of London, the increasing geographic and social mobility, and the new forms of individualistic experimentation. It must be said, however, that the tone of their writings rarely reached a pitch of anxiety and fearfulness comparable to, for example, the diary of the Puritan minister Richard Rogers, endlessly worried about his own "unsettledness." Nostalgia was a more common theme, satire and mockery a more frequent defense among moralists like Thomas Dekker.[19] And the world they would have substituted for Renaissance England was an already romanticized version of medieval England. Not so the Puritans. Their discipline would have established dramatically new forms of association: the anxiety of the minister Rogers led him to join with his brethren in a solemn covenant—and these brethren were neither his immediate neighbors nor his kinfolk.[20]

What Rogers sought from his covenant was a bolstering of his faith, a steeling of his character. "The sixth of this month [December, 1587] we fasted betwixt ourselves," he reported in his diary, ". . . to the stirring up of ourselves to greater godliness." The need for this "stirring up" is so pervasive among the Puritans that one might well imagine that what they feared so greatly was rather in themselves than in the society about them. In fact, what they feared was the image in themselves of the "unsettledness" of their world. Puritan fearfulness is best explained in terms of the actual experiences of exile, alienation, and social mobility about which the saints so often and insistently wrote.[21] Discipline and repression are responses to these experiences, responses which do not aim at a return to some former security, but rather at a vigorous control and a narrowing of energies—a bold effort to shape a personality amidst "chaos." Thus might be explained the extraordinarily regimented life recorded in Margaret Hoby's diary. Mrs. Hoby was a merchant's daughter, married to a gentleman (the son of the Elizabethan ambassador Sir

[18] The report to Walsingham is quoted in Hill, *Puritanism and Revolution,* 234. John Penry, *An Humble Motion with Submission* (Edinburgh, 1590), 72.

[19] The views of the moralists are described in L. C. Knights, *Drama and Society in the Age of Jonson* (London, 1937).

[20] *Two Elizabethan Diaries,* ed. M. Knappen (Chicago, 1933), 69.

[21] They wrote about more than these themes, of course, and even here described more than their own experience, for the outsider is an archetypal figure realized with especial force in Christian thought. The Puritans still lived within a cultural tradition which shaped their expression as it undoubtedly still shaped their experience. . . .

Thomas Hoby, translator of Castiglione) and carried off to a country estate in Yorkshire where all her neighbors were Catholic and, in her eyes, rowdy and sinful men. There she spent her time in earnest conversations with her minister, reading and listening to sermons and laboriously copying them out in her notebook, adhering to a strict routine of public and private prayer, assiduous in her daily self-recrimination:[22]

> I talked of some things not so as I ought when I had considered of them, but I find what is in a man if the Lord's spirit do never so little hide itself . . . but this is my comfort, that my heart is settled to be more watchful hereafter. . . .

How many men have settled since for the same "comfort"!

Undoubtedly, Margaret Hoby's behavior might be differently explained, but not so as to account so well for the similar behavior of her brethren. These people felt themselves exceptionally open to the dangers about them and this must have been, in part, because they were cut off, as were the men who succumbed to chaos—beggars and vagabonds—from the old forms of order and routine. It is this sense of being cut off, alien, that is expressed in the endless descriptions of the saint as a stranger and pilgrim which are so important in Puritan writing.[23] Pilgrimage is, perhaps, one of the major themes in all Christian literature, but it achieves among the Puritans a unique power, a forcefulness and intensity in its popular expression which culminates finally in Bunyan's classic. Over and over again, with the detail which only experience or, perhaps, a continually engaged imagination can give, Puritans describe life as a journey (or, in the image which Hobbes later made famous, as a race) through alien country. And yet, at the same time, they write of the vagabond with venomous hatred: he is a dangerous man because he has not disciplined and prepared himself for his journey. "Wandering beggars and rogues," wrote William Perkins, "that pass from place to place, being under no certain magistracy or ministry, nor joining themselves to any set society in church or commonwealth, are plagues and banes of both, and are to be taken as main enemies of [the] ordinance of God. . . ."[24] The bitterness of this passage suggests the self-hatred of the Puritan pilgrim, pitying and worrying about his own "unsettledness." When the famous preacher Richard Greenham told a Puritan audience "Paradise is our native country," some of his listeners surely

[22] Diary of Lady Margaret Hoby, 1599–1605, ed. D. M. Meads (London, 1930), 97.
[23] See the comments of William Haller on Puritan wayfaring: The Rise of Puritanism (New York, 1957), 147 ff.
[24] William Perkins, Works (London, 1616), III, 539; the passage is quoted in Hill, op. cit., 228.

must have winced to think: *not England.* "We dwell here as in Meshech and as in the tents of Kedar, and therefore we be glad to be at home." It was painful, but inevitable, that the saints should live in tents. Perkins himself wrote in the same vein, for all his hatred of the wanderer: "Alas, poor souls, we are no better than passengers in this world, our way it is in the middle of the sea."[25] For many Puritans, if not for Perkins himself, who grew old in Cambridge, these words must have had a meaning both literal and poignant. Since the days of Mary, exile had been a common experience for the saints. And a generation after Perkins wrote, the "middle of the sea" would become a path for tens of thousands.

The fanatical self-righteousness of that first Puritan John Knox, a Scottish peasant's son, set loose in Europe by war and revolution, is surely in some sense a function of his exile: righteousness was a consolation and a way of organizing the self for survival. The "unsettledness" of Richard Rogers was due in part to his devious struggles with the corporate church and its bishops; but Rogers, who remembered his Essex birthplace as a "dunghill," was ever an outsider, and Puritanism his way of stirring up his heart. When William Whitgift, the future archbishop, cruelly taunted the Puritan leader Thomas Cartwright for "eating at other men's tables," he was perhaps suggesting an important source of Cartwright's vision of congregational unity and holiness. Margaret Hoby's life would have been different indeed had she been raised in a traditional country family: there would, for example, have been dancing at her wedding, and her life thereafter would hardly have allowed for time-consuming religious exercises. Deprived of such a life, because of her social background (and the ideas which were part of it) or, perhaps, because of basic changes in rural life, she willfully sought new comforts.[26] Country gentlemen like John Winthrop and Oliver Cromwell, educated at Cambridge, knowledgeable in London, suddenly turned upon the traditional routine of English life as if it were actually vicious. Half in, half out of that routine, they anxiously sought a new certainty. "Oh, I lived in and loved darkness and hated light; I was a chief, the chief of sinners," wrote Cromwell of his seemingly ordinary and conventional life before conversion. But now, he went on, "my soul is with the congregation of the first born, my body rests in hope;

[25] Greenham, *Works* (London, 1605), 645; Perkins, *op. cit.,* I, 398.
[26] *Two Elizabethan Diaries,* 17; A. F. Scott-Pearson, *Thomas Cartwright and Elizabethan Puritanism* (Cambridge, 1925), 66; *Diary of Margaret Hoby,* 32—at their wedding, the Hoby's sought "only to please the beholders with a sermon and a dinner."

and if here I may honor my God either by doing or by suffering, I shall be most glad."[27]

All this suggests once again the view of Puritanism as a response of particular men to particular experiences of confusion, change, alienation and exile. Now Calvinism obviously made men extremely sensitive to disorder in all its forms. It is more important, however, that it gave meaning to the experience of disorder and provided a way out, a return to certainty. It was an active response, and not a mere reflection of social confusion, for indeed other men responded differently. There is no rigid pattern in these responses. It seems probable that members of a rising middle class most sharply experienced that alienation from old England which drove men to the exercises of sainthood. On the other hand, there were both gentlemen and citizens who certainly enjoyed the new freedoms of mobility, extravagance, individuality and wit, and eagerly sought entrance to the Renaissance court, where freedom was cultivated. And from among these men undoubtedly came many future capitalists. It would not be easy to explain in particular cases why the court held such attractions for some men, while it was vicious and iniquitous in the eyes of others. No more is it readily comprehensible why some of the newcomers to the burgeoning city of London merged into the mob or explored the exciting underworld, while others hated the wickedness of the city and sought out virtuous brethren in the radical conventicles. What is important for the present is that Puritanism was a response to an experience which many men had; it provided one way of understanding the experience and of coping with it.

Coping with it meant being reborn as a new man, self-confident and free of worry, capable of vigorous, willful activity. The saints sometimes took new names to signify their rebirth. If alienation had made them anxious, depressed, unable to work, given to fantasies of demons, morbid introspection or fearful daydreams such as Calvin had suggested were common among fallen men, then sainthood was indeed a transformation.[28] Cromwell's pledge to honor his God "by doing" was no idle boast: he

[27] *Cromwell's Letters and Speeches,* ed. Carlyle (London, 1893), I, 79–80. On Winthrop see E. S. Morgan, *The Puritan Dilemma: The Story of John Winthrop* (Boston, 1958).

[28] Indeed, Calvin thought that commercial competition, with its attendent anxiety, was an aspect of the life of *fallen* man; he pictured him nervously murmuring to himself: "I must use such a mean, I must practise such a feat. I must look into such a business, or otherwise I shall be behindhand in all things. I shall but pine away, I shall not get half my living, if I proceed not in this manner. . . ." *Sermons upon the Fifth Book of Moses* (London, 1583), 821. Presumably the saint would be free from such anxiety.

was obviously capable of just that. Perhaps this transformation gave businessmen the confidence necessary for innovation or freed them from the necessity of feeling guilty about routine connivance, usury, extortion. Thus argue Marxists and Weberians alike. But innovation was more likely due to the recklessness of the speculator than to the self-confidence of the saint; indeed, the saints hated the "projectors" who lived in and about the court, currying favor and waiting for opportunity. The congregational discipline, as has been seen, would have established controls hardly compatible with businesslike hard dealing. Cromwell's "doing" was obviously of a different order, and Cromwell was a representative man. His life suggests that the Puritan experience produced first of all a political activist.

The Puritan new man was active not so that success might reinforce his self-esteem, but in order to transform a world in which he saw his own ever-present wickedness writ large.[29] In a sense, his was a struggle to free himself from temptation by removing all alternatives to godliness, by organizing his own life as a continuous discipline and society as a regiment. His activity was political in that it was always concerned with government—though not only or, perhaps, not most importantly, at the level of the state. Puritans often imagined the congregation as a "little commonwealth," replacing the organic imagery of Anglicans and Catholics with expressions deliberately drawn from the world of coercion and sovereignty. Thus they made manifest their own pervasive concern with *control* rather than with harmony or love.[30] Their treatment of the family was similar: they saw it as a field for the exercise of discipline by a godly father usually described as a "governor." Puritan interest in the family parallels that of Jean Bodin (though, in contrast to Robert Filmer, also a Bodinian, the saints had little to say about paternal affection and benevolence) and probably has the same source. The insistence upon the absolute sovereignty of the father and upon the family as an institution for repressing and disciplining naturally wicked, licentious and rebellious children derives in both cases from an extraordinary fear of disorder and anarchy. Thus two Puritan preachers in a famous treatise on "family government":

[29] Most of the calls for activity in Puritan sermons are put in terms of the struggle against social disorder; activity is rarely described as a way of overcoming the fear of damnation. The clear emphasis of the preachers is on the social effects of hard work, and not, as Weber thought, on success as a spiritual sign. See, for example, the discussion of work in Robert Cleaver and John Dod, *A Godly Form of Household Government* (London, 1621), Sig. P 6 and 7.

[30] See Walter Travers, *A Full and Plain Declaration of Ecclesiastical Discipline out of the Word of God* (n. p., 1574).

The young child which lieth in the cradle [is] both wayward and full of affections: and though his body be but small, yet he hath a great heart, and is altogether inclined to evil. . . . If this sparkle be suffered to increase, it will rage over and burn down the whole house. For we are changed and become good, not by birth, but by education. . . . Therefore parents must be wary and circumspect, that they never smile or laugh at any words or deeds of their children done lewdly . . . naughtily, wantonly . . . they must correct and sharply reprove their children for saying or doing ill. . . .[31]

The father was continually active, warily watching his children; the elders of the congregation were ever alert and vigilant, seeking out the devious paths of sin; so also the godly magistrate. "In you it is now to cleanse, to free your country of villainy," a Puritan minister told the judges of Norwich, ". . . consider your power to reform . . . if you be faithful, and God's power to revenge if you be faithless."[32] In Puritan writings, political activity was described as a form of work: it required systematic application, attention to detail, sustained interest and labor. Much that the godly magistrates undertook might be called, in Marxist terms, progressive; some of their activity, however, would clearly impede free economic activity. But description in these terms is valuable only if one seeks to understand those aspects of Puritan activity which, through a subsequent process of selection, became permanent features of the modern world. In the seventeenth century, Puritan politics obviously had an interest rather different from that suggested by the term "progress." Its immediate purpose was to regain control of a changing world; hence the great concern with method, discipline, and order, and the frequent uneasiness with novelty. When the saints spoke of reform, they meant first of all an overcoming of social instability and all its moral and intellectual concommitants. Godly magistracy was a bold effort to seize control of society, much as sainthood had been an effort to control and organize the self. And the first of these followed from the second: in this way did Puritanism produce revolutionaries. In much the same way, it may be suggested, did the Jacobin man of virtue become an *active citizen,* and the hardened and "steeled" Bolshevik first a *professional* revolutionary and then, in Lenin's words, a "leader," "manager," and "controller."[33]

These revolutionary men do not simply attack and transform the old order as in the Marxist story. The old order is only a part, and often not the most important part, of their experience. They live much of

[31] Cleaver and Dod, *op. cit.,* Sig. S 8; Bodin, *op. cit.,* 9–13.

[32] Thomas Reed, *Moses Old Square for Judges* (London, 1632), 98–99.

[33] Lenin, *The Immediate Tasks of the Soviet Government* (1918) in *Selected Works* (New York, 1935–1937), VII, 332–33.

their lives amidst the breakdown of that order, or in hiding or exile from it. And much of their rebellion is directed against the very "unsettledness" that they know best. The analogy with the Bolsheviks is worth pursuing. Lenin's diatribes against "slovenliness . . . carelessness, untidiness, unpunctuality, nervous haste, the inclination to substitute discussion for action, talk for work, the inclination to undertake everything under the sun without finishing anything" were intended first of all as attacks upon his fellow exiles—whatever their value as descriptions of the "primitive" Russia he hated so much.[34] The first triumph of Bolshevism, as of Puritanism, was over the impulse toward "disorganization" in its own midst: here, so to speak, was Satan at work where he is ever most active—in the ranks of the godly. And it must be said that this triumph was also over the first impulses toward freedom. Thus the Puritans vigorously attacked Renaissance experimentation in dress and in all the arts of self-decoration and hated the free-wheeling vagabonds who "crowd into cities [and] boroughs . . . roll up and down from one lodging to another," never organizing themselves into families and congregations.[35] Similarly, the Jacobin leader Robespierre attacked the economic egotism of the new bourgeoisie and spitefully connected the radical free thought of the Enlightenment with anti-revolutionary conspiracy. Atheism, he declared, is aristocratic.[36] And again Lenin, preaching with all the energy of a secular Calvinist against free love: "Dissoluteness in sexual life is bourgeois, [it] is a phenomenon of decay. The proletariat is a rising class. . . . It needs clarity, clarity and again clarity. And so, I repeat, no weakening, no waste, no destruction of forces."[37]

In fact, Lenin's morality had little to do with the proletariat, and the "dissoluteness" he attacked had little to do with the bourgeoisie. He might as well have talked of saints and worldlings as the Puritans did. The contrast he was getting at was between those men who had succumbed to (or taken advantage of!) the disorder of their time—specu-

[34] *How To Organize Competition* (1917, reprinted Moscow, 1951), 63; also see *Letters,* Trans. and ed. by Elizabeth Hill and Doris Mudie (New York, 1937), 161.

[35] Henry Crosse, *Virtue's Commonwealth* (London, 1603), Sig. L₄ *vers*; Perkins, *Works,* III, 191.

[36] Quoted in A. Aulard, *Christianity and the French Revolution* (Boston, 1927), 113.

[37] Quoted in Klara Zetkin, "Reminiscences of Lenin," in *The Family in the U.S.S.R.,* ed. Rudolf Schlesinger (London, 1949), 78. It should be said that in all the revolutions discussed above, there were men who did not follow the Puritan saints or the vanguard Bolsheviks in their attacks upon human freedom. These men, radical sectarians, secularists, anarchists, libertarians of many sorts, were the products of the same society and the same experience which produced the others. They rarely made good revolutionaries, however, precisely because they never felt the intense need to yield to an organization and a discipline.

lators in philosophy, vagabonds in their sexual life, economic Don Juans —and those men who had somehow pulled themselves out of "unsettledness," organized their lives and regained control. The first group were the damned and the second the saved. The difference between them was not social but ideological.

Puritans, Jacobins and Bolsheviks did tend to come from the same social strata—that is, from the educated middle classes, preachers, lawyers, journalists, teachers, professional men of all sorts. But this is not because such men are representatives of larger social groups whose interests they defend. It has already been shown that the connection between Puritan theory and bourgeois interests is at best a difficult one, which is in no sense implicit in the theory, but is rather worked out later in a long process of corruption, selection and forgetting. Men like the godly ministers speak first of all for themselves: they record most sensitively the experience of "unsettledness" and respond to it most vigorously. For reasons which require further investigation, such men seem less integrated into their society—even in the most stable periods—and more available, as it were, for alienation than are farmers or businessmen. This is not, of course, to reduce their moral discipline (or their radical politics) to the psychological therapy of alienated intellectuals. The alienation which John Knox or Richard Rogers experienced, with all its attendant fearfulness and enthusiasm, sometimes disfiguring and sometimes ennobling, was only a heightened form of the feelings of other men—in a sense, of all men, for ultimately the sociological range of the Puritan response was very wide.

But the historian must also record that "unsettledness" was not a permanent condition and that sainthood was only a temporary role. For men always seek and find not some tense and demanding discipline, but some new routine. The saints failed in their effort to establish a holy commonwealth and, in one way or another, their more recent counterparts have also failed. What this suggests is not that the holy commonwealth was an impractical dream, the program of muddled, unrealistic men. In fact, Puritan ministers and elders (and fathers!) had considerable political experience and the holy commonwealth was in a sense achieved, at least among those men who most needed holiness. Nor is it correct to argue from the failure of the saints that Puritanism in its revolutionary form represents only a temporary triumph of "ideas" over "interest," a momentary burst of enthusiasm.[38] For such moments have their histories, and what needs to be explained is why groups of men,

[38] This is the view of revolutionary enthusiasm suggested in Crane Brinton's book on the French Revolution, *Decade of Revolution* (New York, 1934) and again in his *Anatomy of Revolution* (New York, 1938). The analogy with religion argued in both books is, however, a very suggestive one.

over a fairly long span of time, acquired such an intense interest in ideas like predestination and holiness. Puritan ideology was a response to real experience, therefore a practical effort to cope with personal and social problems. The inability of the saints to establish and maintain their holy commonwealth suggests only that these problems were limited in time to the period of breakdown and psychic and political reconstruction. When men stopped being afraid, or became less afraid, then Puritanism was suddenly irrelevant. Particular elements in the Puritan system were transformed to fit the new routine—and other elements were forgotten. And only then did the saint become a man of "good behavior," cautious, respectable, calm, ready to participate in a Lockeian society.

The Halfway Covenant

EDMUND S. MORGAN

The New England Puritans rationalized their religious and communal life with a series of covenants, called "federal theology." This idiom, derived in large part from the English divines, Ames and Perkins, rather than from Calvin himself, softened the rigor of the Calvinist tenets of unconditional predestination, limited atonement, human inability, the irresistibility of grace, and the perseverance of the saints. These covenants gave fallen men a quasilegal purchase on redemption by reducing the arbitrariness and mystery of an omnipotent God. "The distance between God and the Creature is so great," the New England Puritans argued, "that although reasonable creatures do owe obedience unto him as their Creator, yet they could never have attained the reward of life, but by some voluntary condescension on God's part, which he hath been pleased to express by way of Covenant."

The Bay Colony Puritan was compelled to offer testimony in public to his saving experience of faith. If it were deemed authentic, he would become not only a full communicant of the church but a voting citizen of the state. This peculiarly American ideal of a visible church-state, "a due form of government both civil and ecclesiastical," foreign to Calvin's Geneva as well as to Puritan England, posed a problem for the future. What would happen when fewer and fewer people could testify to an authentic saving experience? The Bay Colony Puritans proposed a practical solution which has become known as "the halfway covenant"—a compromise which historians have traditionally treated as a symptom of declining piety. Edmund S. Morgan challenges this conventional view of the case.

WHEN THEY LEFT ENGLAND IN THE 1630'S, MANY PURITANS ASSUMED that they could and would leave the bad part of the world behind. They soon found that they could not. The fifteen or twenty thousand men and women who disembarked in New England between 1630 and 1640

Edmund S. Morgan, *Visible Saints*, 1963, pp. 120–138. Reprinted by permission of New York University Press. Copyright 1963 by New York University Press.

included large numbers who had to be classified as visibly wicked, so many indeed that some of the founders contemplated a further withdrawal to an isolated area from which this "mixed multitude" should be excluded. The wisest recognized that the world neither could nor should be left behind, and no further exodus occurred. But in the 1630's, by adopting the new strict view of church membership, the New England Puritans executed a spiritual withdrawal from the mixed multitude that amounted almost to an ecclesiastical abdication from the world. They failed to consider, before adopting the new standards of membership, what relation their churches should bear to the mass of men excluded by those standards, and their failure exposed them to even more serious charges of neglect and arrogance than they themselves had formerly made against the Separatists.

Outside the church in New England stood not only the mixed multitude of wicked Englishmen and heathen natives, but also the visibly good, who understood and believed the doctrines of Christianity and lived accordingly but who lacked the final experience of grace. The New England churches made no differentiation among these seemingly different men. Indeed the New England ministers devoted a good deal of time to showing that there was no difference in the eyes of God between the vilest sinner and the "civil" man, who obeyed God's commands outwardly but did not love God in his heart.[1] The only distinction among men in the eyes of God was between those who had saving faith and those who lacked it. Therefore the civil and the uncivil alike were kept outside God's church.

Outside the church in New England, moreover, a man was much farther removed from most of the means of grace than he would have been in the Old World. In England and Holland the establishment of Separatist churches had deprived no one of church membership, for the Separatists were surrounded by other, more comprehensive churches open to all. In New England the Puritans, certain that their way was the only one, forbade the erection of other churches. If a man could not qualify as a visible saint, he was wholly outside any church. He could not be baptized. He could not have his children baptized. He could not take communion. In England both these ordinances were available to everyone and were widely believed to be means of conversion through which God acted on the individual just as He did through preaching of the Gospel. But the New England Puritans did not share this belief and therefore felt obliged to deny baptism and communion

[1] See, for example, Thomas Hooker, *The Christians Two Chiefe Lessons* (London, 1640), p. 213; Thomas Shepard, *Works,* ed. John Albro (3 vols.; Boston, 1853), I, 29.

to the unconverted. In their view both ordinances were seals of the covenant of grace which God extended to his elect. To permit an unbeliever to participate in them would be blasphemous. By this exclusion, however, the church deprived itself of two traditional means of bringing unregenerate men closer to God.

Church discipline, which might also have served this purpose, was similarly confined to those who least needed it. It was used only for recovering or expelling backsliding members. In England, though church discipline was lax, everyone in the community was subject to it. But the New England Puritans assigned to the state the task of disciplining those whom they excluded from their churches.

The absence of ties between the unregenerate part of the community and the church gave the latter an unprecedented purity, but it also placed the very life of the church in jeopardy. The members of the New England churches had themselves come from imperfect churches, in which they had learned the doctrines of Christianity, had taken the sacraments, and received the experience of grace that qualified them for membership in the proper churches of New England. But how would the mass of men who had come to New England unqualified for membership ever become qualified? How would civil men be encouraged to persevere in their outward obedience in the hope of eventual faith? How would the wicked be shown their wickedness? How would the gospel be spread to the heathen? Before leaving for America, many Puritan spokesmen had affirmed a desire to convert the natives. How would they do it with a church designed only for the saved? Without a surrounding of imperfect, unreformed churches, where would the reformed ones obtain a supply of members? How would God's elect be plucked from the mixed multitude?

New Englanders had failed to consider these questions, and when English Puritans asked them, the New Englanders, like the Separatists before them, replied in terms that exposed their failure to recognize the church's mission in the world. John Cotton, for example, the principal spokesman for the New England way, could only ask of his critics: "May there not fall out to be Hypocrites in our Flock? and must wee not preach for their conversion? And are not the children of the Members of our Church, many of them such, as when they grow up stand in need of converting grace? . . . Besides when an Indian or unbeleever commeth into the Church, doe not all the prophets that preach the Word . . . apply their speech to his conviction and conversion?"[2]

The honest answer to the last of these questions was probably no. Nevertheless the New England Puritans did take one measure to fulfill

[2] *The Way of the Congregational Churches Cleared*, p. 74.

the church's evangelical mission. Instead of waiting for unbelievers to wander into the meetinghouse, the civil government of Massachusetts in 1646 passed a law requiring everyone within a town to attend the preaching of the word.[3] Such laws were also passed in the New Haven and Connecticut colonies.[4] The government undoubtedly hoped that compulsory church attendance would improve the colonists not only in godliness but in behavior. Whether the result matched the hope is questionable, for those who attended from compulsion were unlikely to derive from the experience any feeling of kinship to the church. New England preaching, from the point of view of the unregenerate, left much to be desired. Although the Puritans acknowledged preaching to be the principal means through which God converted men, ministers addressed themselves more to saints than to sinners, in sermons designed less to plant the seed of faith than to nourish it where it already grew.[5]

To be sure, not all ministers neglected the unregenerate. Some preachers undoubtedly tried to make new converts from their captive audiences. The surviving sermons of Thomas Hooker, for example, are often addressed to perishing sinners. A few ministers like John Eliot even devoted their spare time to converting the Indians. But for the most part the New England churches, in striving for purity of membership, neglected sinners and heathen and civil men to concentrate on the advancement in grace of those who had already demonstrated saving faith.

If a New Englander did pause to consider the sinners outside the church, he was likely to compromise his insistence on purity of membership. John Eliot, for example, in corresponding with English Puritans about the church's evangelical mission, found himself proposing measures that were inconsistent with New England practice. At one point he advocated admitting everyone in a congregation to the privileges of the church "so as to keep the whole heape of chaff and corne together, only excluding the ignorant and prophane and scandalous." From this undifferentiated mass, there might be simultaneously gathered a special group of "the holy Saints, who are called higher by the grace of Christ," and who might "injoy together a more strickt and select communion" without deserting the regular parochial communion.[6] At another time

---

[3] *Records of the Massachusetts Bay Company*, III, 99.

[4] *Records of the Colony or Jurisdiction of New Haven, from May, 1653, to the Union*, ed. C. J. Hoadly (Hartford, 1858), p. 588; *The Public Records of the Colony of Connecticut, Prior to the Union with New Haven Colony*, ed. J. Hammond Trumbull (Hartford, 1850), p. 524.

[5] E. S. Morgan, *The Puritan Family* (Boston, 1944, 1956), pp. 90–104.

[6] *Correspondence of Baxter and Eliot*, p. 25. Cf. John Eliot, *Communion of Churches* (Cambridge, Mass., 1665).

Eliot proposed transplanting the holiest members of outstanding congregations into other congregations which needed some shining examples to leaven the wicked in their midst.[7]

Eliot never attempted to carry out these novel proposals which he made to Richard Baxter as suggestions for the churches of England. In New England, he and other Puritan ministers continued to exclude from the sacraments all but the proven regenerate. In spite of prodding from English Presbyterians and Anglicans, the New Englanders refused to reverse their withdrawal from the world, and refused any accommodation within the church to the well meaning and well behaved. But the world has its own ways of controlling those who propel themselves too far from it; and the New England churches were eventually brought back to earth, not by the corruptions of the flesh, but by its biology.

The way of the world even in Massachusetts was to be born, grow old, and die. In the process each generation had to beget the next; and children did not spring full-grown and fully educated from their mothers' wombs. They had to be nursed and nurtured mentally and spiritually as well as physically until they were fit to stand by themselves. Somehow the organization of the church had to be accommodated to these facts of life. As the saints died and their children grew up, there had to be a way of getting the new generation into the church.

The Baptists, with a yearning for purity similar to that of the Puritans, solved the problem, or succeeded in ignoring it, by recruiting all new members from adult Christians who had been awakened by Baptist preaching or the preaching of other ministers. As old believers died, newly converted ones would take their places; children were incapable of any kind of membership. The Puritans, both Separatist and non-Separatist, had disclaimed "Anabaptism." Although the most ardent sometimes succumbed to its attractions, the great majority believed that God required the church to baptize not only converted saints previously unbaptized but also the children of saints. Such children became members of the church, but not in the same sense as their parents.

In what sense was a question that troubled the Separatists in England and Holland very little. The younger children of Separatist church members there did not participate in the Lord's Supper, but as they grew to maturity, they could easily qualify for all the privileges of the church, if they wished to, simply by behaving themselves and learning what they were taught. But the Separatist experience could offer no assistance to New Englanders in this matter. New England had prescribed not merely understanding and good behavior but an experience of conversion, an experience beyond the range of human volition, as a qualification for

[7] *Correspondence of Baxter and Eliot*, p. 40.

adult membership. Yet New England still admitted children to this church by baptism, apparently expecting that they would pass from child membership to adult membership when they grew up, just as they had done in the Separatist churches and in the Church of England.[8] It was an arrogant and inconsistent expectation, for it implied a presumption that every child of a saint was destined for salvation and such a presumption was obviously wrong. No Christian could believe that grace was really hereditary.

The Puritans tried to overcome this inconsistency by demanding that when the child of a saint grew up he must demonstrate to the church that he was indeed saved. Until he did so, by the same kind of examination that adults seeking membership were subjected to, he should not be admitted to the Lord's Supper. So said John Cotton, Richard Mather, and the synod of divines who between 1646 and 1648 drafted the exposition of Puritan beliefs and practices which is usually referred to as the Cambridge Platform.[9] But the men who framed the Cambridge Platform did not say what happened to the membership of a child if he grew up and did not experience faith.

Before two decades had passed, the fact was plain that most children of saints did not receive saving faith by the time they were physically mature. To judge from surviving records, it was uncommon for a man or woman to have the requisite religious experience before he was in his twenties. Often it came much later, and many otherwise good men and women never received it.

But if the holy spirit reached these men and women late or not at all, biological urges reached them early. They married young and had large families. When an unconverted child of a church member produced a child of his own, the minister of his church was presented with a problem, the complexity of which had not been foreseen by the architects of the New England system. The new father (or mother) had been in some sense a member of the church. Was he still? If so, was he a member in a different sense than before? What about the child? Was the child a member? Should the child be baptized?

The questions were difficult to answer, because every answer generated several more questions. If a child who grew to physical maturity without

---

[8] The founders of the Salem church evidently shared the Separatists' expectation that the ensuing generations would enter the church as they acquired an adult understanding of the principles of religion. See Morton, *New Englands Memoriall*, p. 77.

[9] Cotton, *The Way of the Congregational Churches Cleared*, pp. 5, 79–80, 111–13; Mather, *Church Government and Church Covenant Discussed*, pp. 20–22; Walker, *Creeds and Platforms*, p. 224.

receiving faith was to be considered no longer a member of tne church, how and when should his expulsion take place? The fact that he had acquired a child before he acquired faith was no sign that he would not eventually attain faith. Should the church meanwhile cast him out? If so, upon what grounds could it be done? The New Englanders, in adopting the new standard of membership, had not correspondingly altered their conception of church discipline. Admonitions and excommunications were still applied only for misconduct or for openly expressed heretical ideas; no one suggested that anyone be excommunicated for failure to display signs of saving faith. When, therefore, a child of a member grew to maturity without faith but without misconduct, it was impossible to find grounds for expelling him. To excommunicate him for having a child in lawful wedlock was palpably absurd. On the other hand, if he remained a member, his child must be entitled to baptism, and if so, why not that child's child too, and so on until the church should cease to be a company of the faithful and should become a genealogical society of the descendants of the faithful.

The Puritans had in fact moved the church so far from the world that it would no longer fit the biological facts of life. Had they been willing to move it a little farther still, by forming monasteries instead of churches, they might have concentrated on their own purity and left to others the task of supplying the church with new members. Had they been willing to abandon infant baptism, they might at least have avoided the embarrassment of trying to adjust spiritual growth to physical. As it was, they had chosen to apply in time and space a conception of the church that could never fit those dimensions. Given both infant baptism and the restriction of church membership to visible saints, it was impossible for the Puritans either to evade the questions just posed or to answer them without an elaborate casuistry that bred dissatisfaction and disagreement. The history of the New England churches during the seventeenth and eighteenth centuries was in large measure a history of these dissatisfactions and disagreements.

In the first decade after the establishment of the more rigorous standard of membership, the questions were not yet urgent. The older children of church members in the new churches had been baptized in England and were perhaps not considered as sharing in their parents' membership. By the late 1640's, however, an increasing number of children who had been baptized in New England churches were coming of age without a religious experience and starting families of their own. The synod which met at Cambridge in 1646–1648 had been asked to decide the status of these persons. Since it failed to do so, every church during the 1650's had to face the question for itself, and most of them seem to have adopted a do-nothing policy by neither expelling the second-generation adults nor baptizing their third-generation children.[10]

By the late 1650's, the preaching of the word was generating few conversions, and with the end of the Great Migration, the overseas supply of saints had been cut off. As the first generation of Puritans died, the churches declined rapidly in membership, and it appeared that a majority of the population would soon be unbaptized.[11] This was an alarming situation for a community which had been founded for religious purposes. It was one thing to create a church of saints; it was another to let those saints carry the church out of the world with them entirely when they died. A meeting of ministers in 1657 and a full-scale synod in 1662 considered the problem and tried to find a solution that would retain a pure membership without destroying the church.

The synod did not address itself to the fundamental problem of the church's relation to the world at large, the problem of how to convert the unconverted. Instead, it confined itself to the more limited question posed by the birth of children to baptized persons who had not or not yet received saving faith. The synod adopted seven propositions, most of which simply affirmed the prevailing New England ideas about infant baptism and the construction of churches from visible saints. But the third, fourth, and fifth propositions settled the problem of the unconverted members and their children, as follows:

[10] The surviving records are not clear on this matter, but the controversial literature following the synod of 1662 seems to support this statement. Jonathan Mitchel charged the opponents of the synod with holding principles that would require the expulsion of "all the adult Children of our Churches that are not come up to full Communion." The implication is that such expulsions had not taken place and would be shocking if they did. (*A Defense of the Answer,* pp. 4–16.) Richard Mather implies that the churches had not generally exercised discipline toward adult children of members: ". . . we know but little of the exercise of Church-discipline towards such." *Ibid.,* p. 60.) Increase Mather in *A Discourse Concerning the Subject of Baptisme* (Cambridge, Mass., 1675) states (p. 29) that churches in Plymouth colony exercised discipline toward children of the church, but (pp. 30–32) that elsewhere it was neglected. But perhaps these statements all refer to excommunication rather than lesser forms of discipline, for Henry Dunster in a letter written about 1652, stated concerning unconverted children of members: ". . . such there be amongst us with whom the Church bears patiently, using means for their Conviction and Conversion. And in case they break out into any unchristian courses, admonish them, and if they continue in them, wholy withdraw from them. But I have not knowne any of these formally excommunicated because they neither cared for nor sought Communion." Jeremiah Chaplin, *Life of Henry Dunster* (Boston, 1872), p. 288.

[11] "It is easie to see that in the way your self and some others go, *the bigger half of the people in this Country will in a little Time be unbaptized.*" Jonathan Mitchel to Increase Mather, appended to Increase Mather, *The First Principles of New England* (Cambridge, Mass., 1675).

Proposition 3d. The Infant-seed of confederate visible Believers, are members of the same Church with their parents, and when grown up, are personally under the Watch, Discipline and Government of that Church.

Proposition 4th. These Adult persons are not therefore to be admitted to full Communion, meerly because they are and continue members, without such further qualifications, as the Word of God requireth thereunto.

Proposition 5th. Church-members who were admitted in minority, understanding the Doctrine of Faith, and publickly professing their assent thereto; not scandalous in life, and solemnly owning the Covenant before the Church, wherein they give up themselves and their Children to the Lord, and subject themselves to the Government of Christ in the Church, their Children are to be Baptized.[12]

The fifth proposition was the crucial one. It meant that if a person born and baptized in the church did not receive faith he could still continue his membership and have his own children baptized, by leading a life free of scandal, by learning and professing the doctrines of Christianity, and by making a voluntary submission to God and His church. This submission, which proposition five calls "owning" the covenant, involved acknowledging the covenant with Christ and the church that had been made for one in infancy by one's parents, acknowledging, that is, so far as it lay within human power to do so. Although Puritan theology made such an acknowledgment meaningless unless it was the product of saving faith, owning the covenant was not intended to imply the genuine participation in the covenant of grace that came from saving faith. Nor was "understanding the Doctrine of Faith" supposed to imply the actual possession of faith. All the actions prescribed by the fifth proposition could be performed without saving faith. All were designed for the well-meaning, well-behaved but faithless offspring of the faithful. By the fifth proposition, these persons could retain their membership in the pure churches of New England simply by fulfilling the conditions which had formerly been required for membership in the Separatist churches of England and Holland.

The membership they retained, however, was not the full membership that had been granted in the Separatist churches. Rather it was the continuation of the membership they had had as children: they could not vote in church affairs, and they could not participate in the Lord's Supper (they were not members in "full communion"). What they gained was two privileges which had probably been hitherto denied them in most New England churches: the application of church discipline (they could be admonished or excommunicated for bad conduct) and baptism for their children. They were "half-way" members, and the synod's whole

12 Walker, *Creeds and Platforms,* pp. 325–28.

solution to the question of their status was dubbed the "half-way covenant."

The term was one of derision, invented by those who thought the synod's solution constituted a lowering of standards. But these opponents of the synod, who were numerous, proposed an absurd alternative to the concept of halfway membership. Faced with the problem of deciding on the status of the adults whom the synod made halfway members, the opponents admitted that the persons whom the synod placed in this category had been members of the church in their minority and also that they were subject to censure and admonition (but not excommunication) when they became adult. Yet, the opponents held, these persons at some undefined point, without action either by themselves or by the church, ceased to be members. They were *"felos de se,"* who cast themselves out of the church. Although the New England churches had never admitted the right of a church member to leave a church unless excommunicated or formally dismissed to another church, grown children were now held to have departed from the church without either themselves or the church knowing it.[13]

Such a view carried the church even farther from the world than the position it had taken in the 1630's. To be sure, the development of restricted membership, from the first Separatists onward, had steadily proceeded toward a greater withdrawal of the church from the world, and this had been accomplished by a continual refinement of doctrine. But the extreme position taken by the opponents of the synod was neither refined nor rational; and most of those who took it must eventually have either retreated to the halfway covenant or moved on to repudiate infant baptism.

The halfway covenant, while wholly insufficient as a recognition of the church's relationship to the world, was probably the most satisfactory way of reconciling the Puritans' conflicting commitments to infant baptism and to a church composed exclusively of saints. Its advocates argued persuasively against their opponents that the establishment of halfway membership was the only way in the long run to preserve the purity of full membership. Unless there was such a category the prospect of declining membership and the desire of parents to have their children baptized might tempt churches to admit persons to membership who were unworthy of the Lord's Supper. Men and women would be encouraged to play the hypocrite or to imagine themselves converted, by a process of wishful thinking, in order to gain baptism for their children. Only by distinguishing between those worthy of baptism and those

---

[13] Charles Chauncy, *Anti-Synodalia Scripta Americana* ([London], 1662); John Davenport, *Another Essay for Investigation of the Truth* (Cambridge, Mass., 1663).

worthy of the Lord's Supper, could the latter be preserved for the truly faithful.[14]

Baptism, it was pointed out, had never been considered as exclusive a sacrament as the Lord's Supper, for Puritans had always recognized baptism in any church, even the Roman Catholic, as valid, and did not repeat the rite for persons converted from that or any other Christian denomination. The drive toward exclusive membership had always aimed primarily at excluding the unworthy from the Lord's Supper. By establishing a category of halfway members, worthy of baptism, the synod hoped to preserve the sanctity of the Lord's Supper.

The supporters of the synod were able to collect a large number of testimonies from the books and manuscripts of the founding fathers, to show that insofar as the fathers considered the problem they had felt the same way about it as the synod. Thomas Shepard, Jr., unearthed and published a manuscript by his father, written three months before the latter's death in 1649. In it the elder Shepard, engaging in the familiar Puritan art of making distinctions, differentiated between the "inward reall holyness" of true saints and "federal holyness, whether externally professed as in grown persons, or graciously promised unto their seed." Only federal holiness was necessary for church membership. The children of saints must be presumed to have this and must be considered as church members until cast out by formal act of the church. Moreover, they must be cast out only if they committed open, outward offenses serious enough to bring the same judgment on any other member who committed them. Shepard, who had once warned against tolerating any known hypocrite in the church, was not dismayed in 1649 by a church in which the majority of members were unregenerate or as yet unregenerate children and children's children. Such a church, he acknowledged, would contain "many chaffy hypocrites and oft times prophane persons." But the same, he said, was true of a church freshly gathered of visible saints: you could never keep out hypocrites.[15]

Increase Mather, who liked to remind people that he was the son of Richard Mather and the son-in-law of John Cotton, at first opposed the halfway covenant. But when he swung round to support it, he produced an abundance of manuscripts from the desks of his father and father-in-law to show that they and their colleagues would have supported it too. Some of the statements adduced by Increase Mather may have antedated the full development of the New England system, but there

---

[14] Jonathan Mitchel and Richard Mather, *A Defence of the Answer*, pp. 45–46; Increase Mather, *Discourse Concerning Baptisme*, p. 52.

[15] Thomas Shepard, *The Church Membership of Children, and their Right to Baptisme* (Cambridge, Mass., 1663) pp. 13–14.

were plenty of later ones to show that when the problem arose, the founders were disposed toward the solution adopted by the synod. Richard Mather, for example, in a letter dated in 1651, had stated his opinion "that the Children of *Church members* submitting themselves to the *Discipline of Christ in the Church,* by an act of their own, when they are grown up to mens and womens Estate, ought to be *watched* over as other *members,* and to have their Infants baptized, but themselves not to be received to the *Lords Table,* nor to *voting* in the *Church,* till by the manifestation of *Faith* and *Repentance,* they shall approve themselves to be fit for the same." Mather had admitted, however, in the same letter, that his church had "not yet thus practiced."[16]

The opponents of the synod did have one founding father on their side: John Davenport of New Haven was still alive and could speak for himself. He was the most articulate and strenuous enemy of the halfway covenant, but his opposition was not as damaging as it might have been because there was published proof that during New England's founding years he had held different views. As a candidate for the ministry in the English church at Amsterdam, Davenport had insisted that he would not baptize all infants presented to him but only those presented by their parents, and then only if the parents submitted to an examination about their beliefs or status. In a lengthy defense of this position printed in 1636 he had explained what he demanded of a parent, and that was simply membership in a Christian church (the Anglican church would do) or profession of the Christian faith. Thus in 1636 he had himself demanded much less than the synod demanded in 1662, and as a result he was not in a strong position to accuse the synod of betraying the standards of the founders.[17]

Although the theological battles of the 1660's were frequently waged with ammunition from the writings of the founding fathers, actually neither Davenport nor the other founders of New England had fully considered the problem of the next generation when in the 1630's they had adopted the test of saving faith for membership. And though historians have followed the opponents of the halfway covenant in hailing it as a betrayal of earlier standards and hence a symptom of the decline of piety, it was no such thing—unless John Calvin, Henry Barrow, Henry Ainsworth, John Robinson, William Perkins, William Ames, and William Bradshaw were all inferior in piety to the minority of New England divines in the 1660's who opposed the measure, unless John Davenport

---

16 Increase Mather, *The First Principles of New England,* pp. 10–11.

17 John Davenport, *An Apologeticall Reply to a booke Called An Answer to the unjust complaint of W. B.* (Rotterdam, 1636); *Another Essay for Investigation of the Truth* (Cambridge, Mass., 1663).

in 1636 was inferior in piety to John Davenport in 1664, unless indeed the founders of New England showed more piety by not facing the problem than their successors did by facing and answering it in 1662.

New England piety may have been declining, but the halfway covenant was *not* a symptom of decline. Rather it was an attempt to answer questions which neither English Puritans nor Separatists had had to face, questions which were created by New England's rigorous new conception of church membership but which the originators of that concept, during their brief experience, had generally been able to evade. By the 1660's the questions could no longer be evaded, but if the clergy and members of the New England churches had really been less pious than their predecessors, those questions might never have arisen. If, for example, they had succumbed to Arminianism, it would have been possible for anyone who wished to do so to join the church, simply by affirming his possession of a faith that lay within the reach of human volition. The halfway covenant became necessary, because New England churches of the second generation did hold to the standards of the first, because they did retain the belief in infant baptism, and because they did insist on the pattern of conversion outlined by Perkins and Hildersam and Ames.

Whether there was a decline of piety in the population at large is another question entirely, for the halfway covenant had nothing to do with the population at large. It is not a question I am prepared to settle, but it may be worth pointing out that though the rate of conversions during the second and third decades of New England's history was probably much lower than the founders had anticipated, this was not necessarily a sign of a decline in piety. The bulk of the population had arrived during the Great Migration of the 1630's and probably a large number of the first church members became so before the new admissions system was completely set up. How many would have become members if they had had to pass the new test we cannot tell. Since the second generation of New Englanders was thus actually the first generation in which every church member did have to pass the new test, a comparison of membership statistics in the first few decades, if they were available, would not solve our problem.

The halfway covenant, I would maintain then, was neither a sign of decline in piety nor a betrayal of the standards of the founding fathers, but an honest attempt to rescue the concept of a church of visible saints from the tangle of problems created in time by human reproduction. Nevertheless, the halfway covenant does mark the end of a phase in Puritan church history during which ministers and church members were so dazzled by the pure new institution they had succeeded in creating that they were for the moment blinded to their obligations to the rest of New England and to the world. The halfway covenant, taken by itself, was a narrow tribal way of recruiting saints, for it wholly neglected the church's evangelical mission to perishing sinners outside the families of its members. But it did turn attention, in however limited a manner, to the problem of propagating the church. As Jonathan Mitchel said, in defending the synod of 1662, "The Lord hath not set up Churches onely that *a few old Christians* may keep one another warm while they live, and then carry away the Church into the cold grave with them when they dye: no, but that they might, with all the care, and with all the Obligations, and Advantages to that care that may be, *nurse up* still successively *another Generation* of Subjects to Christ that may stand up in his *Kingdome* when they are gone, that so he might have a People and Kingdome *successively* continued to him from one Generation to another."[18] With the New England churches' recognition of this obligation, the Puritans' single-minded march toward purity came to rest.

The halfway covenant brought into the open the difficulties that had been lurking in the Puritan conception of church membership from the beginning. From the time when the first Separatists left the Church of England until the establishment in Massachusetts of tests for saving faith, that conception had developed toward making the visible church a closer and closer approximation of the invisible. With the halfway covenant the Puritans recognized that they had pushed their churches to the outer limits of visibility; and the history of the idea we have been tracing reached, if not a stop, at least a turning point.

[18] *Defence of the Answer,* p. 45.

The Great Awakening: Jonathan Edwards

ALAN HEIMERT AND PERRY MILLER

New England Puritanism produced its only original and systematic philosopher in Jonathan Edwards. He made intelligent use of both Locke and Newton, preserved a link to the earlier Puritans by reinstating the Covenant of Grace as a condition for church membership, and formulated a rigorous and passionate theology with which New England theologians had to come to terms for generations after his death. Newton's science stirred Edwards to study atoms, gravity, light, lightning, and planets in order to be "let into a New World of Philosophy." Edwards also used Locke's empirical emphasis on sensations as the source of knowledge to find a new rationale for the entrance of grace into the human soul, shaping his preacher's rhetoric to give his listeners a concrete idea of damnation and of the "sweetness of divine things." A pioneer in the study of the psychology of religion, Edwards played a powerful role in the revivals known as the Great Awakening, beginning in 1734–1735 in his Northampton church, where he had succeeded his grandfather, Solomon Stoddard.

The catalyst of the Awakening was George Whitefield, an Anglican clergyman who toured the colonies in 1739–1740, speaking to large crowds from Georgia to Massachusetts. Revivalist preaching profoundly stirred colonial society, stimulating conservative fears in its rationalist opponents. Alan Heimert and Perry Miller analyze the intellectual and social issues of the Awakening, stressing Edwards' role in arousing a concern for social welfare among saints who lived in the expectation of an imminent millennium.

EDWARDS DID NOT SEE NEW ENGLAND'S TWO ARMIES AS EMBATTLED over ecclesiastical issues, nor was New England in fact ever so clearly divided in this respect as the Presbyterians. This is not to say that the

Alan Heimert and Perry Miller (eds.), *The Great Awakening,* 1967, pp. xxxvii–xliii; xlvi–liv. Copyright © 1967, by the Bobbs-Merrill Company, Inc. Reprinted by permission of the publishers.

New England revival did not pose, nor was seen to pose, a challenge to church order and government. On the contrary, almost from the outset of the revival New Englanders touched by the Spirit began to leave their "unconverted ministers," and, soon, to organize "Separate" congregations totally independent of the "standing order" of Connecticut and Massachusetts. The Separates, one of the few truly new sects to be spawned by the Awakening in America, came in time to serve as the materials of a revitalized and theologically reoriented New England Baptist Church. Itinerancy was also an issue in New England, where the question was raised, whether or not to admit Whitefield, and a host of other wandering spirits, into particular pulpits. Still, the churches of New England, never so closely organized as those of Presbyterianism, were far from uniform in their practices; the role of "associations" and "consociations," and of the clergy in particular churches, differed widely from area to area. Thus the impact of the revival on church policy was so various as to make difficult at first the drawing of any clear inferences as to the ecclesiastical significance of the Awakening.

In New England, enthusiasm, which seemed to build there to an unmatched crescendo, was seen as the most distinctive, and controversial, of the revival's phenomena. Whitefield, Tennent, James Davenport, and the other itinerant exhorters who took *"so great* a Hand in the *religious Stir"* were viewed, by critics and defenders alike, not so much as challenging church order as in terms of the emotional experiences of their auditors. This focus was reflected in the names assumed by the parties that emerged in Connecticut—"New Lights" and "Old Lights"—where the issue was from the outset whether the emotional illumination of the revival experience was a witness of the Holy Spirit, or a flagrant departure from God's declared order of operation in his work of conversion. These party names did not come to prevail universally in Massachusetts, in part because Edwards considered such "epithets" unavailing, in larger part because both he and his chief antagonist, Charles Chauncy of Boston, carried the debate over enthusiasm well beyond the terms employed in the early months of the Awakening. Indeed, *the* question in New England became that of the precise nature of "saving knowledge" and the manner in which it is acquired. On such a question the mind of New England was perhaps disposed to fix, for throughout its century of history it had been always more oriented toward epistemological, even psychological, concerns, than most other Calvinists. Whatever the explanation, the "great debate" in New England centered on the human personality, and out of this debate came the reorientations in religious thought that clearly mark the Great Awakening as the "birth-pangs" of a new epoch in the history of American Protestantism.

The Great Awakening of 1740 was at first hailed by its partisans, we have seen, as a supernatural work. Hence much of the effort in the first delirious months went into formulating the signs or symptoms of authentic conversion, this being still conceived as a seizure from above. The sermon that Edwards delivered on September 10, 1741, at New Haven, entitled *The Distinguishing Marks of a Work of God,* is the best memorial of this early conception, though similar essays were produced by the Tennents. But even in this year, opponents of the Awakening were starting their attack, and everywhere their main charge became that, far from being a supernatural work, the outburst was criminally excited by artificial stimulations. Charles Chauncy's *Seasonable Thoughts on the State of Religion,* published in 1743, is the principal indictment, but the 'Old Lights' and 'Old Side' repeated it again and again. They accused the revivalists of abusing human nature under a pretense that God himself was working the harm. Consequently the revivalists, led by Edwards, were obliged to answer that their techniques did not do violence to the human constitution, either physically or psychologically. Though to the bitter end they contended that the Awakening was a pure act of God, they had progressively so to expound it that in effect they represented Almighty God as accommodating His procedures to the faculties and potentialities of His creature. From the time of Calvin, the focus of Calvinist and of most Protestant thinking had been the will of God; the great divide that we call the Awakening forced both American parties, whether proponents or opponents, to shift the focus of analysis to the nature of man.[1]

The central conflict of the Awakening was thus not theological but one of opposing theories of the human psychology. Edwards' contributions came by way of his reformulation of the propositions of John Locke's *Essay on Human Understanding.* According to Edwards the human personality is an organic unity; its "faculties" are not separate, nor the process of cognition discontinuous. Rather the "understanding" perceives only as the whole being is "affected," and all knowledge—the most important, of course, being "spiritual knowledge"—derives from and ultimately depends on a "sense of the heart." What Edwards accomplished, as he progressively revealed his insights over the course of the revival debate, was to give philosophic substance both to Whitefield's fustian about the "feelings" and to the observable facts of the Awakening. His "ultimate philosophy of the revival," *A Treatise Concerning Religious Affections,* was not published until 1746, but well before then other revivalists (including some, such as Jonathan Dickinson, who had been independently working toward a new psychology) incorporated Edwards' insights into their own thought and sermons.

[1] Perry Miller, "The Great Awakening from 1740 to 1750," *Encounter* (Divinity School, Duke University, Durham, N.C., March, 1956), p. 9.

The Religious Affections has been judged "the most profound exploration of the religious psychology in all American literature." The same
can not be said of any of the "rationalist" contributions to the discussion,
not even those of Edwards' ablest antagonist, Charles Chauncy. "Chauncy
persisted in arguing the whole case on the grounds of the scholastic psychology." Though he quoted Locke's *Understanding* in the first of his
attacks on enthusiasm, Chauncy wrote throughout the 1740's

as though everybody in Christendom assumed that reason, imagination, and
will were distinct 'faculties' and the affections a separate and autonomous
power. He used perception as meaning only to see, and sense was only the
register of the phantasms. Thus he conceived the psychological problem as
it had been conceived since the Middle Ages, that of controlling the imagination and the will by reason, and of subduing the emotions to the will;
hence all intelligible address must be directed to the reason, through which
decisions are always given to the will. Any appeal directly to the passions,
which attempts to bypass speculation, was demonstrably immoral. Whether
this affectation was ignorance or a debater's trick, I cannot say, but it put
Edwards under an immense handicap: in order to make himself understood
he had first to expound a radical and foreign psychology, which few in
New England were prepared to grasp. The irony is that the theological liberal, who in every trait stands for the rational Enlightenment, spoke in the
language of outmoded science, and the defender of Calvinism put his case
upon a modern, dynamic, analytical psychology in which the human organism was viewed, not as a system of gears, but as a living unit.[2]

It may nonetheless be said that Chauncy, no less than Edwards, an-
nounced a new era of religious thought. He laboriously heaped up both
Scriptural and Puritan comments on the perversity of the "passions," but
his point, finally, was that man is, or must be, an essentially rational
creature. "The plain Truth," Chauncy concluded from his reflections on
New England's religious disorders, "is, an enlightened Mind, not raised
Affections, ought always to be the Guide of those who call themselves
Men." Thus out of reaction to revival enthusiasm had emerged a religious
persuasion distinguished not so much by an overt avowal of the freedom
of the human will as by an insistence on the primacy of the "understanding" among the human faculties. Such a rationalism, soon to be
developed in the classrooms of Harvard and Yale as a general philosophy,
was the distinguishing mark of the "Liberal religion" of eighteenth-
century America. Over the next decades Liberals refined their scheme of
salvation, in which "time, exercise, observation, instruction," and the improvement of one's "capacities," were the means of grace—and the only
way, as well, for man to pursue his wordly happiness.

[2] Perry Miller, *Jonathan Edwards* (New York: William Sloane Associates,
1949), pp. 177–178.

Opposed to this philosophy was that inspired by the "joy" of the Awakening and given meaning by Edwards. The experience of conversion, as defined by Edwards, was a delight attendant on the whole being's undifferentiated perception, or "apprehension," as Edwards would have it, of the "excellence of divine things." Man's happiness and his holiness were not achieved through study or by way of a mechanically progressive growth in wisdom, but from a heartfelt "consent" to the "divinity of divinity," an order of being that was, by virtue of its beauty, also essentially good. What this involved is really part of another story— that of Edwards' reconstruction of Calvinist philosophy in the majestic dissertations of the 1750's. There he divested Calvinism of the language and conceptual apparatus of the "covenant theology" and portrayed man's salvation (and the redemption of mankind) as part of the divinely-ordered sequence and "attractions" of the universe. His inspiration was of course the physics of Isaac Newton, from which Edwards derived an interpretation of the "law of nature" quite at odds with the more "mechanical philosophy" of Liberal religion.

Among the opponents of the revival, too, there was a casting off from the safe mooring of Puritan theology. In their case the leap was toward the familiar axioms of the Age of Reason. In the 1750's "the religion of nature" emerged as "the instrument of a group, or of an interest," opposed to the doctrines of Calvinism. Their arguments rested "upon the massive authority of Newton," but specifically they were "directed against domestic opponents"—"against revivalists and enthusiasts, against New Light theologians, against those who still insisted upon a strict construction of the doctrines of total depravity and inherent corruption."[3] Among the consequences of this rationalist assault (which was by no means limited to spokesmen of the Church of England) was a reconsideration of the doctrines of the atonement and of the Trinity. In terms of dogma, the spokesmen of rational religion soon began to flirt with what the defenders of Calvinism called Arian or Socinian heresies.

But it was not so much a doctrinal revolution that the Awakening introduced as a profound shift in the very character, the perspective and focus, of religious thought and discourse. In the years after the revival, the rationalists began to insist that the Bible must be interpreted "reasonably," divested as it were of all its poetry and mystery. The spokesmen of evangelical religion, on the other hand, stressed the "beauty" of the gospel that was revealed to the gracious eye and mind as the inner mean-

[3] Perry Miller, "The Insecurity of Nature. Being the Dudleian Lecture for the Academic Year 1952-1953 . . . ," *Harvard Divinity School Bulletin. Annual Lectures and Book Reviews* (Official Register of Harvard University, Vol. LI, No. 13, Cambridge, Mass. [1954]). pp. 30–31.

ing of the Testaments. But for both parties, Scripture—once for Protestants the ultimate revelation of the Divine Will—was no longer the final source or test of truth. Almost without fully realizing what they were doing, Calvinists and Liberals alike were converting the Bible into a storehouse of rhetorical devices by which to make truths discovered elsewhere compelling. That Scripture was for Calvinists a vast stock of metaphors, and for Liberals, a body of precedents, was less significant than that both had come out of the Awakening to argue, ultimately, from Nature—the nature of the universe, of man, and of society.

. . .

In his *Thoughts on the Revival,* Edwards described the Awakening as an expression of social discontent, and he gave voice to the social aspirations—even goals—of those whom he called "the people of God." Nor was Edwards' *Thoughts on the Revival* simply a defense of "affectionate" religion, for in it he translated the prophetic hopes of the awakened into a program for the redemption of American society. Apart from any assessment of the appropriateness or effectiveness of any of his particular programs (in none of which, Edwards complained, would the "great men" and the "rich men" of colonial society join), it is clear what was implied, in the context of mid-eighteenth-century America, by his prediction that the millennium would "begin in America." The critics of the revival, who from the first moment of the Awakening feared the social implications of the new enthusiasm, were certain that Edwards had issued a call to revolution.

The opponents of the Awakening quickly and consciously strove to strengthen the institutional mechanisms of the colonies and make them over into antipopulist bulwarks against the seemingly seditious energies released in the revival. The most obvious of the pressures being resisted, as also one of the clearest consequences of the revival, was the challenge of the awakened to religious establishments. Everywhere the Awakening issued in a proliferation of religious groups, and a lively competition among them. But in the South the evangelical impulse was resisted by the Episcopal establishment, and so too in New England, where laws were passed, and ministerial resolutions published, denying full freedom to the revival churches. In New England, the separating spirit of the revival gave rise, in most of the larger communities, to two or more competing churches. In many areas critics of the revival formed a new Anglican church; they could not be harassed by colonies which, under royal charter, were obliged to tolerate the Church of England. The weight of the New England establishments fell on the Separates, whose conventicles were formed of those zealously affected by the New Light.

The strictly congregational Separates, like the Baptists who succeeded them in New England, were vocal crusaders for religious freedom. But other partisans of evangelical religion, though they hotly debated with these new sectarians, were likewise champions of religious liberty. For out of the Awakening, and consistent with the revival impulse, emerged the notion of "voluntarism," the assumption that church affiliation was not an obligation to be forced on men but a privilege that must be freely exercised.

The evangelical impulse also worked changes in the definition and constitution of the church. The Awakening brought a resurrection of the seventeenth-century Puritan ideal of church membership limited to the "regenerate." In the immediate post-Awakening years the notion of a "pure" or gathered church was most warmly espoused by the New England Separates and the Baptists of the Middle Colonies, both of which defined the church as a communion of those only who had experienced the converting grace of the Spirit. New Side Presbyterians and the Calvinist leaders of New England Congregationalism loudly disputed with these advocates of such a "pure" church. But the argument, it eventually became clear, was not in fact over the question of whether "saints" alone should be admitted to the privileges of church membership. The inner logic of evangelical religion demanded, as Tennent acknowledged, some distinction between the "precious" and the "vile," and even some sort of separation, for, as Tennent also asked during the Awakening, could the children of light be expected to break bread with the children of darkness?

The same question was also asked by Jonathan Edwards when he came, in the course of the Awakening, to reconsider and at last to publicly repudiate the ecclesiastical theories and practices of his grandfather, Solomon Stoddard. "Stoddardeanism" represented the culmination of the process by which, over the seventeenth century, the gate into the New England church had steadily been made less strait. In the first years of settlement only those were admitted as "saints," and allowed to participate in the sacraments, who satisfied the church with a public "profession of saving faith." Subsequently the examination of "professors" was made less rigorous, and under the provisions of the "Half-Way Covenant," adopted by the Synod of 1662, a descendant of any "saint," though he himself could offer no evidence whatever of regeneration, was allowed to present his children for baptism. Such Half-Way members were in theory barred from the other sacrament, the Lord's Supper, but in the late years of the century this barrier too was removed in many churches. Solomon Stoddard decided to admit all citizens of Northampton, the openly scandalous alone expected, to the Lord's Supper. This practice, along with Stoddard's definition of "visible sainthood" in terms of an evidently sincere assent to the "truth" of the Christian religion, was embraced elsewhere in New England.

All this was challenged by Jonathan Edwards, who decided that both Stoddardeanism and the Half-Way Covenant were inconsistent with the truths and the experience of the revival, which marked some members of every congregation as distinctly "saints." For repudiating Stoddard, Edwards was ejected from Northampton, but his conception of limited church membership was successfully applied in other congregations by his Calvinist colleagues. In time Edwards' system came to be espoused even by many Presbyterians, who thereby broke with that church's tradition of nonexclusion. But such a break had been made at least in part even before the Awakening, when the Tennents had insisted on a much more rigorous examination of applicants for the Lord's Supper. Edwards' polity, however, took the further step of giving to the "saints," and to them alone, not sacramental privileges merely, but the power of governing the church. This power, as Edwards defined it, included disciplining the unregenerate members of the congregation, and distributing, out of a "joint stock" collected from the more prosperous citizens, "charity" to the less fortunate members of society. In sum, Edwards hoped to use the church as an instrument of his (or God's) larger strategy for controlling and redeeming the human community.

Thus Edwards' differences with the Separates were just as significant, and probably more so, than the ideals they held in common. What Edwards shared with the sectarian advocates of a "pure church" was a conviction that the affinities among the elect were much stronger bonds than any of the covenanted relationships into which a man happened to be born. Among the Separates and Baptists this sense of saintly union was expressed in the gathering of "pure" and "independent" churches by way of secession from "corrupt" congregations. Edwards, however, held a vision of the universal Church that transcended local communities and made the godly, wherever they lived or in whatever denomination enrolled, members of a larger Christian commonwealth. Of this greater union the sacrament, defined by Edwards as a "communion" in which was manifested the love of the true saints for each other, was a symbolic reminder—and even a means of making it a reality in human affairs. For "pious union" was, to Edwards, both a taste of millennial felicity and a means of committing the saints to endeavors on behalf of the earthly Kingdom of God. In this respect the Separates were, from Edwards' viewpoint, profoundly irresponsible, for in their communions was expressed, and encouraged, no more than one's sense of difference from (and superiority to) the "impure" neighbors from whom he had withdrawn. Such separated "saints" self-complacently neglected the larger community, except in bewailing its sins and in waiting for God to punish the wicked by intervening in history with the terrors of the Last Judgment. Such an historical pessimism contrasted sharply with Edwards' declaration that "fire from heaven" was not to be looked for, because God intended his kingdom to come into being solely through "natural" cause—by means, that is, of a gradual and progressive improvement in human affairs. To Edwards, the worst of Separate "heresies" was their failure to "fall in" with God's plan (and Edwards') for the redemption of society.

In the Awakening, Edwards believed, God had not simply promised that the millennium would begin in America, but that God had called on his American people to will a reorganized society into being. For Edwards, the ultimate test of sainthood was whether a man was so acting as to "promote" God's historical program. And here precisely was the essential issue as between Edwards and the Separates, which was not ecclesiastical, but doctrinal, and centered on their differing definitions of holiness. Much the same situation prevailed in the Middle Colonies, where the Moravians and the Baptists were persuaded that Gilbert Tennent and Samuel Finley were simply resentful of the competition—and probably envious of the degree to which their more emotional faiths preserved the true spirit of the Awakening, against which, it was charged, the New Side had now turned. The Separates, likewise, thought Edwards had betrayed the warm faith of the revival, and could not understand why he, who had defended "emotional" religion against Charles Chauncy, now referred to the most zealous of the awakened as a "wild, enthusiastical sort of people." The problem was that these sectarians did not understand what Edwards—and the New Side preachers too—had known from the beginning of the Awakening: that true sainthood consisted in much more than unbridled and insubstantial enthusiasm.

Because the Moravians and Baptists seemed to suggest that the regenerate man was released from the obligations of the moral law, Tennent and Edwards identified these enthusiasts as "Antinomians."[4] But such Antinomianism was not to be found, in the post-Awakening years,

---

[4] Antinomianism is not a specific heresy, but a term generally (and almost always loosely) used to characterize the notions of religious "fanatics" who deny the need for subjection to any law, specifically the moral law of the Old Testament. In America, the term is particularly identified with the party that formed around Anne Hutchinson in the New England "Antinomian Crisis" of 1636–1638. Mistress Hutchinson complained that most of the New England ministers preached that fulfillment of the law was a necessary condition of grace. She insisted that grace was not conditional, and in her defeat, the doctrine of "preparation," with which she was contending, became the official orthodoxy of New England. Her critics accused the Antinomians, however, of arguing that the saint was released from any and all "legal" obligations, and it is in this sense, signifying opposition to all laws whatever, that Antinomianism is often employed—as a sort of metaphysical synonym for anarchism.

only among the sectarians. It was a challenge faced in every congregation, including Tennent's and Edwards' own, where there were men and women who had been touched by the Spirit. For everywhere in America there were many who, having "felt" the experience of grace, thereafter simply rejoiced in their good estate and asked no further evidence that they were saved. They believed that their holiness had been assured, and their Christian pilgrimage ended, by the single soul-ravishing experience of the Awakening. It was against such a notion of sainthood—and such an interpretation of the meaning of the Awakening—that Edwards and Tennent and their colleagues were arguing when they rebuked the enthusiasm of the Moravians, Baptists, and Separates. In so arguing against Antinomianism the Calvinists of the colonies evolved a "true religion" which, both in substance and in manner of operation, was one of the most significant of the Awakening's intellectual legacies.

The reconstructed Calvinism of post-Awakening America took for granted the centrality and the necessity of "religious affections," but it condemned as narrow and inadequate any creed that identified holiness with nothing but a momentary emotional experience. The true saint, Tennent insisted, was not so easily comforted; much more was required before he might deem his calling and election sure. In what that "more" consisted was most clearly set forth in the 1740's in Edwards' *Treatise Concerning the Religious Affections,* which provided the Calvinists of all America with the postulates of their more substantial faith. In *The Religious Affections,* Edwards, after defending "affectionate" religion against the barbs of Chauncy, relentlessly exposed as self-deceptive many of the simpler "joys" which the subjects of the Awakening were accepting as proof that they had been saved. Such delight was not, Edwards insisted, the whole of sainthood and was, in fact, if unaccompanied by other affections, presumptive evidence that a man had not been saved at all. Justified happiness, he explained, was attended by a change in man's entire personality (the center of which Edwards called the "heart") and was expressed in the holiest of religious affections, "love." And such holiness of heart must and would manifest itself in a holy "will," as a benevolence, not of thought merely, but of deed.

Having established his principles of psychology, Edwards turned to the question of how a man might know whether he had been so regenerated. In explaining that this could come only by way of "experiment" or "trial," Edwards announced those principles of "experimental religion" which were thereafter to distinguish the evangelical religion of colonial America. To try one's spirit was not to engage in introspective self-examination, but to test the heart by the only appropriate evidence, one's manner of behaving. It was "not in contemplation, but in action,"

that one must prove, to himself or to others, the legitimacy of his claim
to sainthood. "The main and most proper proof of a man's having a
heart to do anything, is his doing of it." This was "experimental religion," in which not a single experience, but man's entire subsequent life,
provided the evidence he was saved. Herein consisted not merely Edwards' difference with the Separates of the 1740's but that which largely
distinguished the evangelical impulse in America from the pietism of
eighteenth-century England and Europe. For "experimental religion," as
defined by Edwards and embraced by other American Calvinists, was not
designed to allow men existential solace in the midst of a troubled world,
but demanded of them strenuous exertions bent on setting the world
aright. The whole of what "experimental religion" required of the saint
was not explicitly revealed by Edwards until his posthumously-published
Dissertation on True Virtue, wherein he identified true sainthood with
total commitment, in heart and in will, to making the social arrangements
of mankind as "excellent," or "beautiful," as God intended them to be.
But in *The Religious Affections* he made it abundantly clear that the
test of sainthood involved endeavors to redeem society and even that the
true saint would and could not rest until the Kingdom of God were
established on earth.

Edwards' definition of sainthood was embraced by many New Side
Presbyterians and, soon after his death, by the Baptists who, under the
leadership of the awakened and self-taught preacher Isaac Backus,
drew most of the New England Separates back into the evangelical fold.
In so regathering, the partisans of "experimental religion" largely ful-
filled one of the best-remembered and most frequently-recalled promises
of the Great Awakening—that of a "more perfect union" of God's
people in America. Such a prospect was revealed early in the revival—
in interdenominational communion services and the exchange of pulpits,
even between preachers of different colonies, among those who favored
the "Work of God." The vision was further illuminated by Edwards'
many efforts to realize the prophecy of the millennium, among them the
device of concurrent prayer, whereby all the "people of God," of whatever denomination or province, might manifest their unity. Although
Edwards' vision extended to all Christendom, it focused most sharply
on the possibility of a union of all the pious "in *America,*" extending
from New England to Georgia. His critics ridiculed Edwards' proposal,
for the opponents of the revival were, by contrast, rigidly sectarian and
parochial, both in thought and in policy. They sought, for example, to
frighten the populace away from Whitefield with the warning that he
was an Episcopal "priest," and to keep evangelical ambassadors from
other colonies out of their local areas. It was two decades after the

Awakening before the spokesmen of rationalism began to evolve their own conception of "union," and when they did, their ideas and program still betrayed the fears aroused by Edwards' suggestion that "God's people" join hands in order to gain "the capacity to act with united strength."

The Cyclical Theory of History

STOW PERSONS

The idea of history which men have is itself an important historical fact, as Carl L. Becker showed in his famous study of "the heavenly city" of the eighteenth-century philosophers. Becker's study of the French *philosophes* emphasized the continuity between them and their Christian ancestors, particularly with respect to the idea of progress, which he understood as a secularization of the Christian story of human redemption in time. Becker did not, however, discriminate between the American and European aspects of the Enlightenment. Looking at the American scene, Stow Persons examines the different ideas of history held by revivalists, their opponents, and the Revolutionary generation. His analysis significantly revises Becker's influential image of the Enlightenment.

A CONCISE STATEMENT OF THE CYCLICAL VIEW OF HISTORY WAS SET forth by Bolingbroke in *The Patriot King* of 1738, as follows:

Absolute stability is not to be expected in any thing human; for that which exists immutably exists alone necessarily, and this attribute of the Supreme Being can neither belong to man, nor to the works of man. The best instituted governments, like the best constituted animal bodies, carry in them the seeds of their destruction: and though they grow and improve for a time, they will soon tend visibly to their dissolution. Every hour they live is an hour the less that they have to live. All that can be done therefore to prolong the duration of a good government, is to draw it back, on every favorable occasion, to the *first good principles* on which it was founded. When these occasions happen often, and are well improved, such governments are prosperous and durable. When they happen seldom, or are ill improved, these political bodies live in pain or in langour, and die soon.[1]

Stow Persons, "The Cyclical Theory of History in Eighteenth Century America," *American Quarterly,* 6 (Summer, 1954), pp. 147–163. Reprinted by permission of the author and the publisher.

[1] Henry Saint-John Bolingbroke, *Letters on the Spirit of Patriotism: on the Idea of a Patriot King: and on the State of Parties, at the Accession of King George the First* (New ed., London: Cadell, 1783), p. 128.

My purpose is to indicate the general currency of such a cyclical theory of history in late eighteenth century America, and to explore its relationship to the idea of progress, which has generally been regarded as the characteristic outlook on history of enlightened thinkers, both in Europe and in America.[2]

As an epoch in the history of thought the American Enlightenment may be taken to have commenced with the reaction to the great religious revival of the 1740's and to have ended with the War of 1812. The function of the revival was to precipitate issues and crystallize parties. Conflicts of interest helped to sharpen objectives and straighten the lines of thought. The Great Awakening presented the first common intellectual issues for Anglo-Americans widely scattered along the continental seaboard, and from it radiate the intellectual traditions that are properly to be called American rather than provincial. Three distinct theories of history were to be found in the thought of the time, with one of which, the cyclical theory, I am particularly concerned.

The investigation involves an approach to the mind of the Enlightenment in America that may seem heretical on at least two counts. On the one hand, it was a complex of ideas which stemmed from the interests of a particular group. We should not be misled by the cosmopolitan content of enlightened thought—its emphasis upon natural law, reason, universal benevolence, and the rights of man. Here was perhaps the first instance of those ambiguous relationships between interest and profession which have given the history of our national ideology its elusive character. To force enthusiastic believers in immediate revelation and special providences to recognize the primacy of natural law and submit to the rule of reason was at the outset precisely the point at issue. On the other hand, by emphasizing the utility of enlightened ideas as weapons in the hands of a class of men in America, I am also risking the charge of ignoring the fact that these ideas were current throughout most of Western civilization in the eighteenth century, with the implication that their analysis in the purely local context must be inadequate. While there is much truth in this, I would nevertheless suggest that the relationship between enlightened thinkers in Europe and in America is one of descent from a common parentage, the English latitudinarians of the previous century, and that the differences between the eighteenth century offspring are to be understood in part at least as the consequence of local controversies. In short, the mind of the American Enlightenment was not a mass mind, but the

---

[2] An earlier version of this paper was presented at the Newberry Library Conference on American Studies, October 13, 1951.

creed of a party, several of whose doctrines are fully understood only as planks in a party platform.

I

The first of the three conceptions of history was that of the revivalists of the Great Awakening. It was a frankly supernaturalist interpretation of history as the unfolding revelation of divine purpose. Human history was conceived to be, in Jonathan Edwards' phrase, the work of redemption, a work which would be completed with the second coming of Christ and the establishment of his millennial kingdom. Many were convinced that the wholesale conversions accomplished by the revival entailed that purification of spirit and morals presumably characteristic of the "latter day" foretold by the prophets. Edwards himself believed that the new world had been reserved for recent discovery and the conversion of the heathen aborigines, in order that a seat might be prepared for the imminent establishment of Christ's kingdom.[3] Night after night expectant revivalists "flew as doves to their windows" to witness the coming of the Lord in clouds of glory.

The relevance of this quaint excitement to our exploration of the moderate and empirical temper of the enlightened mind was suggested twenty years ago by Carl Becker in his study of the French *philosophes.* The idea of progress, Becker observed, is to be understood as a secularization of the millennialist interpretation of history. The conception of the progress of the human race from the earliest primitive horde postulated by Condorcet to its estimable condition in the eighteenth century with its infinitely enticing prospects for the future, is nothing but the pious Christian's account of the work of redemption, with somewhat different characters and emphases, to be sure, but with essentially the same form of plot. Becker's thesis has been employed in a similar analysis of the origins of the idea of progress in America by Professor Rutherford Delmage[4] who has assembled some interesting evidence tracing the transformation of the one view into the other. One may well be reluctant, however, to accept an historical connection established in terms of the similarity of idea-form alone, when in other crucial respects the millennial expectation and the idea of progress represent such sharply contrasting interests and temperaments. The cyclical theory seems to have performed a mediating function in accommodating these theories of history to each other.

[3] Jonathan Edwards, *A History of the Work of Redemption* (3rd. Amer. ed., Worcester: Thomas, 1792), pp. 280–81, 310–11.

[4] Rutherford E. Delmage, "The American Idea of Progress, 1750–1800," *Proceedings of the American Philosophical Society,* XCI (1947), pp. 307–14.

II

A central issue in the controversies arising out of the Great Awakening concerned the method of God's governance of the world. Did he intervene by means of special providences and direct inspiration for the guidance of men in the historical process, or was he content to achieve his ends through those "general and steady laws" known to men through Scripture, experience, and the observation of nature? The revivalists held the former view and their opponents the latter. The millennial expectation was the culminating affirmation of men prepared to commit human history to a transcendent purpose which would in the end give history its meaning. The millennial hope itself, however, could not become a major issue in the conflict because either party insisted upon its Protestant orthodoxy, and all acknowledged the testimony of Scripture that Christ would ultimately return to judge the quick and the dead.[5] The work of the anti-revivalists was less to reject the millennial hope than to reformulate the issues in such a way that the expectation of the second coming would eventually become a radically different concept.

The intellectual spokesmen for the opponents of the revival were the Anglican Alexander Garden, John Thomson the Presbyterian, and Charles Chauncy the Congregationalist.[6] In the controversial tracts of these men, published between 1740 and 1743, and aimed at Whitefield, Tennent, Edwards, and their followers, one finds dressed in religious garb several of the characteristic ideas and attitudes more commonly associated with the secular thinkers of the following generation. As the expression of a group conscious of its interests and of the identity of its foe enlightened ideas in America find their source here.

Fear of the social chaos anticipated in the revivalists' attack upon the privileged position of the established churches was the prime consideration which motivated the counter-attack of the anti-revivalists. All of their doctrinal argument points to this conclusion. Its essence was expressed in Chauncy's dictum that in the work of conversion the divine spirit operates upon the reason, bringing about a change in the temper of mind, and disciplining the unruly passions in accordance with the new and

---

[5] Charles Chauncy, *Seasonable Thoughts on the State of Religion in New England* (Boston: Eliot, 1743), pp. 370–73.

[6] Alexander Garden, *Regeneration, and the Testimony of the Spirit* (Charlestown: Timothy, 1740); *Six Letters to the Rev. Mr. George Whitefield* (2nd ed., Boston: Fleet, 1740). John Thomson, *The Doctrine of Convictions Set in a Clear Light* (Philadelphia: Bradford, 1741); *The Government of the Church of Christ* (Philadelphia: Bradford, 1741). Charles Chauncy, *Enthusiasm Describ'd and Caution'd Against* (Boston: 1742); *Seasonable Thoughts*.

clearer insight into the nature of divine truth.[7] The consequence was to submerge the operation of divine grace within the human process of striving measured in moral terms, to be detected in conduct. By the use of reason and Scripture men were to discover and do God's will, confident that God would not withhold his grace from the truly penitent. This of course implied a merciful and benevolent deity.[8] The evidence of regeneration was not to be found in subjective impressions, ecstatic impulses, or "heightened affections," but in an enrichment of Christian graces, the chief of which was love. Nothing illustrates more clearly the social affiliations of the anti-revivalists than their enumeration of the qualities of the gracious Christian convert. According to Chauncy, believers should display "a spiritual *Likeness* to the LORD JESUS CHRIST, in *Faith;* in *Purity;* in *Lowliness* and *Humility;* in *Love* to GOD, and our *Neighbors;* in *Patience, Meekness,* and *Gentleness;* in *Contempt* of the *World,* Contentedness with their Condition, Resignation to God; and in a Word, a *Zeal* to *honor him,* and *do all the good they can* in the World."[9] The worst that could be said of enthusiasts was that they were "Porters, Cobblers, Barbers, etc. . . . ignorant and impudent wretches," whose restiveness under the disciplined religious leadership of an educated clergy caused them to abandon their proper stations and flock to the revivalists. As the *Boston Evening-Post* observed: "It is one of the main Disorders and Infelicities of the present Age, that many of the *meanest Rank,* and of *Inferior Capacities,* are puffed up with a Pride that is become almost past dealing with. Some of the most contemptible Creatures among us yet think themselves sufficient to direct *Statesmen,* dictate to *Legislators,* and teach *Doctors* and *Divines.*"[10]

The function of reason as the monitor of the moral law is understood in this context. As Chauncy put it, "One of the most *essential* Things necessary in the *new-forming* Men, is the reduction of their *Passions* to a proper Regimen, i.e., the Government of a *sanctified Understanding.* . . . The plain Truth is, an *enlightened Mind,* and not *raised Affections,* ought always to be the Guide of those who call themselves Men."[11] Enlightened thinkers commenced by glorifying reason as a disciplinary agency, and only gradually did the course of events suggest its use as a revolutionary solvent.

---

[7] Chauncy, *Seasonable Thoughts,* pp. 108–19.

[8] Stephen Williams to Eleazer Wheelock, July 18, 1740. Wheelock MSS. *Boston Evening-Post,* April 19, 1742.

[9] Chauncy, *Enthusiasm Describ'd* pp. 8–14. Cf. Thomson, *Doctrine of Convictions,* pp. 21–25.

[10] *Boston Evening-Post,* April 5, 1742. For similar allusions to the class character of the revival see the issues of September 29, October 6, 1740; February 8, 22, 1742; January 24, 1743.

[11] Chauncy, *Seasonable Thoughts,* pp. 324–27.

I have emphasized the circumstances under which the constellation of enlightened ideas was composed because they underline the originally conservative character of the movement. The theory of history which began to emerge from this line of thought I propose to designate the theory of organic cycles. Opponents of the revival acknowledged the biblical authority upon which the millennial hope rested, but they rejected as an enthusiastic delusion the expectation that the revival itself heralded the second coming. Direct inspiration in either of its forms, as subjective impression or as overt historical event, was decisively repudiated, and with it the possibility or relevance of interpreting history as the special revelation of God's will.[12] For the opponents of the revival a pertinent interpretation of history must concern itself with the issues deemed of paramount importance, namely the reasoned and moderate disciplining of the mind and appetites consistently with what had been vouchsafed men to know of the intentions of deity and of their obligations to their fellows.

The new view of history which came into vogue among conservative thinkers in the years following the revival found the source of historical dynamics in the operation of the universal moral law, the effect of which upon history was an endless cyclical movement analogous to the life cycle of the individual organism. Societies and nations rise and fall in endless sequence according as they observe or disregard those universal moral laws ordained of God and graven upon men's consciences for their governance and happiness. Suggestions of the cyclical theme were to be found both in the writers of classical antiquity, especially the historians and moralists, and more recently in the popular English literature of the early eighteenth century. It was subsequently to become a familiar theme in romantic thought. Both John Adams and Jefferson were familiar with the *Patriot King*, where they would have found the passage quoted at the opening of this paper. It is also perhaps pertinent to call attention to the prevalence in contemporary thought of two ideas easily related to the cyclical theme. One was the physiographic notion of primitive corruption and aged refinement, as popularized in the natural histories of Buffon and Raynal. The other was the historical idea of the westward transit of culture. In any event, the universal relevance of the cyclical theory appealed mightily to an age coming to pride itself upon its cosmopolitanism and to view with increasing embarrassment the sectarian limitations of the Christian pretensions. It was held by men many of whom had no immediate interest in the party battles of the revival, but who were at least united with the anti-revivalists in opposition to the emotionalism and democratic inclinations of the religious enthusiasts. The cyclical theory of history

12 *Ibid.*, pp. 183–84, 370–73.

was to become for a brief period one of the distinctive historical conceptions of the dominant social group in America.

The following passage from a sermon of the Rev. David Tappan, Hollis Professor of Divinity at Harvard College, preached in 1798, will serve to illustrate the cyclical view in its most literal form.

Experience proves that political bodies, like the animal economy, have their periods of infancy, youth, maturity, decay, and dissolution. In the early stages of their existence their members are usually industrious and frugal, simple in their manners, just and kind in their intercourse, active and hardy, united and brave. Their feeble, exposed, and necessitous condition in some sort forces upon them this conduct and these habits. The practice of these virtues gradually nourishes them to a state of manly vigor. They become mature and flourishing in wealth and population, in arts and arms, in almost every kind of national prosperity. But when they have reached a certain point of greatness, their taste and manners begin to be infected. Their prosperity inflates and debauches their minds. It betrays them into pride and avarice, luxury and dissipation, idleness and sensuality, and too often into practical and scornful impiety. These, with other kindred vices, hasten their downfall and ruin. [History shows that] virtue is the soul of republican freedom; that luxury tends to extinguish both sound morality and piety; and that the loss of these renders men incapable of estimating and relishing, of preserving or even bearing the blessings of equal liberty.[13]

The special function of the clerical adherents to the cyclical view was to relate it to the divine government of the world. The moral law establishes an irrevocable connection between virtue and happiness on the one hand, and between vice and misery on the other. "The benevolent Ruler of the universe delights in the happiness of his subjects," and while his judgments are for their transgressions, they are also for their instruction.[14] In this most rational and equably governed of worlds sin does not always provoke speedy and sufficient retribution, for if it did there would be no scope for that testing and development of individual character which is necessary to prepare men for the future state.

[13] David Tappan, *A Discourse, Delivered to the Religious Society in Brattle-Street, Boston . . . on April 5, 1798* (Boston: Hall, 1798), pp. 18–19. For similar views of clerics, see Charles Backus, *A Sermon, Preached in Long-Meadow, at the Public Fast, April 17, 1788* (Springfield: Weld and Thomas, 1788), p. 9; Thomas Barnard, *A Sermon, Delivered on the Day of National Thanksgiving, February 19, 1795* (Salem: Cushing, 1795), pp. 21–22; Samuel Stanhope Smith, *The Divine Goodness to the United States of America. A Discourse . . . February 19, 1795* (Philadelphia: W. Young, 1795), pp. 20–21.

[14] Joseph Lathrop, *National Happiness, Illustrated in a Sermon, Delivered at West-Springfield, on February 19, 1795* (Springfield: Hooker and Stebbins, 1795), p. 13.

The actual measures, therefore, of the divine government towards communities and particular persons appear full of wisdom and beauty. While the former receive such a recompense of their conduct, as gives a general, though incomplete display of the governing justice of God; the latter have sufficient advantages and motives to prepare for and confidently expect the ultimate triumph of virtue in the unmixed and endless happiness of its friends, and the final destruction of its obdurate enemies.[15]

Thus it appears that history is virtue teaching by example; and the decline and fall of empires represents a divine judgment upon the corruption of men.

Perhaps because it performed a didactic function in the exhortations of the clergy, we find more explicit expression of the cyclical theme in their writings. But it was widely presupposed by lay thinkers as well, at least before the French Revolution. John Adams, for instance, held it for more than half a century. As early as 1755, he attributed the rise and fall of nations to "some minute and unsuspected cause," a cause which, judging by his reflections upon the fall of Rome, the rise of America, and other great historical events, he assumed to be invariably moral in character.[16] Sixty-four years later he was still harping upon the same theme, challenging Jefferson to cite a single illustration of a nation once corrupted that had been able to cleanse itself and restore political liberty. "Will you tell me," he asked, "how to prevent riches from becoming the effects of temperance and industry? Will you tell me how to prevent riches from producing luxury? Will you tell me how to prevent luxury from producing effeminacy, intoxication, extravagance, vice and folly?"[17] This plaintive cry reminds us of John Wesley's inexorable cycle of piety, virtue, riches, and corruption before which the great evangelical for all his zeal for souls stood helpless. In fact, the thoroughly moralistic character of enlightened social theory is so striking that it is remarkable that in an age as remote from this concern as is our own it has been so seldom commented upon.

If the cyclical view of history was as widely entertained as I have assumed, we are provided with a possible explanation of why it was that the enlightened mind in America did not express itself in any more important measure in the historiographical form. In the final analysis history can only reiterate its great theme; the same yesterday, today, and forever. There was nothing to be learned from it that could not be found in one's personal experience, or in the life of one's own time. In his treatise de-

---

[15] Tappan, *Discourse, April 5, 1798,* pp. 24–25.
[16] Adams to Nathan Webb, October 12, 1755. *Works* (C. F. Adams, ed.), I, 23.
[17] Paul Wilstach, ed., *Correspondence of John Adams and Thomas Jefferson* (Indianapolis: Bobbs-Merrill, 1925), pp. 169–70 (December 18, 1819).

voted specifically to the philosophy of history, the *Discourses on Davila,* John Adams tells us that the "key . . . to the rise and fall of empires" is found in the universal operation of the human passion for distinction, in its various forms of emulation, ambition, jealousy, envy and vanity.[18] This was the psychological source and motivation of those dynamic cycles which constitute the course of history. It appears to have been assumed that the connection ordained of God between nature, personality, and history was so tight as to deprive history of that range of possibilities which alone is capable of endowing it with more than passing interest. "Such is our unalterable moral constitution," wrote Adams, "that an internal inclination to do wrong is criminal; and a wicked thought stains the mind with guilt, and makes it tingle with pain." Hence of necessity history unfolds the perennial struggle between "the cause of liberty, truth, virtue, and humanity," on the one hand, and slavery, ignorance, misery, and despotism on the other; virtue prevailing during the great days of Roman culture, darkness and misery from the fourth to the fourteenth century. Once we have grasped the principle further study will merely substantiate the thesis.[19]

Jefferson also conceived of history as a series of cyclical fluctuations within a larger static framework, at least until his last years. Like Adams he also found the source of historical change to reside in the moral nature. Reflecting upon the revolutionary experiences of his own state, he expressed the opinion in the *Notes on Virginia* that when a state of public virtue prevails it is high time to erect safeguards for the protection of liberty, since "the spirit of the times may alter, will alter," and corrupt men will arise to persecute their fellows.[20] Anticipating Lord Acton's dictum that power corrupts, he appealed to history for proof that even the best governments are eventually perverted into tyrannies by those entrusted with power. To forestall this sad fate in Virginia he drafted the celebrated Bill for the More General Diffusion of Knowledge (1778), the preamble of which expresses the conviction that education aids the citizen in recognizing "ambition" and thus defeating its aims.[21] It was, in other words, the constant uniformities or repetitions of history, not its unique occurrences, that impressed Jefferson as being of value.[22] He was still of the same opinion many years later when he wrote to Adams that "in fact, the terms of whig and tory belong to natural as well as civil history. They denote

---

[18] Adams, *Works,* VI, 239, 232–34.
[19] *Ibid.,* IV (*Novanglus and Massachusettensis*), 44, 17–18.
[20] Adrienne Koch and William Peden, eds., *The Life and Selected Writings of Thomas Jefferson* (New York: Modern Library, 1944), p. 277.
[21] Jefferson, *Papers* (Boyd, ed.), II, 526–27.
[22] Koch and Peden, p. 265.

the temper and constitution of mind of different individuals."[23] Such a point of view was well adapted to nurture a distinguished political science —as indeed it did—but it was not conducive to a fruitful investigation of history.

It would not do, however, to leave the reader with the impression that the cyclical conception of history was merely a convenient device whereby enlightened thinkers were enabled to concentrate their attention elsewhere. It had an integral part in the conception which the age entertained of itself, and its projection into the future suggested an attitude towards human and social possibilities that was one of the most distinctive features of the enlightened mind. Those who employed the cyclical idea were uniformly agreed that the America of their day belonged in the youthful stage of growth approaching maturity. The Rev. Thomas Barnard of Salem, for instance, comparing the prospects of the new United States with those of older European countries which had nothing to look forward to except "decline and mortification, according to the course of human affairs," remarked upon the opportunities for growth and progress which lay before her. "I should prefer youth and early manhood, ever employed, lively, and full of hope, to complete manhood and old age, when we every day become less active, and less pleased. I should prefer the present period of our nation, for my life, to the more perfect state to which it will gradually advance."[24] Sometimes the cyclical idea is employed in the appraisal of specific issues, as when President Samuel Stanhope Smith of the College of New Jersey warns the country against involvement in the French revolutionary wars on the ground that peace is especially important to a "young and growing country not yet enervated by luxury, nor sunk into effeminacy and sloth. These vices indeed sometimes require the purifying flame of war to purge them off; and the state emerges from its fires regenerated, as it were, and new created."[25] Or it is used to justify the spirit and form of political institutions in America, as when the Rev. Samuel Williams opined that "on all accounts, a *free and equal government* is best suited to our infant and rising state."[26]

The self-consciousness with which the Enlightened age identified itself was in part at least the consequence of a theory of history which presupposed a series of epochs alternating in character. General Washington's letter to the state governors at the end of the Revolution is characteristic of this spirit. "The foundation of our empire," he wrote,

[23] Wilstach, p. 59.

[24] Barnard, *Sermon, February 19, 1795*, pp. 21–22.

[25] Smith, *Divine Goodness*, pp. 20–21.

[26] Samuel Williams, *A Discourse on the Love of Our Country; Delivered on a Day of Thanksgiving, December 15, 1774* (Salem: S. & E. Hall, 1775), p. 18.

"was not laid in the gloomy age of ignorance and superstition; but at an epocha when the rights of mankind were better understood and more clearly defined, than at any former period."[27] Similar sentiments are frequently encountered, and if taken out of the cyclical context may be misunderstood to indicate a belief in unlimited progress. Actually, most enlightened thinkers had a keen sense of the precariousness of the felicity which they enjoyed, of the moral and social conditions which would make its continuation possible, and of the ultimate likelihood of its dissipation. The cyclical conception of history was the crystallization of their hopes and fears. By reading back into their thought ideas which more commonly belong to their descendants we may seriously misunderstand their point of view.

The function of the cyclical idea can perhaps be most briefly and effectively illustrated from the field of thought in which the enlightened mind achieved its supreme expression, political theory. The conservative, defensive character of that theory is now pretty generally recognized. Liberty, the supreme good, could be achieved only if men exercised those moral virtues enjoined by the anti-revivalists, the practical fruit of which was the accumulation of property. The economic basis of enlightened political theory is aptly illustrated in the famous syllogism of President John Augustine Smith of William and Mary college, an ardent Jeffersonian Republican: since ninety-nine per cent of all legislation relates to property; and since it is the essence of republicanism that laws should emanate from those upon whom they bear; then restriction of the franchise to men of property is good republicanism. But property was more than an arbitrary qualification for political participation; it was an index of the moral health of the community. Unfortunately, property as we have seen was presumed to entail its own peculiar corruptions, the avoidance of which constituted a major preoccupation of political theorists. Jefferson pinned his faith to agriculture, writing to Madison in 1787 that Americans could be expected to preserve their liberties "as long as we remain virtuous, and I think we shall be so, as long as agriculture is our principal object, which will be the case, while there remain vacant lands in any part of America. When we get piled upon one another in large cities, as in Europe, we shall become corrupt as in Europe, and go to eating one another, as they do there."[28] These rural loyalties of the republican political theorists are not to be understood entirely in economic or regional terms, but perhaps primarily in moral terms. Even Benjamin Franklin, incorrigible cosmopolite, shared this sentimental agrarianism. The American counterpart of the European

[27] Washington, *Writings* (Ford ed.), X, 256.
[28] Jefferson, *Writings* (1903 ed.), VI, 392–93.

myth of the noble savage, living under the full light of nature, and uncorrupted by the vices of urban life, was of course the freehold farmer, whose virtuous life was the one sure foundation of national felicity.

Sound social and political institutions were, however, but temporary bulwarks against the inexorable processes of nature and history. The cyclical theory was perfectly compatible with the anticipated transformation of sturdy farmers into a landless proletariat, and with the degeneration of republican liberty into democratic license and ultimately to the tyranny of dictatorship. In his old age, John Adams looked back upon the eighteenth century and pronounced it to be, on the whole, the century "most honorable to human nature;" but he had no inclination to assume that the nineteenth century would be even more so. "My duties in my little infinitesimal circle," he wrote, "I can understand and feel. The duties of a son, a brother, a father, a neighbor, a citizen, I can see and feel, but I trust the ruler with his skies."[29]

In view of the typical emphasis upon moral conditions as the agents of cyclical change one might well question the appropriateness or significance of the use of the organic analogy. But I think the association is worth preserving in our descriptive terminology if only because it serves to illustrate the intimate connection between nature and value, which was perhaps the most distinctive feature of enlightened thought. The transmutation of natural law into natural right was the neatest trick of the age, and although we in our time can understand it with difficulty and may even suspect fraud, we cannot fail to admire the assurance and virtuosity with which the trick was performed. The inexorable rise and fall of nations might well be ordained of God after the pattern of the life cycle of organisms, but from the creature's point of view the Deity in his beneficent wisdom has provided that our own vices and virtues, wisdom and folly, shall register a proximate if not immediate effect upon the course of human events. This we can understand, and we trust the ruler with his skies.

III

The third conception of history to be found in the thought of eighteenth century America was embodied in the idea of progress. I shall not attempt to document the rise of this idea in America, but will merely indicate what I understand to be its impact upon the revolutionary generation. To put it bluntly: the notion of progress was repugnant to the characteristic convictions and temper of the class of men who in the

[29] Adams to Jefferson, November 13, 1815; September 15, 1813. Wilstach, pp. 118, 86.

generation prior to the Revolution had synthesized enlightened ideas in America. But at the same time it held a fatal fascination for them. Much of their practical experience recommended its validity. With diminishing reluctance they accommodated themselves to the idea, and in the end those of them who lived long enough, like Adams and Jefferson, embraced it heartily. But in so doing they signed, as it were, articles of intellectual abdication, and the enlightened mind thus became something else.

From a genetic point of view the idea of progress as it appeared in America was the offspring of a union of the millennial hope with the moralism of the cyclical view of history. The womb in which the progeny was nurtured was the excitement of the revolutionary struggle. The respects in which the Revolution involved a domestic class struggle have been familiar to students of American history for a generation, and it is possible that the competition between these attitudes towards history might be fruitfully related to the social class struggle. In any event, certain modifications in either theory of history looking towards a rapprochement may be indicated.

As contemplated by the revivalists of the seventeen-forties, the imminent coming of the Lord represented the divine will imposed upon history. It was that not-so-far-off divine event towards which the whole creation moved; and the events of the revival, including the saving or hardening of sinners, were to be understood as but reflex actions of that mighty upheaval. But as revival enthusiasm within the Reformed churches rapidly ebbed after 1745 its proponents were placed on the defensive by a changing mood and by the extravagances of fanatics. Leading evangelicals now realized that their millennial expectations had been at best premature, and that if the hope were to be kept alive it must not disregard historical possibilities. The survival of the millennial vision was made possible, among the more intellectually respectable of the clergy at least, by measuring progress towards the final event in moral terms.[30]

To illustrate this significant tendency, again in its most literal form, I have chosen a sermon of the Rev. Ebenezer Baldwin of Danbury, Connecticut, preached in 1775 on the eve of hostilities with Britain. Baldwin looked hopefully beyond the dark days immediately ahead to a glorious future. He anticipated that the colonies were to be the "foundation of a great and mighty Empire; the largest the World ever saw, to be founded on such Principles of Liberty and Freedom, both civil and

---

[30] See the sermon by Samuel Langdon, *Joy and Gratitude to God for the Long Life of a Good King, and the Conquest of Quebec. A Sermon Preached . . . November 10, 1759* (Portsmouth: Fowle, 1760).

religious, as never before took place in the World; which shall be the principal Seat of that glorious Kingdom, which Christ shall erect upon Earth in the latter Days." When Baldwin delivered his sermon to the printer he appended a long footnote in amplification of this prediction in which he observed that the American population, then numbering some three million souls, was doubling every twenty-five years. This rate of increase could be expected to continue for about a century, with a somewhat lesser rate of increase for a second century, at the end of which time (i.e., 1975) a unified North American empire would contain a population of some 192 millions, a curiously accurate prediction. Because this late twentieth century empire would be the product of natural growth rather than of conquest its original principles of civil and religious liberty would have survived intact. Baldwin then reminded his readers of the common Christian conviction that Christ would establish his millennial kingdom on earth before the end of the world, and that calculations based on the prophecies in Daniel and Revelation fixed the date of the second advent at about 2000 A.D., when America would be at the height of its glory, and Europe sunk beneath tyranny, corruption, and luxury. Christ's kingdom must of course be established upon a system of civil liberty; it could not be compatible with despotism or tyranny. Since by the end of the twentieth century it would be highly improbable that liberty would prevail anywhere but in America was it "chimerical to suppose America will largely share in the Happiness of this glorious Day, and that the present Scenes are remotely preparing the Way for it?"[31] The significant features of this revised form of millennial hope are first the deferment of the great event to the remote future; but more important, the estimation of conditions under which its consummation would occur in moral terms. One could now measure the advance of mankind towards the millennium in terms of the state of civil and religious liberty.

Essentially similar sentiments were expressed a few months later in more succinct and secular terms in the greatest of revolutionary tracts, Tom Paine's *Common Sense.* "We [Americans]," cried Paine, "have it in our power to begin the world over again. A situation, similar to the present, hath not happened since the days of Noah until now. The birth day of a new world is at hand."[32] Whether Baldwin or Paine entertained the more extravagant hopes we are not required to determine. Our attention is directed to the lengthened historical perspective in which thinkers were beginning to frame their judgments. The life cycle of empires, or the "Revolution of Ages," in the phrase of the pre-revolu-

[31] Ebenezer Baldwin, *The Duty of Rejoicing under Calamities and Afflictions* (New York: Hugh Gaine, 1776), pp. 38–40 and note.
[32] Thomas Paine, *Writings* (Conway ed.), I, 118–19.

tionary historian William Douglass, gave way to *the* revolution which marks off all history since Noah, or to the cumulative effect of specified factors pointing towards the millennium in 2000 A.D.

The "poet of the Revolution," Philip Freneau, in a Princeton commencement poem of 1771, paid his respects to the intellectual conventions of the age with an even more comprehensive synthesis. He succeeded in combining the ideas of the cyclical rise and fall of states, the westward passage of empire from Asia across Europe to the new world, and the final establishment of the millennial kingdom in America.[33]

Passages from the correspondence of Adams and Jefferson, chiefly during the second decade of the nineteenth century, both illustrate the weakening of the cyclical theory, and suggest the character of the new point of view. In their discussion of the sources of political power, Adams was inclined to stress such Machiavellian forces as selfishness, physical or psychological energy, or economic power. Jefferson, on the other hand, influenced perhaps in his later years by the French thinkers, pointed out that certain innovations of an apparently permanent character were rendering Adams' analysis obsolete. The invention of gun powder had deprived the physically strong of their primordial advantage. In the United States at least, where labor was properly rewarded, economic power was more widely distributed than ever before, with consequent equalization of political power. Even in Europe, which was lagging behind America in these respects, a sensible change was occurring. "Science," Jefferson reported, "has liberated the ideas of those who read and reflect, and the American example has kindled feelings of right in the people. An insurrection has consequently begun, of science, talents, and courage, against rank and birth, which have fallen into contempt. . . . Science is progressive, and talents and enterprise on the alert."[34] In similar vein, he was now prepared to redefine republicanism as the conviction of those who believe in the "improvability of the condition of man, and who have acted on that behalf, in opposition to those who consider man as a beast of burden made to be rode by him who has genius enough to get a bridle into his mouth."[35] We readily recognize these ideas—the cumulative character of technology, the liberating power of science, the kindling of feelings of right, and the improvement of the condition of mankind—to be authentic features of the new faith in human progress.

Franklin was perhaps the first American to use these doctrines in such a way as to suggest a unilinear conception of history. The invention

[33] "The Rising Glory of America," in F. L. Pattee, ed., *The Poems of Philip Freneau* (3 vols. Princeton: University Library, 1902), I, 49–84.
[34] Wilstach, pp. 93–94.
[35] Jefferson to Joel Barlow, January 24, 1810. *Writings* (Ford ed.), IX, 269.

of printing, the accumulation and dissemination of knowledge, and the consequent strengthening of the spirit of liberty were coming to be regarded as unique occurrences which could not be properly evaluated within a pattern of cyclical repetition. We find these views frequently recurring in Franklin's correspondence during the 1780's.[36] In later years, the aged Jefferson agreed with Adams' favorable judgment of the eighteenth century, but he pointed out that the operation of those characteristics which rendered it notable could be traced back at least as far as the fifteenth century.[37] The age of enlightenment was not therefore to be regarded as a cyclical episode, but as a phase of a secular trend extending far back in history, and one which would conceivably project indefinitely into the future.

It is worth noting that in these early expressions of the idea of progress the moral element is strongly emphasized, and that there is nothing of the note of complacent inevitability which Ekirch, in his study of the use of the idea after 1815, finds to be one of its most prominent features. I am inclined to suspect that the enlightened theory of divine benevolence, with its associated conviction that this is the best of all possible worlds, was itself paradoxically the strongest barrier against the idea of human progress. The idea of progress was to be the fighting faith of men with a mission to perform, whether to feed the hungry, convert the heathen, or accumulate one's pile. It connoted a certain discontent with the prevailing state of affairs. Its inevitability in the minds of its nineteenth century disciples was no more incompatible with energetic effort than were the similar features of inevitability in Puritan or Marxist thinking. But such a temper of mind was largely alien to the American Enlightenment, and certain changes had to occur before the new point of view could recommend itself with any force.

We can see one such change occurring in the increasing discontent of John Adams towards the end of his life with the hedonic calculus which was a characteristic feature of the thought of his generation. The preponderance of pleasure over pain, he concluded, is not in itself sufficient to make life endurable, even for the most fortunate. Only from the hope of a future heavenly life free from pain could he draw the strength to face the ills of earthly existence. "Without the supposition of a future state," he remarked, "mankind and this globe appear to me the most sublime and beautiful bubble and bauble that imagination can conceive."[38] For Adams the future state had become what it has been to most Christian Americans ever since: an otherworldly heaven eternally

---

[36] *Writings* (Smyth ed.), IX, 102, 657; X, 66–67. I am obliged to Professor Delmage for these references, *op. cit.*, note 4 above.

[37] Wilstach, pp. 119–20.

[38] Wilstach, pp. 136–37.

removed from earth to which souls repair after death, and where the ultimate balance of pleasure over pain is assured by divine benevolence. The "heaven" of modern Christianity thus came to the rescue of a faltering hedonism, which was not quite sure after all whether the balance of earthly pleasure over pain was worth the candle.

But what had all of this to do with attitudes towards history? It simply indicated that for at least one representative of the age the idea that the creation was infinitely good and that evil or pain had a sufficient function in displaying that goodness was no longer convincing. Human experience, individually and collectively, was both incomplete and imperfect, and while for personal fulfillment one looked to heaven beyond the grave, for social fulfillment one anticipated the steady advance of morals and intellect. These matters were rather elaborately developed in the famous deistic tract, *Reason the Only Oracle of Man* (1784), traditionally ascribed to Ethan Allen. But to find the argument in the last letters of John Adams, who in earlier life had been such a staunch representative of enlightened modes of thought, suggests the pervasiveness of the new point of view. Christians, Jews, Mohammedans, and Hindoos, Adams observed, all share a similar hope for a future state analogous to the Christian millennium. But "you and I," he wrote to Jefferson in 1821, "hope for splendid improvements in human society, and vast amelioration in the condition of mankind. Our faith may be supposed by more rational arguments than any of the former. I own I am very sanguine in the belief of them, as I hope and believe you are."[39]

When he had earlier employed the cyclical view of history Adams would hardly have called it a "faith." His emotions had not then been attached to a future which would right current evils, which was incidentally one reason why his interest in history had revealed such a different quality from that found in nineteenth century romantics who searched the past for confirmation of their faith in the future.

Thus the reaction to the millennialism of enthusiastic revivalists was a theory of cyclical fluctuation within a static historical continuum. The dynamic element within the cycle was the moral factor. But the implicit conservatism of this view, and the countervailing weight of American experience, seriously limited its utility in the revolutionary environment of the seventeen-seventies and eighties. The new synthesis which began to emerge after the revolution, the idea of progress, drew from millennialism its sense of the irreversible secular trend of the historical process, and from the moralism of the cyclical theory the assumption that the rôle of the individual in history is a purposive and creative one.

39 Wilstach, pp. 176–77.

Sober Philosophe:
Benjamin Franklin

GERALD STOURZH

Inspired by Newton's physics, men of the Enlightenment dreamed of reordering society in the light of Natural Law and Reason. The movement from the Puritan past to the new age of the Enlightenment is dramatized in the life of Benjamin Franklin. As colonial agent, he had spent eighteen years in London, where he enjoyed membership in the scientific Royal Society and nursed his vision of a British Empire in which an expanding America would be the brightest jewel. Franklin was as contemptuous of theology as he was absorbed with morality, public affairs, and natural science. A cosmopolitan, whose worldly wit and literary skill added to the luster of his reputation abroad as a scientist and republican, Franklin was also a child of New England Puritanism. The sober flavor of the early American Enlightenment is evident in Franklin's thought, which historians have too often merged with glib generalizations about the Age of Reason.

PERHAPS NO PERIOD OF MODERN HISTORY HAS BEEN MORE A VICTIM OF generalization than the Age of Enlightenment. The worship of reason and progress and belief in the essential goodness and perfectibility of human nature are most commonly associated with the 18th century climate of opinion. Many of the stereotypes which have been applied to it have automatically been transferred to Benjamin Franklin. Already to contemporaries of his old age, Franklin seemed the very personification of the Age of Reason. Condorcet, who had known Franklin personally, summed up his description of Franklin's political career as follows: "In a word, his politics were those of a man who believed in the power of reason and the reality of virtue."[1] In Germany, an admirer was even

Gerald Stourzh, "Reason and Power in Benjamin Franklin's Political Thought," *American Political Science Review*, 47, no. 4 (1953), pp. 1092–1115. Reprinted by permission of the author and the publisher.

[1] *Oeuvres du Marquis de Condorcet*, eds. A. Condorcet O'Connor and M. F. Arago, 2nd ed., 12 vols. (Paris, 1847–49), Vol. 3, p. 420.

more enthusiastic: "Reason and virtue, made possible through reason alone, consequently again reason and nothing but reason, is the magic with which Benjamin Franklin conquered heaven and earth."[2] This is also the judgment of posterity. F. L. Mott and Chester E. Jorgensen, who have so far presented the most acute analysis of Franklin's thought and its relationship to the intellectual history of his time, do not hesitate to call him "the completest colonial representative" of the Age of Enlightenment.[3] Unanimous agreement seems to exist that Franklin was "in tune with his time."[4]

This essay will attempt to show that these generalizations, instead of illuminating the essence of Franklin's moral and political philosophy, tend rather to obscure some of the mainsprings of his thought and action. Our investigation rests upon the assumption that man's understanding of politics is inseparable from his conception of human nature. Consequently, this reappraisal of Franklin's political thought will subject his views on human nature to close scrutiny; it is hoped that this procedure may lead to a rejection of some of the cliches to which he has fallen victim.

I. THE "GREAT CHAIN OF BEING"

Many of the notions which are commonly applied to the 18th century, such as the belief in progress and in the perfectibility of human nature, are significant chiefly with respect to the currents of thought and action related to the American and French Revolutions, and do little to deepen our understanding of earlier developments. So it is to the first half of the 18th century that we must now turn. We are prone to overlook the extraordinary difference in age which separated Franklin from the other Founding Fathers of the Republic. Franklin was born in 1706, twenty-six years before Washington, twenty-nine years before John Adams, thirty-seven years before Jefferson, thirty-nine years before John Jay, forty-five years before James Madison, and fifty-one years before Alexander Hamilton.

---

[2] Georg Forster, "Erinnerungen aus dem Jahre 1790," in "Kleine Schriften," *Georg Forsters saemmtliche Schriften*, ed. by his daughter, 9 vols. (Leipzig, 1843), Vol. 6, p. 207.

[3] *Benjamin Franklin, Representative Selections with Introduction, Bibliography, and Notes*, eds. F. L. Mott and Chester E. Jorgenson (New York, 1936), p. xiii.

[4] Carl Becker, review of the Franklin Institute's *Meet Dr. Franklin*, in *American Historical Review*, Vol. 50, p. 142 (Oct., 1944). Cf. Henry Steele Commager's statement that it was the faith in reason which gave unity to Franklin's life. "Franklin, the American," review of Carl Van Doren's *Benjamin Franklin*, in *New York Times Book Review*, Oct. 9, 1938, p. 1. Charles A. Beard explicitly referred to Franklin as an outstanding example of American writers on progress. Introduction to J. B. Bury, *The Idea of Progress* (New York, 1932), p. xxxvii.

Franklin's fame as a social and natural philosopher rests mainly on the achievements of his middle and late years. One needs to remember, however, that he was a moral philosopher long before he became a natural philosopher and before he advised his fellowmen how to acquire wealth.[5] At the age of twenty-two, he formed a "club for mutual improvement,"[6] the Junto, where great emphasis was laid on moral or political problems. Whether self-interest was the root of human action, whether man could attain perfection, whether "encroachments on the just liberties of the people"[7] had taken place—all these things were matters of discussion at Franklin's club. Already at the age of nineteen, during his first stay in London, he had printed his first independent opus, *A Dissertation on Liberty and Necessity, Pleasure and Pain.*[8] This piece showed that no trace was left of his Presbyterian family background. The secularization of his thought had been completed.[9] Gone were the Puritan belief in revelation and the Christian conception of

[5] Even after having achieved world-wide fame as a natural philosopher, he observed that we deserve reprehension if "we neglect the Knowledge and Practice of essential Duties" in order to attain eminence in the knowledge of nature. *The Writings of Benjamin Franklin,* ed. Henry Albert Smyth, 10 vols. (New York, 1905–7), Vol. 4, p. 22. (Hereafter cited as *Writings.*)

[6] *Autobiography, Writings,* Vol. I, p. 22.

[7] James Parton, *Life and Times of Benjamin Franklin,* 2d ed., 2 vols. (Boston, 1897), Vol. I, p. 160. See also *Writings,* Vol. 2, p. 89. The authors who so far have most closely scrutinized Franklin's political thought do not see the relevance of many of the younger Franklin's remarks on human nature, arbitrary government, or the nature of political dispute to his concept of politics. See M. R. Eiselen, *Franklin's Political Theories* (Garden City, N. Y., 1928), p. 13; R. D. Miles, "The Political Philosophy of Benjamin Franklin," unpub. diss. (Univ. of Michigan, 1949), p. 36; *Benjamin Franklin, Representative Selections* (cited in note 3), p. lxxxii. The most recent work in this field, Clinton Rossiter's "The Political Theory of Benjamin Franklin," *Pennsylvania Magazine of History and Biography,* Vol. 76, pp. 259–93 (July, 1952), pays no attention to Franklin's conception of human nature and his attitude towards the problem of power and the ends of political life. Rossiter's contention (p. 268) is that Franklin "limited his own thought process to the one devastating question: *Does it work?,* or more exactly, *Does it work well?*" Franklin, however, like everybody else, had certain ends and goals in view, and the question "Does it work?" is meaningless without the context of certain basic desiderata.

[8] This little work has been omitted in the Smyth edition of Franklin's writings, because "the work has no value, and it would be an injury and an offence to the memory of Franklin to republish it." *Writings,* Vol. 2, p. vi. It is, however, reprinted as an appendix to Parton, *op. cit.,* Vol. 1, and has since been republished independently with a bibliographical note by Lawrence C. Wroth (New York, 1930).

[9] See Herbert Schneider, "The Significance of Benjamin Franklin's Moral Philosophy," *Columbia University Studies in the History of Ideas,* Vol. 2, p. 298 (1918).

human nature which, paradoxically, included the notion of the depravity of man, as well as of his uniqueness among all created beings.[10] Franklin's *Dissertation* shows that he was thoroughly acquainted with the leading ideas of his time. The early decades of the 18th century were characterized by the climate of opinion which has been aptly called "cosmic Toryism."[11] Pope's *Essay on Man* and many pages of Addison's *Spectator*—both of which Franklin admired—most perfectly set forth the creed of a new age. Overshadowing everything else, there was joy about the discoveries of the human mind, which had solved the enigma of creation:

> Nature and Nature's Laws lay hid in Night:
> GOD said, *Let Newton be!* and all was Light.[12]

The perfection of that Great Machine, the Newtonian universe, filling humanity with admiration for the Divine Watchmaker, seemed to suggest that this world was indeed the best of all possible worlds. Everything was necessary, was good. Pope's "Whatever is, is right," is the key phrase of this period. The goodness of the Creator revealed itself in His giving existence to all possible creatures. The universe "presented

---

[10] In his *Autobiography,* Franklin acknowledges his debt to Shaftesbury and Collins for becoming "a real doubter in many points of our religious doctrine." *Writings,* Vol. 1, p. 244. The question of Franklin's attitude toward the great moral philosophers and of their influence upon him is considerably more difficult to determine than the same question with regard to John Adams or Thomas Jefferson. With the exception of authors named in the *Autobiography,* comments on books Franklin read are extremely rare. His library has not been preserved; there is, however, a list of books known to have been in Franklin's library at the time of his death (compiled by Dr. George Simpson Eddy in Princeton University; photostat in the library of the American Philosophical Society in Philadelphia). See also Mr. Eddy's article, "Dr. Benjamin Franklin's Library," *Proceedings of the American Antiquarian Society,* new series, Vol. 34, pp. 206–26 (Oct., 1924). Except for comments in some English pamphlets, there exist nothing like the voluminous marginal notes of John Adams and Jefferson. Also he was not able to keep up a correspondence like Adams' or Jefferson's, discussing great problems from the perspective of a long life in retirement after the great events of their lives had taken place. Immersed in public business almost until his death, Franklin does not seem to have had much time left over for reading. Benjamin Rush told John Adams that "Dr. Franklin thought a great deal, wrote occasionally, but read during the middle and later years of his life very little." October 31, 1807, in Benjamin Rush, *The Letters of Benjamin Rush,* ed. L. H. Butterfield, 2 vols. (Princeton, 1951), Vol. 2, p. 953. For a compilation of the authors with whom Franklin was acquainted, see Lois Margaret MacLaurin, *Franklin's Vocabulary* (Garden City, N.Y., 1928), Ch. 1, and *Benjamin Franklin, Representative Selections* (cited in note 3), p. lv.

[11] Basil Willey, *The Eighteenth Century Background* (London, 1940), Ch. 3, *passim.*

[12] Pope's epitaph intended for Newton's tomb.

the spectacle of a continuous scale or ladder of creatures, extending without a break from the worm to the seraph."[13] Somewhere in this "Great Chain of Being," to use a favorite phrase of the period,[14] there must be a place for Man. Man, as it were, formed the "middle link" between lower and higher creatures. No wonder, then, that Franklin chose as a motto for his *Dissertation* the following lines of Dryden:

> Whatever is, is in its Causes just,
> Since all Things are by Fate; but purblind Man
> Sees but a part o' th' Chain, the nearest Link,
> His Eyes not carrying to the equal Beam
> That poises all above.[15]

The consequences of the conception of the universe as a "Great Chain of Being" for Franklin's understanding of human nature are highly significant. To be sure, man had liberated himself from the oppression of Original Sin, and in his newly established innocence he hailed the Creator and praised the Creation. But if the depravity of human nature had been banished, so had man's striving for redemption, man's aspiration for perfection. There was nothing left which ought to be redeemed. Indeed, in the new rational order of the universe, it would not seem proper to long for a higher place in the hierarchy of beings. Man's release from the anguish of Original Sin was accompanied by a lowering of the goals of human life. "The imperfection of man is indispensable to the fullness of the hierarchy of being." Man had, so to speak, already attained the grade of perfection which belonged to his station. From the point of view of mortality, then, what this amounted to was a "counsel of imperfection—an ethics of prudent mediocrity."[16]

[16] Lovejoy, *op. cit.,* pp. 199, 200.

Quiet contentment with, and enjoyment of, one's place in the Great Chain of Being must have been a comforting creed for the wealthy and educated classes of the Augustan Age:

[13] Willey, *op. cit.,* pp. 47–48.

[14] See A. O. Lovejoy, *The Great Chain of Being* (Cambridge, Mass., 1936). This brilliant analysis of that complex of ideas has been applied to Franklin only once, although it offers important clues for an understanding of Franklin's conception of human nature. Arthur Stuart Pitt in "The Sources, Significance, and Date of Franklin's 'An Arabian Tale,' " *Publications of the Modern Language Association,* Vol. 57, pp. 155–68 (March, 1942), applies Lovejoy's analysis to one piece of Franklin's and does not refer to relevant writings of Franklin's youth in which this idea may also be found. Pitt's article is valuable in pointing out the sources from which Franklin could have accepted the idea directly, namely Locke, Milton, Addison, and Pope.

[15] Parton, *Life and Times of Benjamin Franklin* (cited in note 7), Vol. 1, p. 605.

> Order is Heav'n's first law; and this confest,
> Some are, and must be, greater than the rest,
> More rich, more wise.[17]

This was not the optimism of progress, which we usually associate with the eighteenth century. It was an optimism of acceptance;[18] for the rich and complacent, the real and the good seemed indeed to coincide.

Not so for Benjamin Franklin. Late in his life, in 1771, he referred to "the poverty and obscurity in which I was born and bred." His innate desire for justice and equality, his keen awareness of existing conditions of injustice and inequality, finally his own experience of things which he could not possibly call just or good—for instance, he tells us that his brother's "harsh and tyrannical treatment of me might be a means of impressing me with that aversion to arbitrary power that has stuck to me through my whole life"[19]—all this contravened the facile optimism of the Augustan Age.

Franklin, indeed, accepted the cosmological premises of his age (as witness the above quoted motto of the *Dissertation*). But his conclusions make the edifice of "Cosmic Toryism"—so imposing in Pope's magnificent language—appear a mockery and an absurdity. Franklin's argumentation was simple enough: God being all-powerful and good, man could have no free will, and the distinction between good and evil had to be abolished. He also argued that pain or uneasiness was the mainspring of all our actions, and that pleasure was produced by the removal of this uneasiness. It followed that *"No State of Life can be happier than the present, because Pleasure and Pain are inseparable."* The unintentional irony of this brand of optimism cannot be better expressed than in young Franklin's conclusion:

I am sensible that the Doctrine here advanc'd, if it were to be publish'd, would meet with but an indifferent Reception. Mankind naturally and generally love to be flatter'd: Whatever sooths our Pride, and tends to exalt our Species above the rest of the Creation, we are pleas'd with and easily believe, when ungrateful Truths shall be with the utmost Indignation rejected. "What! bring ourselves down to an Equality with the Beasts of the Field! With the meanest part of the Creation! 'Tis insufferable!" But, (to use a Piece of *common* Sense) our *Geese* are but *Geese* tho' we may think 'em *Swans;* and Truth will be Truth tho' it sometimes prove mortifying and distasteful.[20]

---

[17] Alexander Pope, "An Essay on Man," Epistle 4, in *Selected Works,* Modern Library ed. (New York, 1948), p. 127.

[18] Willey, *op. cit.,* p. 56.

[19] *Autobiography, Writings,* Vol. 1, pp. 226, 247 (n. 1).

[20] Parton, *op. cit.,* Vol. 1, p. 617.

The dilemma which confronted him at the age of nineteen is characteristic of most eighteenth-century philosophy: "If nature is good, then
there is no evil in the world; if there is evil in the world, then nature
so far is not good."[21]

Franklin cut this Gordian knot by sacrificing "Reason" to "Experience."
He turned away from metaphysics for the quite pragmatic reason that his
denial of good and evil did not provide him with a basis for the attain-
ment of social and individual happiness:

> Revelation had indeed no weight with me, as such; but I entertain'd an
> opinion that, though certain actions might not be bad *because* they were
> forbidden by it, or good *because* it commanded them, yet probably these
> actions might be forbidden *because* they were bad for us, or commanded
> *because* they were beneficial to us. . . .[22]

To achieve useful things rather than indulge in doubtful metaphysical
speculations, to become a doer of good—these, then, became the principal
aims of Franklin's thought and action.[23]

This fundamental change from the earlier to the later Enlightenment—
from passive contemplation to improvement, from a static to a dynamic
conception of human affairs—did contribute to the substitution of the
idea of human perfectibility for the idea of human perfection—a very
limited kind of perfection, as we have seen; but it was by no means
sufficient to bring about the faith in the perfectibility of human nature.
Something else was needed: proof that "social evils were due neither to
innate and incorrigible disabilities of the human being nor the nature
of things, but simply to ignorance and prejudices."[24] The associationist
psychology, elaborating Locke's theory of the malleability of human
nature, provided the basis for the expansion of the idea of progress
and perfectibility from the purely intellectual domain into the realm
of moral and social life in general. The Age of Reason, then, presents
us with a more perplexing picture than we might have supposed.

Reason, after all, may mean three different things: reason as a faculty
of man; reason as a quality of the universe; and reason as a temper
in the conduct of human affairs.[25] We might venture the generalization

21 Carl Becker, *The Heavenly City of the Eighteenth Century Philosophers* (New
Haven, 1932), p. 69.

22 *Autobiography, Writings,* Vol. 1, p. 296. See also *Writings,* Vol. 7, p. 412.

23 See *Writings,* Vol. 1, p. 341; Vol. 2, p. 215; Vol. 3, p. 145; Vol. 9, p. 208;
Vol. 10, p. 38

24 Bury, *The Idea of Progress* (cited in note 4), p 128.

25 This distinction is Roland Bainton's. See his "The Appeal to Reason and the
American Revolution," in *The Constitution Reconsidered,* ed. Conyers Read (New
York, 1938), p. 121.

that the earlier Enlightenment stressed reason as the quality of the New-tonian universe, whereas the later Enlightenment, in spite of important exceptions, exalted the power of human reason to mold the moral and social life of mankind.[26] Franklin's "reason," as we shall see presently, is above all a temper in the conduct of human affairs.

This discussion is important for a correct understanding of Franklin's position in the center of the cross-currents of the Age of Enlightenment. The fact that the roots of his thought are to be found in the early Enlightenment is not always realized, or, if realized, not always suffi-ciently explained. Julian P. Boyd, in his introduction to Carl Becker's biographical sketch of Franklin, states that Franklin and Jefferson believed "that men would be amenable to rational persuasion, that they would thereby be induced to promote their own and their fellows' best interests, and that, in the end, perfect felicity for man and society would be achieved."[27] These ideas are certainly suggestive of the later Enlighten-ment, and appear to be more applicable to Jefferson than to Franklin. Carl Becker himself asserts, somewhat ambiguously and with undue generalization, that Franklin "was a true child of the Enlightenment, not indeed of the school of Rousseau, but of Defoe and Pope and Swift, of Fontenelle and Montesquieu and Voltaire."[28] There is little evidence that this school prophesied the achievement of perfect felicity for man and society.

Bernard Mandeville, a personal acquaintance of Franklin, joined the chorus of those who proclaimed the compatibility of human imperfection and the general harmony. "Private Vices, Public Benefits" was the sub-title of his famous *Fable of the Bees,* which Franklin owned and prob-ably read. Mandeville's paradoxical doctrines must have been a powerful challenge to Franklin's young mind. "The Moral Virtues," Mandeville asserted in terms reminiscent of Machiavelli, "are the Political Offspring which Flattery begot upon Pride." While arguing that men are actuated by self-interest and that this self-interest promotes the prosperity of society as a whole, Mandeville maintains a rigorous standard of virtue, declaring those acts alone to be virtuous "by which Man, contrary to the impulse of Nature, should endeavour the Benefit of others, or the

---

[26] Cf. A. O. Lovejoy's statement: "The authors who were perhaps the most influential and the most representative in the early and mid-eighteenth century, made a great point of reducing man's claims to 'reason' to a minimum." " 'Pride' in Eighteenth Century Thought," in *Essays in the History of Ideas* (Baltimore, 1948), p. 68.

[27] Carl Becker, *Benjamin Franklin* (Ithaca, 1946), p. ix.

[28] *Ibid.,* p. 31.

Conquest of his own Passions out of a Rational Ambition of being good."[29]

By making ethical standards so excessively rigorous, Mandeville rendered them impossible of observance, and indirectly (though intentionally) pointed out their irrelevance for practical life. The very rigor of his ethical demands in contrast to his practical devices suggests that Mandeville lacked "idealism." This was not the case with Franklin. The consciously paradoxical Mandeville could offer no salvation for the young Franklin caught on the horns of his own dilemma. Shaftesbury, Mandeville's *bête noire*—whose works were already familiar to Franklin —had a more promising solution. In his *Inquiry Concerning Virtue or Merit* (1699), Shaftesbury had asserted that man by nature possesses a faculty to distinguish and to prefer what is right—the famous "moral sense."

Franklin's option for Shaftesbury was made clear from his reprinting two dialogues "Between Philocles and Horatio, . . . concerning Virtue and Pleasure" from the *London Journal* of 1729 in the *Pennsylvania Gazette* of 1730. In the second dialogue, reason was described as the chief faculty of man, and reasonable and morally good actions were defined as actions preservative of the human kind and naturally tending to produce real and unmixed happiness. These dialogues until recently have been held to be Franklin's own work; however, a reference in the *Autobiography* to a "Socratic dialogue" and "a discourse on self-denial," traditionally interpreted as concerning the two dialogues between Philocles and Horatio, recently has been shown to concern two pieces published in the *Pennsylvania Gazette* of 1735. The first piece is a dialogue between Crito and Socrates, never before correctly attributed to Franklin, in which he asserted that the "SCIENCE OF VIRTUE" was "of more worth, and of more consequence" to one's happiness than all other knowledge put together; in the second piece, a discourse on self-denial, Franklin combated the (Mandevillean) idea that "the greater the *Self-Denial* the greater the Virtue." Thirty-three years later, Franklin was still following Shaftesbury when he exhorted: "Be in general virtuous, and you will be happy." However, we shall see later that Franklin, in the last analysis, was not as far removed from Mandeville's pessimism as these cheerful views would suggest. His was a sort of middle position between Mandeville's "realism" and Shaftesbury's "idealism."[30]

[29] Bernard Mandeville, *The Fable of the Bees,* ed. F. B. Kaye, 2 vols. (Oxford, 1924), Vol. 1, pp. 48–49, 51. Franklin owned Mandeville's work, according to a list in the Mason-Franklin Collection of the Yale University Library. He was introduced to Mandeville during his first stay in London. *Writings,* Vol. 1, p. 278.

[30] The proof that the two dialogues between Philocles and Horatio were not written by Franklin and the identification of the two other pieces have been

II. The Idea of Progress

The restraining influence of the idea of the Great Chain of Being retained its hold on Franklin after his return to a more conventional recognition of good and evil. In his "Articles of Belief" of 1728 he said that "Man is not the most perfect Being but one, rather as there are many Degrees of Beings his Inferiors, so there are many Degrees of Beings superior to him."[31] Franklin presented the following question and answers to the discussions in the Junto:

Can a man arrive at perfection in his life, as some believe; or is it impossible, as others believe?

Answer. Perhaps they differ in the meaning of the word *perfection.* I suppose the perfection of any thing to be only the greatest the nature of the thing is capable of. . . .

If they mean a man cannot in this life be so perfect as an angel, it may be true; for an angel, by being incorporeal, is allowed some perfections we are at present incapable of, and less liable to some imperfections than we are liable to. If they mean a man is not capable of being perfect here as he is capable of being in heaven, that may be true likewise. But that a man is not capable of being so perfect here, is not sense. . . . In the above sense, there may be a perfect oyster, a perfect horse, a perfect ship; why not a perfect man? That is, as perfect as his present nature and circumstance admit.[32]

We note here the acknowledgment of man's necessarily "imperfect" state of perfection. However, it is striking to see that Franklin refused to employ this theory as a justification of the status quo. Within certain bounds, change, or progress for the better, was possible. Many years later, Franklin was to use exactly the same argument in the debate on the status of America within the British Empire. A pro-English writer had presented the familiar argument of "Cosmic Toryism" (and of conservatism in general, of course): "To expect perfection in human institutions is absurd." Franklin retorted indignantly: "Does this justify

---

furnished by Alfred O. Aldridge, "Franklin's 'Shaftesburian' Dialogues Not Franklin's: A Revision of the Franklin Canon," *American Literature,* Vol. 21, pp. 151–59 (May, 1949). See also *Writings,* Vol. 1, p. 343; Vol. 2, pp. 168–69. The discourse on self-denial is printed in *The Complete Works of Benjamin Franklin,* ed. John Bigelow, 10 vols. (New York, 1887–88), Vol. 1, pp. 414–17. The last quote, written in 1768, is in *Writings,* Vol. 5, p. 159.

[31] *Writings,* Vol. 2, p. 92; see also Vol. 10, p. 124 and note 14, above.

[32] *The Works of Benjamin Franklin,* ed. Jared Sparks, 10 vols. (Boston, 1836–40), Vol. 2, p. 554.

any and every Imperfection that can be invented or added to our Constitution?"[33]

This attitude differs from the belief in moral progress and perfectibility. There are, however, some passages in Franklin's later writings, better known than the preceding ones, which seem to suggest his agreement with the creed of moral progress and perfectibility. Two years before his death, looking with considerable satisfaction upon the achievements of his country and his own life, he explained to a Boston clergyman his belief in "the growing felicity of mankind, from the improvements in philosophy, morals, politics"; he also stressed "the invention and acquisition of new and useful utensils and instruments" and concluded that "invention and improvement are prolific. . . . The present progress is rapid." However, he immediately added: "I see a little absurdity in what I have just written, but it is to a friend, who will wink and let it pass."[34]

There remains, then, a wide gulf between this qualified view of human progress and the exuberant joy over the progress of man's rational and moral faculties so perfectly expressed in the lines of a good friend of Franklin's, the British non-conformist clergyman and philosopher, Joseph Priestley:

> Whatever was the beginning of this world, the end will be glorious and paradisiacal beyond what our imaginations can now conceive. Extravagant as some people may suppose these views to be, I think I could show them to be fairly suggested by the true theory of human nature and to arise from the natural course of human affairs.[35]

Franklin himself was well aware of this gulf. He distinguished sharply between man's intellectual progress and the steadily increasing power of man over matter, on the one hand, and the permanency of moral imperfection, on the other. He wrote to Priestley in 1782:

> I should rejoice much, if I could once more recover the Leisure to search with you into the works of Nature; I mean the *inanimate,* not the *animate* or moral part of them, the more I discover'd of the former, the more I admir'd them; the more I know of the latter, the more I am disgusted with them. Men I find to be a Sort of Beings very badly constructed, as they are generally more easily provok'd than reconcil'd, more disposed to do Mischief to each other than to make Reparation, much more easily deceiv'd than undeceiv'd, and having more Pride and even Pleasure in killing than in begetting one another.

---

[33] Franklin's marginal notes in [Matthew C. Wheelock], *Reflections Moral and Political on Great Britain and the Colonies* (London, 1770), p. 48. Franklin's copy in the Jefferson Collection of the Library of Congress.

[34] *Writings,* Vol. 9, p. 651. See also Vol. 9, pp. 489, 530; Vol. 1, p. 226.

[35] Quoted by Bury, *The Idea of Progress* (cited in note 4), pp. 221–22.

He had begun to doubt, he continued, whether "the Species were really worth producing or preserving. . . . I know, you have no such Doubts because, in your zeal for their welfare, you are taking a great deal of pains to save their Souls. Perhaps, as you grow older, you may look upon this as a hopeless Project."[36]

One is struck by the remarkable constancy of Franklin's views on human nature. In 1787 he tried to dissuade the author of a work on natural religion from publishing it. In this famous letter, we may find the quintessence of Franklin's concept of human nature. There is little of the trust in human reason which is so generally supposed to be a mark of his moral teachings:

> You yourself may find it easy to live a virtuous Life, without the Assistance afforded by Religion; you having a clear perception of the Advantages of Virtue, and the Disadvantages of Vice, and possessing a Strength of Resolution sufficient to enable you to resist common Temptations. But think how great a Proportion of Mankind consists of weak and ignorant Men and Women, and of inexperienc'd, and inconsiderate Youth of both Sexes, who have need of the Motives of Religion to restrain them from Vice, and support their Virtue, and retain them in the Practice of it till it becomes *habitual,* which is the Great Point for its Security. . . . If men are so wicked as we now see them *with religion,* what would they be *if without it?*[37]

One is reminded of Gibbon's approval of conditions in the Rome of the Antonines, where all religions were considered equally false by the wise, equally true by the people, and equally useful by the magistrates.

III: THE BELIEF IN "REASON"

Reason as a temper in the conduct of human affairs counted much with Franklin, as we shall see later. However, reason as a faculty of the human mind, stronger than our desires or passions, counted far less. Often Franklin candidly and smilingly referred to the weakness of reason. In his *Autobiography,* he tells us of his struggle "between principle and inclination" when, on his first voyage to Philadelphia, his vegetarian principles came into conflict with his love of eating fish. Remembering that greater fish ate the smaller ones, he did not see any reason why he should not eat fish: "So convenient a thing it is to be a *reasonable creature,* since it enables one to find or make a reason for every thing one has a mind to do."[38]

[36] *Writings,* Vol. 8, pp. 451–52.
[37] *Writings,* Vol. 9, pp. 521–22. See also Vol. 2, pp. 203, 393, and Vol. 9, pp. 600–1.
[38] *Writings,* Vol. 1, p. 267. See also Vol. 5, p. 225, and Vol. 9, p. 512.

Reason as a guide to human happiness was recognized by Franklin only to a limited degree.

> Our Reason would still be of more Use to us, if it could enable us to *prevent* the Evils it can hardly enable us to *bear.*—But in that it is so deficient, and in other things so often misleads us, that I have sometimes been almost tempted to wish we had been furnished with a good sensible Instinct instead of it.[39]

Trial and error appeared to him more useful to this end than abstract reasoning. "We are, I think, in the right Road of Improvement, for we are making Experiments. I do not oppose all that seem wrong, for the Multitude are more effectually set right by Experience, than kept from going wrong by Reasoning with them." Another time he put it even more bluntly: "What assurance of the *Future* can be better founded than that which is built on Experience of the *Past?*"[40] His scepticism about the efficacy of "reason" also appears in his opinion that "happiness in this life rather depends on internals than externals; and that, besides the natural effects of wisdom and virtue, vice and folly, there is such a thing as a happy or an unhappy constitution."[41]

There remains one problem with regard to Franklin's rather modest view of the power of human reason in moral matters: his serenity—some might call it complacency—in spite of his awareness of the disorder and imperfection of human life. Sometimes, it is true, he was uneasy:

> I rather suspect, from certain circumstances, that though the general government of the universe is well administered, our particular little affairs are perhaps below notice, and left to take the chance of human prudence or imprudence, as either may happen to be uppermost. It is, however, an uncomfortable thought, and I leave it.[42]

But on another occasion Franklin felt obliged to quiet the anxieties of his sister, who had been upset by his remark that men "are devils to one another":

[39] *The Letters of Benjamin Franklin & Jane Mecom,* ed. Carl Van Doren (Princeton, 1950), p. 112.

[40] *Writings,* Vol. 9, p. 489, and Vol. 4, p. 250. On another occasion Franklin acknowledged the weakness of reason by the use of a pungent folk saying: "An Answer now occurs to me, for that Question of Robinson Crusoe's Man Friday, which I once thought unanswerable, *Why God no kill the devil?* It is to be found in the Scottish Proverb, *'Ye'd do little for God an the Dell' were dead.'* " To John Whitehurst, New York, June 27, 1763. Unpub. letter in the Mason-Franklin Collection of the Yale University Library. Cf. also Vol. 3, pp. 16–17, Vol. 4, p. 120, and Vol. 6, p. 424.

[41] *Writings,* Vol. 3, p. 457. See also Vol. 9, p. 548.

[42] Rev. L. Tyerman, *Life of the Rev. George Whitefield,* 2 vols. (London, 1876), Vol. 2, pp. 540–41, quoted in *Benjamin Franklin, Representative Selections* (cited in note 3), p. cxxxvi.

I meant no more by saying Mankind were Devils to one another, than that being in general superior to the Malice of the other Creatures, they were not so much tormented by them as by themselves. Upon the whole I am much disposed to like the World as I find it, & to doubt my own Judgment as to what would mend it. I see so much Wisdom in what I understand of its Creation and Government, that I suspect equal Wisdom may be in what I do not understand: and thence have perhaps as much Trust in God as the most pious Christian.[43]

Indeed, Franklin's pessimism does not contain that quality of the tragic sense of life which inevitably presents itself wherever a recognition of the discrepancy between man's actual depravity and the loftiness of his aspirations exists.

We suggest a threefold explanation for this phenomenon: first of all, as we have pointed out, the complex of ideas associated with the concept of the "Great Chain of Being," predominant at the time of Franklin's youth, worked in favor of bridging this gulf by lowering the goals of human endeavor. Secondly, the success story of his own life taught him that certain valuable things in human life can be achieved. Thirdly, we cannot help thinking that Franklin himself was endowed with that "happy constitution" which he deemed a requisite for true happiness in this life.

IV. THE PASSION OF PRIDE

Having discovered that Franklin acknowledged the imperfection of human reason and consequently the existence and importance of the passions to a greater degree than one might have supposed, let us specify in greater detail his insight into the nature of the two outstanding passions of social life, the desire for wealth and the desire for power—avarice and ambition. "That I may avoid Avarice and Ambition . . .—Help me, O Father," was Franklin's prayer in the "Articles of Belief" of 1728.[44]

The universal fame of Poor Richard and the description of Franklin's own "way to wealth" in his *Autobiography* (Franklin's account of his life ends with his arrival in London in 1757 for the first of his three great public missions in Europe) have led many people to see in Franklin only the ingenious businessman pursuing thrift for thrift's sake and money for money's sake. Nothing could be further from the truth than this conception. To be sure, he recognized the existence and the nature

43 *The Letters of Benjamin Franklin & Jane Mecom* (cited in note 39), pp. 124, 125–26. See also *Writings,* Vol. 2, p. 61; Vol. 4, p. 388; Vol. 9, p. 247.
44 *Writings,* Vol. 2, p. 99.

of avarice in unequivocal terms: "The Love of Money is not a Thing of certain Measure, so as that it may be easily filled and satisfied. Avarice is infinite; and where there is not good Oeconomy, no Salary, however large, will prevent Necessity."[45] He denied, however, that desire for more wealth actuated his work. His early retirement from business (1748) to devote himself to the higher things of life—chiefly to public service and scientific research—seems to prove this point.

Franklin considered wealth essentially as means to an end. He knew that it was not easy "for an empty sack to stand upright." He looked upon his fortune as an essential factor in his not having succumbed to corruption.[46] In a famous and often quoted letter to his mother, Franklin said that at the end of his life he "would rather have it said, *He lived usefully* than *He died Rich.*" At about the same time (two years after his retirement) he wrote to his printer friend William Strahan in England: "London citizens, they say, are ambitious of what they call *dying worth* a great sum. The very notion seems to me absurd."[47]

On the other hand, the motive of power and prestige found much earlier recognition in Franklin's writings; he even confessed candidly that he himself was not free from this desire and from the feeling of being superior to his fellowmen. At the age of sixteen, in his first secret contributions to his brother's *New-England Courant* (he wrote under the pseudonym Mrs. Dogood), he gave a satisfactory definition of what we nowadays would call lust for power, and what was in the eighteenth century called Pride:

Among the many reigning Vices of the Town which may at any Time come under my Consideration and Reprehension, there is none which I am more inclin'd to expose than that of *Pride.* It is acknowledged by all to be a Vice the most hateful to God and Man. Even those who nourish it themselves, hate to see it in others. The proud Man aspires after Nothing less than an unlimited Superiority over his Fellow-Creatures.[48]

As Arthur O. Lovejoy has pointed out, the idea of Pride was frequently contemplated during the earlier half of the eighteenth century.[49] There are two different, though not unrelated, conceptions of Pride. First of all, it means "the most powerful and pervasive of all passions,"

---

[45] *Writings,* Vol. 5, p. 325.

[46] *The Letters of Benjamin Franklin & Jane Mecom* (cited in note 39), p. 123.

[47] *Writings,* Vol. 3, pp. 5, 6. Cf. Benjamin Rush to John Adams: "The Doctor was a rigid economist, but he was in every stage of his life charitable, hospitable, and generous." August 19, 1811, in *Letters of Benjamin Rush* (cited in note 10), Vol. 2, p. 1093.

[48] *Writings,* Vol. 2, pp. 18–19.

[49] Lovejoy, " 'Pride' in Eighteenth Century Thought," (cited in note 26), p. 62–68.

which manifests itself in two forms: self-esteem and desire for the admiration of others. The second conception is closely connected with the idea of the Scale of Being; it means the generic Pride of man as such, the sin against the laws of order, of gradation, the revolt of man against the station which has been allotted to him by the Creator.

These different conceptions of Pride are indeed inseparable. In Franklin's own writings, the accent is on the first rather than on the second meaning. This topic runs through his work like a red thread. In 1729, at the age of 23, he wrote that "almost every Man has a strong natural Desire of being valu'd and esteem'd by the rest of his Species."[50] Observations in a letter written in 1751 testify to his keen psychological insight:

What you mention concerning the love of praise is indeed very true; it reigns more or less in every heart, though we are generally hypocrites, in that respect, and pretend to disregard praise. . . . Being forbid to praise themselves, they learn instead of it to censure others; which is only a roundabout way of praising themselves. . . . This fondness for ourselves, rather than malevolence to others, I take to be the general source of censure. . . .[51]

Quite revealing with regard to our discussion is Franklin's well-known account of his project of an "Art of Virtue." His list of virtues to be practiced contained at first only twelve: "But a Quaker friend having kindly informed me that I was generally thought proud . . . I added *Humility* to my list. . . . I cannot boast of much success in acquiring the *reality* of this virtue, but I had a good deal with regard to the *appearance* of it."[52] His account of his rise in Pennsylvania's public life and politics reflects his joy and pride about his career. In 1737 he was appointed Postmaster of Philadelphia and Justice of the Peace; in 1744 he established the American Philosophical Society; in 1748 he was chosen a member of the Council of Philadelphia; in 1749 he was appointed Provincial Grandmaster of the Colonial Masons; in 1750 he was appointed one of the commissioners to treat with the Indians in Carlisle; and in 1751 he became a member of the Assembly of Pennsylvania. He was particularly pleased with this last appointment, and he admitted candidly that his ambition was "flatter'd by all these promotions; it certainly was; for, considering my low beginning, they were great things to me."[53]

There is no change of emphasis with respect to Pride during his long

50 *Writings*, Vol. 2, p. 108.
51 *Writings*, Vol. 3, pp. 54–55.
52 *Writings*, Vol. 1, p. 337.
53 *Writings*, Vol. 1, p. 374. For Franklin's acknowledgment of his own political ambition, see *Writings*, Vol. 5, pp. 148, 206, 357; Vol. 9, pp. 488, 621.

life. The old man of 78 denounces the evil of Pride with no less fervor, though with more self-knowledge, than the boy of 16:

In reality, there is, perhaps, no one of our natural passions so hard to subdue as *pride*. Disguise it, struggle with it, beat it down, stifle it, mortify it as much as one pleases, it is still alive, and will every now and then peep out and show itself; you will see it, perhaps, often in this history; for even if I could conceive that I had compleatly overcome it, I should probably be proud of my humility.[54]

Furthermore, the experience of English political life which he acquired during his two protracted stays in England (from 1757 to 1762, and from 1765 to 1775) made an indelible impression on his mind. The corruption and venality in English politics and the disastrous blunders of English politicians which Franklin traced back to this cause[55] probably were the main reasons why he advocated at the Federal Convention of 1787 what he himself said some might regard as a "Utopian Idea": the abolition of salaries for the chief executive. The reason he gave for advocating such a step has hitherto not been appreciated as being of crucial importance for an understanding of his political thought:

There are two Passions which have a powerful Influence in the Affairs of Men. These are *Ambition* and *Avarice;* the Love of Power and the Love of Money. Separately, each of these has great Force in prompting Men to Action; but when united in View of the same Object, they have in many minds the most violent Effects. Place before the Eyes of such Men a Post of *Honour,* that shall at the same time be a Place of *Profit,* and they will move Heaven and Earth to obtain it.[56]

It has never been pointed out that this scheme of what might be called the "separation of passions" had been ripening in Franklin's mind for several years. The first expression of it is to be found early in 1783.[57] In 1784 he mentioned it several times, and it is in these statements that we find one of the few allusions to the concept of checks and balances in Franklin's thought. He recommended: "Make every place of *honour* a place of *burthen.* By that means the effect of one of the passions above-mentioned would be taken away and something would be added to counteract the other."[58]

[54] *Autobiography* (end of the part written in Passy, France, 1784), *Writings,* Vol. 1, p. 339.

[55] *Writings,* Vol. 10, p. 62. See also Vol. 5, pp. 100, 112, 117, 133. See also *Benjamin Franklin's Letters to the Press, 1758–1775,* ed. Verner W. Crane (Chapel Hill, 1950), pp. 59, 164, 232.

[56] *Writings,* Vol. 9, p. 591.

[57] *Writings,* Vol. 9, p. 23.

[58] *Writings,* Vol. 9, p. 170. See also *ibid.,* pp. 172 and 260.

V. THE NATURE OF POLITICS

Franklin's frequent praise of the general welfare did not blind him to the fact that most other people had a much narrower vision than his own. "Men will always be powerfully influenced in their Opinions and Actions by what appears to be their particular Interest," he wrote in his first tract on political economy, at the age of twenty-three.[59] Fortunately, one of the very few memoranda and notes dealing with the studies and discussions of young Franklin which have come to our knowledge directly concerns this problem. Franklin himself, in his *Autobiography*, gives us the text of *"Observations* on my reading history, in Library, May 19th, 1731" which, in his words, had been "accidentally preserv'd":

That the great affairs of the world, the wars, revolutions, etc., are carried on and affected by parties.

That the view of these parties is their present interest, or what they take to be such.

That the different views of these different parties occasion all confusion.

That while a party is carrying on a general design, each man has his particular private interest in view.

That as soon as a party has gain'd its general point, each member becomes intent upon his particular interest; which, thwarting others, breaks that party into divisions, and occasions more confusion.

That few in public affairs act from a mere view of the good of their country, whatever they may pretend; and, tho' their actings bring real good to their country, yet men primarily considered that their own and their country's interest was united, and did not act from a principle of benevolence.

That fewer still, in public affairs, act with a view for the good of mankind. . . .[60]

These lines do not mirror Shaftesbury's benevolent altruism; Franklin's contention that men act primarily from their own interest "and . . . not . . . from a principle of benevolence," "tho' their actings bring real good to their country," strongly suggests the general theme of Mandeville's work: "Private vices, public benefits."

Many decades after the foregoing observations, the contrast between Franklin's views on politics and those of the enlightened rationalism of contemporary France is clearly expressed in a discussion with the French physiocrat Dupont de Nemours. Dupont had suggested that the Federal Convention be delayed until the separate constitutions of the member states were corrected—according to physiocratic principles, of course.

[59] *Writings,* Vol. 2, p. 139.
[60] *Writings,* Vol. 1, pp. 339–40. Cf. also Vol. 2, p. 196, and Vol. 4, p. 322.

Franklin mildly observed that "we must not expect that a new government may be formed, as a game of chess may be played." He stressed that in the game of politics there were so many players with so many strong and various prejudices, "and their particular interests, independent of the general, seeming so opposite," that "the play is more like *tric-trac* with a box of dice."[61] In public, and when he was propagandizing for America in Europe, Franklin played down the evils of party strife: after the end of the War of Independence he conceded somewhat apologetically that "it is true, in some of the States there are Parties and Discords." He contended now that parties "are the common lot of Humanity," and that they exist wherever there is liberty; they even, perhaps, help to preserve it. "By the Collision of different Sentiments, Sparks of Truth are struck out, and Political Light is obtained."[62]

In private, Franklin did not conceal his suspicion that "unity out of discord" was not as easily achieved as his just quoted method of obtaining "political light" might suggest. But he certainly did not believe that passions and prejudices always, or even usually, overrule enlightened self-interest. He held that "there is a vast variety of good and ill Events, that are in some degree the Effects of Prudence or the want of it."[63] He believed that "reasonable sensible Men, can always make a reasonable scheme appear such to other reasonable Men, if they take Pains, and have Time and Opportunity for it. . . ." However, this dictum is severely limited by the conclusion: ". . . unless from some Circumstance their Honesty and Good Intentions are suspected."[64] That Franklin thought those circumstances to exist frequently, we learn from a famous message to George Washington, written in France in 1780. He told Washington how much the latter would enjoy his reputation in France, "pure and free from those little Shades that the Jealousy and Envy of a Man's Countrymen and Cotemporaries are ever endeavouring to cast over living Merit."[65]

Although Franklin himself talked so much about "Common Interests," he could be impatient when others built their arguments on this point. He observed that "it is an Insult on common sense to affect an Appearance of Generosity in a Matter of obvious Interest."[66] This belief in self-interest as a moving force of politics appears with rare clarity in marginal notes in a pamphlet whose author argued that "if the Interests

[61] *Writings*, Vol. 9, p. 659; see also p. 241.
[62] *Writings*, Vol. 10, pp. 120–21. See also Vol. 4, p. 35.
[63] *Writings*, Vol. 7, p. 358.
[64] *Writings*, Vol. 3, pp. 41–42.
[65] *Writings*, Vol. 8, p. 28. Cf. the expression of the same idea 36 years earlier in *Writings*, Vol. 2, p. 242.
[66] *Benjamin Franklin's Letters to the Press* (cited in note 55), p. 183.

of Great Britain evidently raise and fall with those of the Colonies, then the Parliament of Great Britain will have the same regard for the Colonists as for her own People." Franklin retorted:

All this Argument of the Interest of Britain and the Colonies being the *same* is fallacious and unsatisfactory. Partners in Trade have a *common* Interest, which is the same, the Flourishing of the Partnership Business: But they may moreover have each a *separate* Interest; and in pursuit of that *separate* Interest, one of them may endeavour to impose on the other, may cheat him in the Accounts, may draw to himself more than his Share of the Profits, may put upon the other more than an equal Share of the Burthen. Their having a common Interest is no Security against such Injustice. . . .[67]

VI. DEMOCRACY

It is fair to ask how Franklin's views on the above matters square with his avowal of radically democratic notions after 1775. In view of the foregoing, Franklin would not, it seems, agree with the underlying assumptions of Jeffersonian democracy, stated by Jefferson himself: "Nature hath implanted in our breasts a love of others, a sense of duty to them, a moral instinct, in short, which prompts us irresistibly to feel and to succor their distresses. . . ." It was also Jefferson who believed "that man was a rational animal, endowed by nature with rights, and with an innate sense of justice."[68] On this faith in the rationality and goodness of man, the theory of Jeffersonian democracy has been erected. Vernon L. Parrington said of Franklin that "he was a forerunner of Jefferson, like him firm in the conviction that government was good in the measure that it remained close to the people."[69] Charles A. Beard, discussing the members of the Federal Convention, tells us that Benjamin Franklin "seems to have entertained a more hopeful view of democracy than any other member of that famous group."[70] All this must seem rather strange in view of the none too optimistic conception of human

---

[67] Marginal comments in *Good Humour, or, A Way with the Colonies* (London, 1766), pp. 26–27. Franklin's copy is in the library of the Historical Society of Pennsylvania, Philadelphia. This comment is reprinted in *A Collection of the Familiar Letters and Miscellaneous Papers of Benjamin Franklin,* ed. Jared Sparks (Boston, 1833), p. 229.

[68] Jefferson to Thomas Law, June 13, 1814, and to Judge William Johnson, June 12, 1823, quoted by Adrienne Koch, *The Philosophy of Thomas Jefferson* (New York, 1943), pp. 19, 139.

[69] Vernon L. Parrington, *The Main Currents of American Thought*, 3 vols. (New York, 1930), Vol. 1, pp. 176–77.

[70] Charles A. Beard, *An Economic Interpretation of the Constitution* (New York, 1913), p. 197.

nature which we have found in Franklin. His radically democratic views after 1775—before that time his outlook seemed essentially conservative —baffled contemporary observers as it has later students.

There is, as a matter of fact, plenty of evidence of Franklin's sincere devotion to monarchy during the greater part of his life. It was the most natural thing for him to assure his friend, the famous Methodist preacher George Whitefield, that a settlement of colonies on the Ohio would be blessed with success "if we undertook it with sincere Regard to . . . the Service of our gracious King, and (which is the same thing) the Publick Good."[71] Franklin loved to contrast the corruption of Parliament and the virtues of George III. To an American friend, he said that he could "scarcely conceive a King of better Dispositions, of more exemplary virtues, or more truly desirous of promoting the Welfare of all his Subjects."[72]

Another "conservative" aspect of Franklin which cannot be glossed over lightly is his acceptance of the Puritan and mercantilistic attitude towards the economic problems of the working class. Throughout his life he was critical of the English Poor Laws. He deplored "the proneness of human nature to a life of ease, of freedom from care and labour," and he considered that laws which *"compel the rich to maintain the poor"* might possibly be "fighting against the order of God and Nature, which perhaps has appointed want and misery as the proper punishments for, and cautions against, as well as necessary consequences of, idleness and extravagance."[73] This was written in 1753. But as late as 1789, long after he had come out for the political equality of the poor and for a radical theory of property, he still confirmed to an English correspondent that "I have long been of your opinion, that your legal provision for the poor is a very great evil, operating as it does to the encouragement of idleness."[74]

Franklin's endorsement of democracy is most emphatically revealed in his advocacy of a unicameral legislature for the Commonwealth of Pennsylvania, as well as for the federal government. The issue of unicameral versus bicameral legislative bodies—an issue much discussed in

[71] *Writings*, Vol. 3, p. 339. See also Vol. 2, pp. 377–78; Vol. 4, pp. 94, 213.

[72] *Writings*, Vol. 5, p. 204. See also Vol. 5, p. 261. Another sign of Franklin's antiradical attitude during his stay in England is his disgust with the Wilkes case. See *Writings*, Vol. 5, pp. 121, 133, 134, and 150. Also *Letters and Papers of Benjamin Franklin and Richard Jackson, 1753–1785*, ed. Carl Van Doren (Philadelphia, 1947), p. 139.

[73] *Letters and Papers of Benjamin Franklin and Richard Jackson, op. cit.*, pp. 34, 35.

[74] *Writings*, Vol. 10, p. 64. See for an elaboration of his arguments "On the Labouring Poor," *Writings*, Vol. 5, pp. 122–27, and "On the Price of Corn, and Management of the Poor," *Writings*, Vol. 5, pp. 534–39.

the latter decades of the eighteenth century—reflected faithfully, as a rule, the clash of views of two different theories of human nature and of politics. The bicameral system was based on the principle of checks and balances; a pessimistic view of human nature naturally would try to forestall the abuse of power in a single and all-powerful assembly. On the other hand, most of those who trusted in the faculties of human reason did not see the necessity for a second chamber to check and harass the activities of a body of reasonable men.

In the case of Franklin, however, this correspondence of political convictions with views on human nature is lacking. He was the president of the Pennsylvania Convention of 1776 which—almost uniquely among the American states—set up a unicameral system. This, of course, filled many of the French *philosophes* with great joy. Franklin, they supposed, had secured a triumph of enlightened principles in the new world. Condorcet, in his "Éloge de Franklin," had this to say:

Franklin's voice alone decided this last provision. He thought that as enlightenment would naturally make rapid progress, above all in a country to which the revolution had given a new system, one ought to encourage the devices of perfecting legislation, and not to surround them with extrinsic obstacles. . . . The opinion contrary to his stands for that discouraging philosophy which considers error and corruption as the habitual state of societies and the development of virtue and reason as a kind of miracle which one must not expect to make enduring. It was high time that a philosophy both nobler and truer should direct the destiny of mankind, and Franklin was worthy to give the first example of it.[75]

As a matter of fact, it has since been shown that Franklin, who at the time of the Pennsylvania Convention also served in the Continental Congress, played a minor role in the adoption of the unicameral system. The unicameral legislature was rooted in the historical structure of Pennsylvania's proprietary government.[76] This, however, is irrelevant from our point of view, since Franklin endorsed and defended the unicameral system in his "Queries and Remarks respecting Alterations in the Constitution of Pennsylvania," written in November, 1789.[77]

In the opposition to checks and balances and a second chamber, Franklin's most famous companion was Thomas Paine, author of *The Age of Reason*. This similarity of views between Franklin and one of the most vocal spokesmen of the creed of reason and the perfectibility

[75] *Oeuvres de Condorcet* (cited in note 1), Vol. 3, pp. 401–2.

[76] See J. Paul Selsam, *The Pennsylvania Constitution of 1776* (Philadelphia, 1926), and Charles M. Andrews, *The Colonial Period of American History*, 4 vols. (New Haven, 1934–38), Vol. 3, p. 320.

[77] *Writings*, Vol. 10, pp. 54–60.

of man perhaps contributes to the misinterpretation of Franklin's position among the eighteenth-century philosophers. Paine's arguments against the system of checks and balances and for a single house were characteristic of the later Enlightenment:

> Freedom is the associate of innocence, not the companion of suspicion. She only requires to be cherished, not to be caged, and to be beloved is, to her, to be protected. Her residence is in the undistinguished multitude of rich and poor, and a partisan to neither is the patroness of all.[78]

This argument, of course, presupposes the rationality and goodness of human nature. We might perhaps agree with Paine that "no man was a better judge of human nature than Franklin,"[79] but Paine certainly did not have Franklin's conception of human nature.

The reasons for Franklin's almost radical attitude in 1776 and 1787 appear in his own writings. One thing seems certain: belief in the goodness and the wisdom of the people is *not* at the root of his democratic faith. This idea is quite foreign to Franklin. Discussing the Albany Plan of Union in 1754, he thought that "it is very possible, that this general government might be as well and faithfully administered without the people, as with them."[80] Nor did he fundamentally change his view in the last years of his life. "Popular favour is very precarious, being sometimes *lost* as well as *gained* by good actions." In 1788, he wrote publicly that "popular Opposition to a public Measure is no Proof of its Impropriety."[81] What a strange democrat it was who told the Federal Convention that "there is a natural Inclination in Mankind to kingly Government."[82] The most plausible and popular reason for belief in democracy, then, is eliminated.

On the other hand, Franklin did not believe in the intrinsic goodness of the wealthy or the wisdom of the powerful; he had no liking for aristocratic government, be it by an aristocracy of wealth or an aristocracy of birth. He was scornful of the House of Lords and thought "Hereditary Professors of Mathematicks" preferable to hereditary legislators because they could do less mischief.[83]

---

[78] "A Serious Address to the People of Pennsylvania on the Present Situation of their Affairs" (Dec., 1778), in *The Complete Writings of Thomas Paine,* ed. Philip S. Foner, 2 vols. (New York, 1945), Vol. 2, p. 284.

[79] "Constitutional Reform" (1805), *ibid.,* pp. 998–99.

[80] *Writings,* Vol. 3, p. 231. See also p. 309.

[81] *Writings,* Vol. 9, pp. 564, 702. In 1788, Franklin repeatedly said that there was at present the "danger of too little obedience in the *governed,*" although in general the opposite evil of "giving too much power to our *governors*" was more dreaded. *Writings,* Vol. 9, p. 638; and Vol. 10, p. 7.

[82] *Writings,* Vol. 9, p. 593.

[83] *Writings,* Vol. 6, pp. 370–71. For other attacks on the principle of hereditary honors and privileges, in connection with the Order of the Cincinnati, see *Writings,* Vol. 9, pp. 162, 336.

It is noteworthy that in the whole of Franklin's work only one reference to Montesquieu can be found; and that concerns his ideas on criminal law. Separation of powers, the role of the aristocracy in a healthy society —these are doctrines which never took possession of Franklin's mind.

The antithesis between Adams, under the influence of Harrington, and Franklin, chiefly influenced by his own experience, is remarkably complete. Adams wrote:

> It must be remembered that the rich are *people* as well as as the poor; that they have rights as well as others; they have as clear and as *sacred* a right to their large property as others have to theirs which is smaller; that oppression to them is as possible and wicked as to others. . . .[84]

Franklin mounts a formidable counterattack:

> And why should the upper House, chosen by a Minority, have equal Power with the lower chosen by a majority? Is it supposed that Wisdom is the necessary concomitant of Riches . . . and why is Property to be represented at all? . . . The Combinations of Civil Society are not like those of a Set of Merchants, who club their Property in different Proportions for Building and Freighting a Ship, and may therefore have some Right to Vote in the Disposition of the Voyage in a greater or less Degree according to their respective Contributions; but the important ends of Civil Society, and the personal Securities of Life and Liberty, these remain the same in every member of the Society; and the poorest continues to have an equal Claim to them with the most opulent. . . .[85]

It is this strong objection against the attempt to use—openly or covertly —a second chamber as a tool of class rule which seems to underlie Franklin's disapproval of the bicameral system. Franklin, it should be pointed out, was aware of the necessity and inevitability of poises and counter-poises. This is shown by his attempt, referred to above, to create a sort of balance of passions, checking avarice with ambition. There exist some, though quite rare, allusions to a balance of power concept in his utterances on imperial and international relations. The most pointed and direct reference to the idea of checks and balances, however, may be found in an unpublished letter to a well-known figure of Pennsylvania politics, Joseph Galloway, in 1767. Franklin discussed and welcomed a

[84] Quoted by Zoltan Haraszti, *John Adams and the Prophets of Progress* (Cambridge, Mass., 1952), p. 36.

[85] "Queries and Remarks . . . ," *Writings,* Vol. 10, pp. 58–61. For Franklin's disagreement with the bicameral system of the United States Constitution, see *Writings,* Vol. 9, pp. 645, 674. The paradox of Franklin's attitude is thrown into relief if one considers that even Jefferson, in his *Notes on Virginia,* raised his voice against the dangers of an "elective despotism," and exalted "those benefits" which a "proper complication of principles" would produce. *The Works of Thomas Jefferson,* ed. Paul Leicester Ford (New York and London, 1904-5), Vol. 4, p. 19.

new Circuit Bill for the judges of Pennsylvania. He suggested and encouraged an increase in the salaries to be granted by the Assembly for the judges to offset the nominating and recalling powers of the Proprietor: "From you they should therefore receive a Salary equal in Influence upon their Minds, to be held during your Pleasure. For where the Beam *is moveable,* it is only by equal Weights in opposite scales that it can possibly be kept even."[86]

Consequently, the arguments of Thomas Paine or the French *philosophes,* which derive their validity from assumptions about the goodness or rationality of human nature, do not hold in the case of Franklin. In a brilliant recent essay it has been suggested that "despite the European flavor of a Jefferson or a Franklin, the Americans refused to join in the great Enlightenment enterprise of shattering the Christian concept of sin, replacing it with an unlimited humanism, and then emerging with an earthly enterprise as glittering as the heavenly one that had been destroyed."[87] As far as Franklin is concerned, however, the alternatives of Calvinist pessimism and the "unlimited humanism" of the European Enlightenment do not really clarify the essential quality of his political thought. His thought is rooted in a climate of opinion which combined the rejection of the doctrine of original sin with a rather modest view of human nature.

It seems, then, that the desire for equality, rather than any rationalistic concepts, offers the clue to an adequate understanding of those elements in Franklin's political thought which at first sight appear inconsistent with his not too cheerful view of human goodness. His striving for equality also suggests a solution to the thorny problem of reconciling his democratic views after he had decided for American independence with his faithful loyalty to the Crown before that date. The American interest obliged him to fight against Parliament—an aristocratic body in those days—while remaining loyal to the King; in recognizing the King's sovereignty while denying the Parliament's rights over the Colonies, Franklin by necessity was driven into a position which —historically speaking—seemed to contradict his Whig principles. The complaining Americans spoke, as Lord North rightly said, the "language of Toryism."[88] During the decade before 1775 Franklin fought for the equal rights of England and the Colonies under the Crown. But his desire for equality went deeper than that. In his "Some good Whig Principles," while conceding that the government of Great Britain ought

[86] April 14, 1767, in the William L. Clements Library, Ann Arbor, Michigan.

[87] Louis Hartz, "American Political Thought and the American Revolution," this REVIEW, Vol. 46, pp. 321–42, at p. 324 (June, 1952).

[88] Quoted by G. H. Guttridge, *English Whiggism and the American Revolution* (Berkeley, 1942), p. 62.

to be lodged "in the hands of King, Lords of Parliament, and Representatives of *the whole body* of the freemen of this realm," he took care to affirm that *"every man* of the commonalty (excepting infants, insane persons, and criminals) is, of common right, and by the laws of God, *a freeman"* and that "the poor man has an *equal* right, but *more* need, to have representatives in the legislature than the rich one."[89] It has not been widely known that Franklin, in a conversation with Benjamin Vaughan, his friend and at the same time emissary of the British Prime Minister Lord Shelburne during the peace negotiations of 1782, has confirmed this view. Vaughan reported to Shelburne that "Dr. Franklin's opinions about *parliaments* are, that people should not be rejected as electors because they are at *present* ignorant"; Franklin thought that "a statesman should meliorate his people," and Vaughan supposed that Franklin "would put this, among other reasons for extending the privilege of election, that it *would* meliorate them." It was Franklin's opinion, Vaughan thought, "that the lower people are as we see them, because oppressed; & then their situation in point of manners, becomes the reason for oppressing them."[90] The fact is that Franklin's overriding concern for equality foreshadows the attacks of the socialism of later generations on the absolute sanctity of private property:

All the Property that is necessary to a Man, for the Conservation of the Individual and the Propagation of the Species, is his natural Right, which none can justly deprive him of: But all Property superfluous to such purposes is the Property of the Publick, who, by their Laws, have created it, and who may therefore by other Laws dispose of it, whenever the Welfare of the Publick shall demand such Disposition.[91]

Franklin's previously quoted speech in the Federal Convention provides us with an essential insight: he expressed belief in "a natural Inclination in Mankind to kingly Government." His reasons are revealing: "It sometimes relieves them from Aristocratic Domination. They had rather one Tyrant than 500. It gives more of the Appearance of Equality among Citizens; and that they like."[92] Equality, then, is not incompatible with monarchy.

From all this a significant conclusion may be drawn. It is an oversimplification to speak of Franklin's "conservatism" before 1775 and of

[89] *Writings,* Vol. 10, p. 130.

[90] Benjamin Vaughan to Lord Shelburne, November 24, 1782. Benjamin Vaughan Papers in the American Philosophical Society, Philadelphia. Photostat in the Benjamin Vaughan Collection in the William L. Clements Library, Ann Arbor, Michigan.

[91] *Writings,* Vol. 9, p. 138 (written in 1783). See also Vol. 10, p. 59.

[92] *Writings,* Vol. 9, p. 539.

his "radicalism" after 1775. Professor MacIver illustrates the conservative character of the first stage of American political thought preceding the appeal to natural rights by reference to Franklin, who, in spite of his later attacks on the Order of the Cincinnati, "nevertheless clung to the principle of a hereditary, though constitutional monarchy, until the tide of revolution rendered it untenable."[93] The term "conservative" does not do justice to the possibility of paying faithful allegiance to a monarchy and still disliking aristocracies of heredity or wealth. Because of his innate desire for equality, as well as his defense of the American cause against the encroachments of Parliament, Franklin found it much easier to be a monarchist. Monarchy, rather than aristocracy, was compatible with those elements of his thought which after 1775 made him a democrat.

Another of the factors which, while not incompatible with monarchical feelings, contributed greatly to Franklin's acceptance of democracy, is the belief which he shared with Hume that power, in the last analysis, is founded on opinion. "I wish some good Angel would forever whisper in the Ears of your great Men, that Dominion is founded in Opinion, and that if you would preserve your Authority among us, you must preserve the Opinion we us'd to have of your Justice."[94] He thought that "Government must depend for it's Efficiency either on Force or Opinion." Force, however, is not as efficient as Opinion: "Alexander and Caesar . . . received more faithful service, and performed greater actions, by means of the love their soldiers bore them, than they could possibly have done, if, instead of being beloved and respected, they had been hated and feared by those they commanded." Efficiency, then, became an argument for democracy. "Popular elections have their inconvenience in some cases; but in establishing new forms of government, we cannot always obtain what we may think the best; for the prejudices of those concerned, if they cannot be removed, must be in some degree complied with."[95]

It has rarely been noticed how detached Franklin, the greatest champion of democracy in the Federal Convention, was from the problem of the best government. His speech at the conclusion of the deliberations of the Constitutional Convention may give us a clue to the perplexing problem of why he gave comparatively little attention to the theoretical questions of political philosophy and devoted almost all his time to the solution of concrete issues. He stated his disagreement with several points of the

---

[93] R. M. MacIver, "European Doctrines and the Constitution," in *The Constitution Reconsidered* (cited in note 25), p. 55.

[94] *Letters and Papers of Benjamin Franklin and Richard Jackson* (cited in note 72), p. 145 (written in 1764). See also *Writings,* Vol. 6, p. 129; Vol. 9, p. 608.

[95] *Benjamin Franklin's Letters to the Press* (cited in note 55), p. 193; *Writings,* Vol. 2, p. 56; Vol. 3, p. 228. See also Vol. 3, 231; Vol. 5, p. 79.

Constitution, nevertheless urging general allegiance and loyalty to its principles. Asking his colleagues to doubt a little their feeling of infallibility, Franklin summed up the experience of his life: "I think a general Government necessary for us, and there is no *form* of government but what may be a blessing to the people, if well administered."[96] Perhaps in speaking these words he was thinking of one of the favorite writers of his younger days, Alexander Pope:

> For Forms of Government let fools contest;
> Whate'er is best administer'd is best.[97]

VII. THE DUALITY OF FRANKLIN'S POLITICAL THOUGHT

There are two outstanding and sometimes contradictory factors in Franklin's political thought. On the one hand, we find an acute comprehension of the power factor in human nature, and, consequently, in politics. On the other hand, Franklin always during his long life revolted in the name of equality against the imperfections of the existing order. He himself stated the basic antithesis of his political thought: Power versus Equality.

Fortunately, Franklin's notes on the problem at hand have been preserved; they are to be found in his marginal comments to Allen Ramsay's pamphlet, *Thoughts on the Origin and Nature of Government*, which presents the straight view of power politics. Franklin rebelled against the rationalization and justification of the power factor. "The natural weakness of man in a solitary State," Ramsay proclaimed, "prompts him to fly for protection to whoever is able to afford it, that is to some one more powerful, than himself; while the more powerful standing equally in need of his service, readily receives it in return for the protection he gives." Franklin's answer is unequivocal: *"May not Equals unite with Equals for common Purposes?"*[98]

In the last analysis, Franklin looked upon government as the trustee of the people. He had stated this Whig principle in his very first publication as a sixteen-year-old boy[99] and he never deviated from it. So in opposition to Ramsay's doctrine, according to which the governed have

---

[96] *Writings,* Vol. 9, p. 607.

[97] Pope, "Essay on Man," Epistle 3, *Selected Works* (cited in note 17), p. 124.

[98] [Allen Ramsay], *Thoughts on the Origin and Nature of Government* (London, 1769), p. 10. Franklin's copy in the Jefferson Collection of the Library of Congress. (My italics.)

[99] "Dogood Papers," *Writings,* Vol. 2, p. 26. Cf. *Benjamin Franklin's Letters to the Press* (cited in note 55), p. 140.

no right of control whatsoever, once they have agreed to submit themselves to the sovereign, Franklin declared the accountability of the rulers:

> If I appoint a Representative for the express purpose of doing a business for me that is for *my* Service and that of others, & to consider what I am to pay as my Proportion of the Expense necessary for accomplishing that Business, I am then tax'd by my own Consent.—A Number of Persons unite to form a Company for Trade, Expences are necessary, Directors are chosen to do the Business & proportion those Expences. They are paid a Reasonable Consideration for their Trouble. Here is nothing of weak & Strong. Protection on one hand, & Service on the other. The Directors are the Servants, not the Masters; their Duty is prescrib'd, the Powers they have is from the members & returns to them. The Directors are also accountable.[100]

Franklin refused to recognize that power alone could create right. When Ramsay declared that according to nature's laws every man "in Society shall rank himself amongst the Ruling or the Ruled, . . . all Equality and Independence being by the Law of Nature strictly forbidden . . . ," Franklin rejoined indignantly, "I do not find this Strange Law among those of Nature. I doubt it is forged. . . ." He summarized Ramsay's doctrine as meaning that "He that is strongest may do what he pleases with those that are weaker," and commented angrily: "A most Equitable Law of Nature indeed."[101]

On the other hand, Franklin's grasp of the realities of power inevitably involved him in moral and logical ambiguities of political decision. At times he expressed the tragic conflict of ethics and politics. Characteristic of the peculiar contradiction within his political thought was this statement three years before the Declaration of Independence on England's prospects in the Anglo-American conflict: "*Power* does not infer *Right;* and, as the *Right* is nothing, and the *Power* (by our Increase) continually diminishing, the one will soon be as insignificant as the *other.*"[102] In this instance, obviously, he was trying to make the best of both worlds. But there were times when he was only too well aware of the conflict of these two worlds. In a passage which seems to have escaped the notice of most students of his political thought, Franklin observed that "*moral and political Rights sometimes differ, and sometimes are both subdu'd by Might.*"[103]

The measured terms of Franklin's political thinking present a striking contrast to the optimism and rationalism which we usually associate with the Age of Enlightenment. Franklin's insight into the passions of pride

---

[100] Marginal notes to Ramsay, *op. cit.,* pp. 33–34.
[101] *Ibid.,* pp. 12, 13.
[102] *Writings,* Vol. 6, p. 87.
[103] *Writings,* Vol. 8, p. 304. (My italics.)

and power prevented him from applying the expectation of man's scientific and intellectual progress to the realm of moral matters. To be sure, he would not deny the influence of scientific insights upon politics, and he thought that a great deal of good would result from introducing the enlightened doctrines of free trade and physiocracy into international politics. But Franklin, unlike many of his friends in France, was never inclined to consider these and other ideas as panaceas. The mutual adjustment of interests would always remain the chief remedy of political evils. It was in this domain that reason, as a temper in the conduct of human affairs, made its greatest contribution to his political thought. Moderation and equity, so he had been taught by his experience (rather than by abstract reasoning) were true political wisdom. His belief that the rulers ought to be accountable, together with his more pragmatic conviction that force alone, in the long run, could not solve the great problems of politics, brought forth his declaration of faith that "Government is not establish'd merely by *Power;* there must be maintain'd a general Opinion of its *Wisdom* and *Justice* to make it firm and durable."[104]

---

[104] *Benjamin Franklin's Autobiographical Writings,* ed. Carl Van Doren (New York, 1945), pp. 184–85. Cf. *Writings,* Vol. 4, p. 269; Vol. 7, p. 390.

Democracy and The Federalist

MARTIN DIAMOND

The major American contribution to political theory was made by the
carefully wrought essays of James Madison and Alexander Hamilton, who
wrote under the pressure of emergency to persuade voters to ratify the new
Constitution drawn up at Philadelphia. Hamilton would have preferred a
system more closely modelled on the British monarchy, but he subordinated
his desires in defense of a republicanism achieved in American terms.
Madison later collaborated with Jefferson to build the Republican Party,
while Hamilton led a Federalist party built upon his program for economic
nationalism, manufacturing, and a powerful central government, propped by
judicial review of state legislation and by the economic interests of the substantial men of property. In *The Federalist,* however, both men cooperated
in an argument which was remarkably consistent.

Historians in the Progressive period, like J. Allen Smith and Charles A.
Beard, painted the portrait of the framers as antidemocrats. By giving more
careful attention to the precise meaning they gave to republicanism, Martin
Diamond challenges this view of the framers.

I

OUR MAJOR POLITICAL PROBLEMS TODAY ARE PROBLEMS OF DEMOCRACY;
and, as much as anything else, the *Federalist* papers are a teaching about
democracy. The conclusion of one of the most important of these papers
states what is also the most important theme in the entire work: the
necessity for "a republican remedy for the diseases most incident to
republican government."[1] The theme is clearly repeated in a passage
where Thomas Jefferson is praised for displaying equally "a fervent

Martin Diamond, "Democracy and *The Federalist:* A Reconsideration of the
Framer's Intent," *American Political Science Review,* 53 (March, 1959), pp. 53–
68. Reprinted by permission of the author and the publisher.
[1] *Federalist,* No. 10, p. 62. All references are to the Modern Library edition, ed.
E. M. Earle.

attachment to republican government and an enlightened view of the dangerous propensities against which it ought to be guarded."[2] *The Federalist,* thus, stresses its commitment to republican or popular government, but, of course, insists that this must be an enlightened commitment.

But *The Federalist* and the Founding Fathers generally have not been taken at their word. Predominantly, they are understood as being only quasi- or even anti-democrats. Modern American historical writing, at least until very recently, has generally seen the Constitution as some sort of apostasy from, or reaction to, the radically democratic implications of the Declaration of Independence—a reaction that was undone by the great "democratic breakthroughs" of Jeffersonianism, Jacksonianism, etc. This view, I believe, involves a false understanding of the crucial political issues involved in the founding of the American Republic. Further, it is based implicitly upon a questionable modern approach to democracy and has tended to have the effect, moreover, of relegating the political teaching of the Founding Fathers to the pre-democratic past and thus of making it of no vital concern to moderns. The Founding Fathers themselves repeatedly stressed that their Constitution was wholly consistent with the true principles of republican or popular government. The prevailing modern opinion, in varying degrees and in different ways, rejects that claim. It thus becomes important to understand what was the relation of the Founding Fathers to popular government or democracy.

I have deliberately used interchangeably their terms, "popular government" and "democracy." The Founding Fathers, of course, did not use the terms entirely synonymously and the idea that they were less than "democrats" has been fortified by the fact that they sometimes defined "democracy" invidiously in comparison with "republic." But this fact does not really justify the opinion. For their basic view was that *popular government was the genus, and democracy and republic were two species* of that genus of government. What distinguished popular government from other genera of government was that in it, political authority is "derived from the great body of the society, not from . . . [any] favoured class of ·it."[3]

[2] *Federalist,* No. 49, p. 327.

[3] *Federalist,* No. 39, p. 244. Here Madison speaks explicity of the republican form of government. But see on the same page how Madison compares the republican form with "every *other popular* government." Regarding the crucial question of the lodgement of political authority, Madison speaks of republic, democracy and popular government interchangeably. Consider that, in the very paper where he distinguishes so precisely between democracies and republics regarding direct versus representative rule, Madison defines his general aim both as a search for "a republican remedy" for republican diseases *and* a remedy that will "preserve the spirit and the form of *popular* government." (p. 58.) Interestingly, on June 6

With respect to this decisive question, of where political authority is lodged, democracy and republic—as *The Federalist* uses the terms—differ not in the least. Republics, equally with democracies, may claim to be wholly a form of popular government. This is neither to deny the difference between the two, nor to depreciate the importance *The Federalist* attached to the difference; but in *The Federalist*'s view, the difference does not relate to the essential principle of popular government. Democracy means in *The Federalist* that form of popular government where the citizens "assemble and administer the government in person."[4] Republics differ in that the people rule through representatives and, of course, in the consequences of that difference. The crucial point is that republics and democracies are equally forms of popular government, but that the one form is vastly preferable to the other because of the substantive consequences of the difference in form. Those historians who consider the Founding Fathers as less than "democrats," miss or reject the Founders' central contention that, while being perfectly faithful to the *principle* of popular government, they had solved the *problem* of popular government.

In what way is the Constitution ordinarily thought to be less democratic than the Declaration? The argument is usually that the former is characterized by fear of the people, by preoccupation with minority interests and rights, and by measures therefore taken against the power of majorities. The Declaration, it is true, does not display these features, but this is no proof of a fundamental difference of principle between the two. Is it not obviously possible that the difference is due only to a difference in the tasks to which the two documents were addressed? And is it not further possible that the democratic principles of the Declaration are not only compatible with the prophylactic measures of the Constitution, but actually imply them?

The Declaration of Independence formulates two criteria for judging whether any government is good, or indeed legitimate. Good government must rest, procedurally, upon the consent of the governed. Good government, substantively, must do only certain things, *e.g.,* secure certain rights. This may be stated another way by borrowing a phrase from Locke, appropriate enough when discussing the Declaration. That "the people shall be judge" is of the essence of democracy, is its peculiar form or method of proceeding. That the people shall judge rightly is the substantive problem of democracy. But whether the procedure will bring about the

---

at the Federal Convention, Madison's phrasing for a similar problem was the search for "the only defense against the inconveniences of democracy consistent with the *democratic* form of government." Madison, *Writings,* ed. G. Hunt, Vol. 3 (G. P. Putnam's Sons, New York, 1902), p. 103. Italics supplied throughout.

[4] *Federalist,* No. 10, p. 58.

substance is problematic. Between the Declaration's two criteria, then, a tension exists: consent can be given or obtained for governmental actions which are not right—at least as the men of 1776 saw the right. (To give an obvious example from their point of view: the people may freely but wrongly vote away the protection due to property.) Thus the Declaration clearly contained, although it did not resolve, a fundamental problem. Solving the problem was not its task; that was the task for the framers of the Constitution. But the man who wrote the Declaration of Independence and the leading men who supported it were perfectly aware of the difficulty, and of the necessity for a "republican remedy."

What the text of the Declaration, taken alone, tells of its meaning may easily be substantiated by the testimony of its author and supporters. Consider only that Jefferson, with no known change of heart at all, said of *The Federalist* that it was "the best commentary on the principles of government which was ever written."[5] Jefferson, it must be remembered, came firmly to recommend the adoption of the Constitution, his criticisms of it having come down only to a proposal for rotation in the Presidency and for the subsequent adoption of a bill of rights. I do not, of course, deny the peculiar character of "Jeffersonianism" nor the importance to many things of its proper understanding. I only state here that it is certain that Jefferson, unlike later historians, did not view the Constitution as a retrogression from democracy. Or further, consider that John Adams, now celebrated as America's great conservative, was so enthusiastic about Jefferson's draft of the Declaration as to wish on his own account that hardly a word be changed. And this same Adams, also without any change of heart and without complaint, accepted the Constitution as embodying many of his own views on government.

The idea that the Constitution was a falling back from the fuller democracy of the Declaration thus rests in part upon a false reading of the Declaration as free from the concerns regarding democracy that the framers of the Constitution felt. Perhaps only those would so read it who take for granted a perfect, self-subsisting harmony between consent (equality) and the proper aim of government (justice), or between consent and individual rights (liberty). This assumption was utterly foreign to the leading men of the Declaration.

II

The Declaration has wrongly been converted into, as it were, a super-democratic document; has the Constitution wrongly been converted in the modern view into an insufficiently democratic document? The only

[5] *The Works of Thomas Jefferson*, ed. Paul L. Ford (The Federal Edition), Vol. 5 (G. P. Putnam's Sons, New York, 1904), p. 434.

basis for depreciating the democratic character of the Constitution lies in its framers' apprehensive diagnosis of the "diseases," "defects" or "evil propensities" of democracy, and in their remedies. But if what the Founders considered to be defects *are* genuine defects, and if the remedies, without violating the principles of popular government, *are* genuine remedies, then it would be unreasonable to call the Founders anti- or quasi-democrats. Rather, they would be the wise partisans of democracy; a man is not a better democrat but only a foolish democrat if he ignores real defects inherent in popular government. Thus, the question becomes: are there natural defects to democracy and, if there are, what are the best remedies?

In part, the Founding Fathers answered this question by employing a traditional mode of political analysis. They believed there were several basic possible regimes, each having several possible forms. Of these possible regimes they believed the best, or at least the best for America, to be popular government, but only if purged of its defects. At any rate, an unpurged popular government they believed to be indefensible. They believed there were several forms of popular government, crucial among these direct democracy and republican—or representative—government (the latter perhaps divisible into two distinct forms, large and small republics). Their constitution and their defense of it constitute an argument for that form of popular government (large republic) in which the "evil propensities" would be weakest or most susceptible of remedy.

The whole of the thought of the Founding Fathers is intelligible and, especially, the evaluation of their claim to be wise partisans of popular government is possible, only if the words *"disease," "defect,"* and *"evil propensity"* are allowed their full force. Unlike modern "value-free" social scientists, the Founding Fathers believed that true knowledge of the good and bad in human conduct was possible, and that they themselves possessed sufficient knowledge to discern the really grave defects of popular government and their proper remedies. The modern relativistic or positivistic theories, implicitly employed by most commentators on the Founding Fathers, deny the possibility of such true knowledge and therefore deny that the Founding Fathers *could* have been actuated by knowledge of the good rather than by passion or interest. (I deliberately employ the language of *Federalist* No. 10. Madison defined faction, in part, as a group "united and actuated by . . . passion, or . . . interest." That is, factions are groups *not*—as presumably the authors of *The Federalist* were—actuated by reason.) How this modern view of the value problem supports the conception of the Constitution as less democratic than the Declaration is clear. The Founding Fathers did in fact seek to prejudice the outcome of democracy; they sought to alter, by certain restraints, the likelihood that the majority would decide certain political issues in bad ways. These restraints the Founders justified as mitigating the natural defects of democracy. But, say the moderns, there are no "bad" political decisions, wrong-in-themselves, from reaching which the majority ought to be restrained. Therefore, ultimately, nothing other than the specific interests of the Founders can explain their zeal in restraining democracy. And inasmuch as the restraints were typically placed on the many in the interest of the propertied, the departure of the Constitution is "anti-democratic" or "thermidorean." In short, according to this view, there cannot be what the Founders claimed to possess, "an *enlightened* view of the dangerous propensities against which [popular government] . . . ought to be guarded," the substantive goodness or badness of such propensities being a matter of opinion or taste on which reason can shed no light.

What are some of the arrangements which have been considered signs of "undemocratic" features of the Constitution? The process by which the Constitution may be amended is often cited in evidence. Everyone is familiar with the arithmetic which shows that a remarkably small minority could prevent passage of a constitutional amendment supported by an overwhelming majority of the people. That is, bare majorities in the thirteen least populous states could prevent passage of an amendment desired by overwhelming majorities in the thirty-six most populous states. But let us, for a reason to be made clear in a moment, turn that arithmetic around. Bare majorities in the thirty-seven least populous states can pass amendments against the opposition of overwhelming majorities in the twelve most populous states. And this would mean in actual votes today (and would have meant for the thirteen original states) constitutional amendment by a minority against the opposition of a majority of citizens. My point is simply that, while the amending procedure does involve qualified majorities, the qualification is not of the kind that requires an especially large numerical majority for action.

I suggest that the real aim and practical effect of the complicated amending procedure was not at all to give power to minorities, but to ensure that passage of an amendment would require a *nationally* distributed majority, though one that legally could consist of a bare numerical majority. It was only adventitious that the procedure has the theoretical possibility of a minority blocking (or passing) an amendment. The aim of requiring nationally distributed majorities was, I think, to ensure that no amendment could be passed simply with the support of the few states or sections sufficiently numerous to provide a bare majority. No doubt it was also believed that it would be difficult for such a national majority to form or become effective save for the decent purposes that could command national agreement, and this difficulty was surely deemed a great virtue of the amending process. This is what I think *The Federalist* really means when it praises the amending process and says that "it guards equally against that extreme facility, which would render the Constitution too mutable; and that extreme difficulty, which might perpetuate its discovered faults."[6] All I wish to emphasize here is that the actual method adopted, with respect to the numerical size of majorities, is meant to leave all legal power in the hands of ordinary majorities so long as they are national majorities. The departure from simple majoritarianism is, at least, not in an oligarchic or aristocratic direction. In this crucial respect, the amending procedure does conform strictly to the principles of republican (popular) government.

Consider next the suffrage question. It has long been assumed as proof of an anti-democratic element in the Constitution that the Founding Fathers depended for the working of their Constitution upon a substantially limited franchise. Just as the Constitution allegedly was ratified by a highly qualified electorate, so too, it is held, was the new government to be based upon a suffrage subject to substantial property qualifications. This view has only recently been seriously challenged, especially by Robert E. Brown, whose detailed researches convince him that the property qualifications in nearly all the original states were probably so small as to exclude never more than twenty-five per cent, and in most cases as little as only five to ten per cent, of the adult white male population.[7] That is, the property qualifications were not designed to exclude the mass of the poor but only the small proportion which lacked a concrete—however small—stake in society, *i.e.,* primarily the transients or "idlers."

The Constitution, of course, left the suffrage question to the decision of the individual states. What is the implication of that fact for deciding what sort of suffrage the Framers had in mind? The immediately popular branch of the national legislature was to be elected by voters who "shall have the qualifications requisite for electors of the most numerous branch of the State Legislature." The mode of election to the electoral college for the Presidency and to the Senate is also left to "be prescribed in each State by the legislature thereof." At a minimum, it may be stated that the Framers did not themselves attempt to reduce, or prevent the expansion of, the suffrage; that question was left wholly to the states—and these were, ironically, the very hotbeds of post-revolutionary democracy from the rule of which it is familiarly alleged that the Founders sought to escape.[8]

---

[6] *Federalist,* No. 43, p. 286.

[7] *Middle Class Democracy and the Revolution in Massachusetts, 1691–1780.* (Cornell University Press, Ithaca, 1955).

[8] Madison must have thought that he had established this point beyond misinterpretation in *The Federalist,* No. 57. "Who are to be the electors of the

In general, the conclusion seems inescapable that the states had a far broader suffrage than is ordinarily thought, and nothing in the actions of the Framers suggests any expectation or prospect of the reduction of the suffrage. Again, as in the question of the amending process, I suggest that the Constitution represented no departure whatsoever from the democratic standards of the Revolutionary period, or from any democratic standards then generally recognized.[9]

What of the Senate? The organization of the Senate, its terms of office and its staggered mode of replacement, its election by state legislatures rather than directly by the people, among other things, have been used to demonstrate the undemocratic character of the Senate as intended by the Framers. Was this not a device to represent property and not people, and was it not intended therefore to be a non-popular element in the government? I suggest, on the contrary, that the really important thing is that the Framers thought they had found a way to protect property *without* representing it. That the Founders intended the Senate to be one of the crucial devices for remedying the defects of democracy is certainly true. But *The Federalist* argues that the Senate, as actually proposed in the Constitution, was calculated to be such a device as would operate only in a way that "will consist . . . with the genuine principles of republican government."[10] I believe that the claim is just.

Rather than viewing the Senate from the perspective of modern experience and opinions, consider how radically democratic the Senate appears when viewed from a pre-modern perspective. The model of a divided legislature that the Founders had most in mind was probably the

---

federal representatives? Not the rich, more than the poor; not the learned, more than the ignorant; not the haughty heirs of distinguished names, more than the humble sons of obscurity and unpropitious fortune. The electors are to be the great body of the people of the United States. They are to be the same who exercise the right in every State of electing the corresponding branch of the legislature of the State" (p. 371).

[9] This is not to deny the importance of the existing property qualifications for the understanding of the Founders' political theory. The legal exclusion from the franchise of even a very small portion of the adult population may have enormous significance for the politics and life of a country. This is obvious in the case of a racial, ethnic or religious minority. And the exclusion of otherwise eligible adult males on the grounds of poverty may be equally important. The property qualification clearly praises and rewards certain virtues, implies that the voter must possess certain qualities to warrant his exercise of the franchise, and aims at excluding a "rabble" from the operations of political parties. But important, therefore, as the property qualification was, it does not demonstrate that the Founding Fathers departed radically from the most important aspects of the principle of majority rule.

[10] *Federalist*, No. 62, p. 403.

English Parliament. There the House of Lords was thought to provide some of the beneficial checks upon the popular Commons which it was hoped the Senate would supply in the American Constitution. But the American Senate was to possess none of the qualities which permitted the House of Lords to fulfill its role; *i.e.,* its hereditary basis, or membership upon election by the Crown, or any of its other aristocratic characteristics.[11] Yet the Founding Fathers knew that the advantages of having both a Senate and a House would "be in proportion to the dissimilarity in the genius of the two bodies."[12] What is remarkable is that, in seeking to secure this dissimilarity, they did not in any respect go beyond the limits permitted by the "genuine principles of republican government."

Not only is this dramatically demonstrated in comparison with the English House of Lords, but also in comparison with all earlier theory regarding the division of the legislative power. The aim of such a division in earlier thought is to secure a balance between the aristocratic and democratic elements of a polity. This is connected with the pre-modern preference for a *mixed* republic, which was rejected by the Founders in favor of a *democratic* republic. And the traditional way to secure this balance or mixture was to give one house or office to the suffrages of the few and one to the suffrages of the many. Nothing of the kind is involved in the American Senate. Indeed, on this issue, so often cited as evidence of the Founders' undemocratic predilections, the very opposite is the case. The Senate is a constitutional device which *par excellence* reveals the strategy of the Founders. They wanted something like the advantages earlier thinkers had seen in a mixed legislative power, but they thought this was possible (and perhaps preferable) without any introduction whatsoever of aristocratic power into their system. What pre-modern thought had seen in an aristocratic senate—wisdom, nobility, manners, religion, etc.—the Founding Fathers converted into stability, enlightened self-interest, a "temperate and respectable body of citizens." The qualities of a senate having thus been altered (involving perhaps comparable changes in the notion of the ends of government), it became possible to secure these advantages through a Senate based wholly upon popular principles. Or so I would characterize a Senate whose membership required no property qualification and which was appointed (or elected in the manner prescribed) by State legislatures which, in their own turn, were elected annually or biennially by a nearly universal manhood suffrage.

The great claim of *The Federalist* is that the Constitution represents the fulfillment of a truly novel experiment, of "a revolution which has no parallel in the annals of society," and which is decisive for the happiness

11 *Federalist*, No. 63, p. 415.
12 *Federalist*, No. 62, p. 403.

of "the whole human race."[13] And the novelty, I argue, consisted in solving the problems of popular government by means which yet maintain the government "wholly popular."[14] In defending that claim against the idea of the Constitution as a retreat from democracy I have dealt thus far only with the easier task: the demonstration that the constitutional devices and arrangements do not derogate from the legal power of majorities to rule. What remains is to examine the claim that the Constitution did in fact remedy the natural defects of democracy. Before any effort is made in this direction, it may be useful to summarize some of the implications and possible utility of the analysis thus far.

Above all, the merit of the suggestions I have made, if they are accurate in describing the intention and action of the Founders, is that it makes the Founders available to us for the study of modern problems. I have tried to restore to them their *bona fides* as partisans of democracy. This done, we may take seriously the question whether they were, as they claimed to be, wise partisans of democracy or popular government. If they were partisans of democracy and if the regime they created was decisively democratic, then they speak to us not merely about bygone problems, not from a viewpoint—in this regard—radically different from our own, but as men addressing themselves to problems identical in principle with our own. They are a source from within our own heritage which teaches us the way to put the question to democracy, a way which is rejected by certain prevailing modern ideas. But we cannot avail ourselves of their assistance if we consider American history to be a succession of democratizations which overcame the Founding Fathers' intentions. On that view it is easy to regard them as simply outmoded. If I am right regarding the extent of democracy in their thought and regime, then they are not outmoded by modern events but rather are tested by them. American history, on this view, is not primarily the replacement of a pre-democratic regime by a democratic regime, but is rather a continuing testimony to how the Founding Fathers' democratic regime has worked out in modern circumstances. The whole of our national experience thus becomes a way of judging the Founders' principles, of judging democracy itself, or of pondering the flaws of democracy and the means to its improvement.

III

What was the Founding Fathers' view of the good life? Upon what fundamental theoretical premises did that view of the good life depend? How comprehensive was their understanding of the dangers against which

[13] *Federalist*, No. 14, p. 85.
[14] *Ibid.*, p. 81.

popular government was to be guarded? How efficacious were their remedies and what may have been the unanticipated costs of those remedies? These questions are clearly too vast to answer here and now. What follows is only a series of notes which bear upon the problems raised, and which I think may serve as general guides to what it is important to seek in studying the Founding Fathers.

The Federalist does not discuss systematically, as would a theoretical treatise, the question of the ends or purposes of government. That is, it does not deal systematically with philosophical issues. This is not to say that its authors did not have a view in such matters. But what that view was, and what are its implications for the understanding of the Constitution, is a subject on which I find it difficult to speak with confidence. I must still regard as open the question whether the authors of *The Federalist,* or the other leading founders, had themselves fully reflected on these matters, or whether they treated them as settled by thinkers like Locke and Montesquieu, or whether crucial premises in their thought were unreflectively taken for granted. But men cannot act on a political scale so vast as they did without having and employing a view of the politically fundamental; and it is this view which provides the crucial perspective for the understanding of their particular actions and thoughts.

Perhaps the most explicit fundamental utterance of *The Federalist* is the statement regarding

the great principle of self-preservation . . . the transcendent law of nature and of nature's God, which declares that the safety and happiness of society are the objects at which all political institutions aim, and to which all such institutions must be sacrificed.[15]

But self-preservation, it is made clear, includes more than mere preservation. This passage, which interestingly echoes the Declaration of Independence on the "laws of nature and of nature's God," emphasizes that preservation includes "happiness" as well as "safety." That is, *The Federalist* is aware of and explicitly rejects the kind of regime that would follow from a narrower view of self-preservation. For example, *The Federalist* seems explicitly to be rejecting Hobbes when, in another context, it rejects the view that "nothing less than the chains of despotism can restrain [men] from destroying and devouring one another."[16] But while it rejects the "chains of despotism," *i.e.,* the Hobbesean solution to the problem of self-preservation, it nonetheless seems to accept the Hobbesean statement of the problem. As it were, the primary fears of *The Federalist* are Hobbesean, that is, fears of "foreign war and domestic con-

[15] *Federalist,* No. 43, p. 287.
[16] *Federalist,* No. 55, p. 365.

vulsion." Rejecting a despotic solution, the great aim of *The Federalist* is to supply a liberal and republican solution to the same problem. But while there is a great difference, never to be underestimated, between a liberal and a repressive, a republican and a monarchical solution, it may be that in making the same dangers and their solution *the* desideratum for the structure and functions of government much of the Hobbesean view is preserved.

The main object of *The Federalist* was to urge the necessity of a firm and energetic Union. The utility of such a Union, and therefore the chief ends it will serve, is that it will strengthen the American people against the dangers of "foreign war" and secure them from the dangers of "domestic convulsion." These functions of government are the most frequently discussed and the most vehemently emphasized in the whole work. To a very great extent, then, *The Federalist* determines the role of government with reference only, or primarily, to the extremes of external and internal danger. It is to avoid the pre-civil forms of these dangers that men form government and it is the civil solution of these dangers which, almost exclusively, determines the legitimate objects of government. But again, *The Federalist* repeatedly emphasizes that a "novel" solution is at hand. The means now exist—and America is uniquely in a position to employ them—for a republican solution which avoids the extremes of tyranny and anarchy. But notice that, on this view, liberalism and republicanism are not the means by which men may ascend to a nobler life; rather they are simply instrumentalities which solve Hobbesean problems in a more moderate manner. It is tempting to suggest that if America is a "Lockean" nation, as is so often asserted, it is true in the very precise sense that Locke's "comfortable preservation" displaces the harshness of the Hobbesean view, while not repudiating that view in general.

To be sure, *The Federalist* does make other explicit statements regarding the ends of government. For example: "Justice is the end of government. It is the end of civil society."[17] But this statement, to the best of my knowledge, is made only once in the entire work; and the context suggests that "justice" means simply "civil rights" which in turn seems to refer primarily to the protection of economic interests. That justice has here this relatively narrow meaning, as compared with traditional philosophical and theological usage, is made more probable when we take account of the crucial statement in *Federalist* No. 10. There the "first object of government" is the protection of the diverse human faculties from which arise the "rights of property" and the unequal distribution of property. The importance of this statement of the function of government is underscored when it is recalled how large a proportion of *The Fed-*

17 *Federalist*, No. 51, p. 340.

eralist deals with the improvements in "commerce" made possible by the new Constitution. For example, in a list of the four "principal objects of federal legislation,"[18] three (foreign trade, interstate trade, and taxes) deal explicitly with commerce. The fourth, the militia, also deals with commerce insofar as it largely has to do with the prevention of "domestic convulsion" brought on by economic matters.

The very great emphasis of *The Federalist* on commerce, and on the role of government in nurturing it, may not be at all incompatible with the theme of "happiness" which is the most frequently occurring definition of the "object of government." The most definite statement is the following:

A good government implies two things: first, fidelity to the object of government, which is the happiness of the people, secondly, a knowledge of the means by which that object can be best obtained.[19]

The Federalist is not very explicit in defining happiness. But there are firm indications that what it had in mind has little in common with traditional philosophical or theological understandings of the term. At one place, *The Federalist* indicates that happiness requires that government "provide for the security, advance the prosperity, [and] support the reputation of the commonwealth."[20] In another, happiness seems to require "our safety, our tranquility, our dignity, our reputation."[21] Part of what these words mean is made clear by the fact that they summarize a lengthy indictment of the Articles of Confederation, the particulars of which deal in nearly every case with commercial shortcomings. Happiness, "a knowledge of the means" to which *The Federalist* openly claims to possess, seems to consist primarily in physical preservation from external and internal danger *and* in the comforts afforded by a commercial society; which comforts are at once the dividends of security and the means to a republican rather than repressive security.

What is striking is the apparent exclusion from the functions of government of a wide range of non-economic tasks traditionally considered the decisive business of government. It is tempting to speculate that this reduction in the tasks of government has something to do with *The Federalist's* defense of popular government. The traditional criticism of popular government was that it gave over the art of government into the hands of the many, which is to say the unwise. It would be a formidable reply to reduce the complexity of the governmental art to dimensions more commensurate with the capacity of the many. I use two statements by

18 *Federalist*, No. 53, p. 350–51.
19 *Federalist*, No. 62, p. 404.
20 *Federalist*, No. 30, p. 186.
21 *Federalist*, No. 15, p. 88.

Madison, years apart, to illustrate the possibility that he may have had something like this in mind. "There can be no doubt that there are subjects to which the capacities of the bulk of mankind are unequal."[22] But on the other hand, "the confidence of the [Republican party] in the capacity of mankind for self-government"[23] is what distinguished it from the Federalist party which distrusted that capacity. The confidence in mankind's capacities would seem to require having removed from government the subjects to which those capacities are unequal.

IV

So far as concerns those ends of government on which *The Federalist* is almost wholly silent, it is reasonable to infer that what the Founders made no provision for they did not rank highly among the legitimate objects of government. Other political theories had ranked highly, as objects of government, the nurturing of a particular religion, education, military courage, civic-spiritedness, moderation, individual excellence in the virtues, etc. On all of these *The Federalist* is either silent, or has in mind only pallid versions of the originals, or even seems to speak with contempt. The Founders apparently did not consider it necessary to make special provision for excellence. Did they assume these virtues would flourish without governmental or other explicit provision? Did they consciously sacrifice some of them to other necessities of a stable popular regime—as it were, as the price of their solution to the problem of democracy? Or were these virtues less necessary to a country when it had been properly founded on the basis of the new "science of politics"? In what follows I suggest some possible answers to these questions.

The Founding Fathers are often criticized for an excessive attention to, and reliance upon, mechanical institutional arrangements and for an insufficient attention to "sociological" factors. While a moderate version of this criticism may finally be just, it is nonetheless clear that *The Federalist* pays considerable and shrewd attention to such factors. For example, in *Federalist* No. 51, equal attention is given to the institutional and non-institutional strengths of the new Constitution. One of these latter is the solution to the "problems of faction." It will be convenient to examine *Federalist* No. 10 where the argument about faction is more fully developed than in No. 51. A close examination of that solution

[22] Letter to Edmund Randolph, January 10, 1788.
[23] Letter to William Eustis, May 22, 1823. The letters to Randolph and Eustis were brought to my attention by Ralph Ketcham's article, "Notes on James Madison's Sources for the Tenth Federalist Paper," *Midwest Journal of Political Science,* Vol. 1 (May, 1957).

reveals something about *The Federalist's* view of the virtues necessary to the good life.

The problem dealt with in the tenth essay is how "to break and control the violence of faction." "The friend of popular governments never finds himself so much alarmed for their character and fate, as when he contemplates their propensity to this dangerous vice." Faction is, thus, *the* problem of popular government. Now it must be made clear that Madison, the author of this essay, was not here really concerned with the problem of faction generally. He devotes only two sentences in the whole essay to the dangers of *minority* factions. The real problem in a popular government, then, is *majority* faction, or, more precisely, *the* majority faction, *i.e.,* the great mass of the little propertied and unpropertied. This is the only faction that can "execute and mask its violence under the forms of the Constitution." That is, in the American republic the many have the legal power to rule and thus from them can come the greatest harm. Madison interprets that harm fairly narrowly; at least, his overwhelming emphasis is on the classic economic struggle between the rich and the poor which made of ancient democracies "spectacles of turbulence and contention." *The* problem for the friend of popular government is how to avoid the "domestic convulsion" which results when the rich and the poor, the few and the many, as is their wont, are at each others' throats. Always before in popular governments the many, armed with political power, invariably precipitated such convulsions. But the friend of popular government must find only "a republican remedy" for this disease which is "most incident to republican government." "To secure the public good and private rights against the danger of . . . [majority] faction, and at the same time to preserve the spirit and the form of popular government, is then the great object to which our inquiries are directed."

Without wrenching Madison's meaning too greatly, the problem may be put crudely this way: Madison gave a beforehand answer to Marx. The whole of the Marxian scheme depends upon the many—having been proletarianized—causing precisely such domestic convulsion and usurpation of property as Madison wished to avoid. Madison believed that in America the many could be diverted from that probable course. How will the many, *the* majority, be prevented from using for the evil purpose of usurping property the legal power which is theirs in a popular regime? "Evidently by one of two [means] only. Either the existence of the same passion or interest in a majority at the same time must be prevented, or the majority, having such co-existent passion or interest, must be rendered, by their number and local situation, unable to concert and carry into effect schemes of oppression." But "we well know that neither moral nor religious motives can be relied on" to do these things. The "circumstance principally" which will solve the problem is the "greater number of citizens and extent of territory which may be brought within the compass" of large republican governments rather than of small direct democracies.

Rather than mutilate Madison, let me complete his thought by quoting the rest of his argument before commenting on it:

The smaller the society, the fewer probably will be the distinct parties and interests, the more frequently will a majority be found of the same party; and the smaller the number of individuals composing a majority, and the smaller the compass within which they are placed, the more easily will they concert and execute their plans of oppression. Extend the sphere and you take in a greater variety of parties and interests; you make it less probable that a majority of the whole will have a common motive to invade the rights of other citizens; or if such a common motive exists, it will be more difficult for all who feel it to discover their own strength, and to act in unison with each other.

I want to deal only with what is implied or required by the first of the two means, i.e., preventing the majority from having the same "passion or interest" at the same time. I would argue that this is the more important of the two remedial means afforded by a large republic. If the majority comes to have the same passion or interest and holds to it intensely for a period of only four to six years, it seems certain that it would triumph over the "extent of territory," over the barriers of federalism, and separation of powers, and all the checks and balances of the Constitution. I do not wish to depreciate the importance of those barriers; I believe they have enormous efficacy in stemming the tide Madison feared. But I would argue that their efficacy depends upon a prior weakening of the force applied against them, upon the majority having been fragmented or deflected from its "schemes of oppression." An inflamed Marxian proletariat would not indefinitely be deterred by institutional checks or extent of territory. The crucial point then, as I see it, is the means by which a majority bent upon oppression is prevented from ever forming or becoming firm.

Madison's whole scheme essentially comes down to this. The struggle of classes is to be replaced by a struggle of interests. The class struggle is domestic convulsion; the struggle of interests is a safe, even energizing, struggle which is compatible with, or even promotes, the safety and stability of society. But how can this be accomplished? What will prevent the many from thinking of their interest as that of the Many opposed to the Few? Madison, as I see it, implies that nothing can prevent it in a small democratic society where the many are divided into only a few trades and callings: these divisions are insufficient to prevent them from conceiving their lot in common and uniting for oppression. But in a large republic, numerous and powerful divisions will arise among the many to prevent that happening. A host of interests grows up "of necessity in civilized nations, and divide[s] them into different classes, actuated by different sentiments and views." "Civilized nations" clearly means here large, commercial societies. In a large commercial society the interest of the many can be fragmented into many narrower, more limited interests. The mass will not unite as a mass to make extreme demands upon the few, the struggle over which will destroy society; the mass will fragment into relatively small groups, seeking small immediate advantages for their narrow and particular interests.

If the Madisonian solution is essentially as I have described it, it becomes clear that certain things are required for the solution to operate. I only mention several of them. First, the country in which this is to take place will have to be profoundly democratic. That is, all men must be free—and even encouraged—to seek their immediate profit and to associate with others in the process. There must be no rigid class barriers which bar men from the pursuit of immediate interest. Indeed, it is especially the lowly, from whom the most is to be feared, who must feel most sanguine about the prospects of achieving limited and immediate benefits. Second, the gains must be real; that is, the fragmented interests must from time to time achieve real gains, else the scheme would cease to beguile or mollify. But I do not want to develop these themes here. Rather, I want to emphasize only one crucial aspect of Madison's design: that is, the question of the apparently narrow ends of society envisaged by the Founding Fathers. Madison's plan, as I have described it, most assuredly does not rest on the "moral and religious motives" whose efficacy he deprecated. Indeed there is not even the suggestion that the pursuit of interest should be an especially enlightened pursuit. Rather, the problem posed by the dangerous passions and interests of the many is solved primarily by a reliance upon passion and interests themselves. As Tocqueville pointed out, Americans employ the principle of "self-interest rightly understood."

The principle of self-interest rightly understood is not a lofty one, but it is clear and sure. It does not aim at mighty objects, but it attains . . . all those at which it aims. By its admirable conformity to human weaknesses it easily obtains great dominion; nor is that dominion precarious, since the principle checks one personal interest by another, and uses, to direct the passions, the very same instrument that excites them.[24]

Madison's solution to his problem worked astonishingly well. The danger he wished to avert has been averted and largely for the reasons he

[24] *Democracy in America,* ed. Phillips Bradley (Knopf, New York, 1951) Vol. 2, pp. 122–23.

gave. But it is possible to question now whether he did not take too narrow a view of what the dangers were. Living today as beneficiaries of his system, we may yet wonder whether he failed to contemplate other equally grave problems of democracy, or whether his remedy for the one disease has not had some unfortunate collateral consequences. The Madisonian solution involved a fundamental reliance on ceaseless striving after immediate interest (perhaps now immediate gratification). Tocqueville appreciated that this "permanent agitation . . . is characteristic of a peaceful democracy,"[25] one might even say, the price of its peace. And Tocqueville was aware of how great might be the price. "In the midst of this universal tumult, this incessant conflict of jarring interests, this continual striving of men after fortune, where is that calm to be found which is necessary for the deeper combinations of the intellect?"[26]

V

There is, I think, in *The Federalist* a profound distinction made between the qualities necessary for Founders and the qualities necessary for the men who come after. It is a distinction that bears on the question of the Founding Fathers' view of what is required for the good life and on their defense of popular government. Founding requires "an exemption from the pestilential influence of party animosities";[27] but the subsequent governing of America will depend on precisely those party animosities, moderated in the way I have described. Or again, founding requires that "reason" and not the passions," "sit in judgment."[28] But, as I have argued, the society once founded will subsequently depend precisely upon the passions, only moderated in their consequences by having been guided into proper channels. The reason of the Founders constructs the system within which the passions of the men who come after may be relied upon.

Founders need a knowledge of the newly improved "science of politics" and a knowledge of the great political alternatives in order to construct a durable regime; while the men who come after need be only legislators who are but interested "advocates and parties to the causes they determine."[29] *The Federalist* speaks, as has often been observed, with harsh realism about the shortcomings of human nature, but, as has not so often been observed, none of its strictures can characterize the Founders; they must be free of these shortcomings in order to have had disinterested and true knowledge of political things. While "a nation of philosophers is

25 *Ibid.,* p. 42.
26 *Idem.*
27 *Federalist,* No. 37, p. 232.
28 *Federalist,* No. 49, p. 331.
29 *Federalist,* No. 10, p. 56.

as little to be expected as the philosophical race of kings wished for by Plato,"[30] it is tempting to speculate that *The Federalist* contemplates a kind of philosopher-founder the posthumous duration of whose rule depends upon "that veneration which time bestows on everything,"[31] and in particular on a regime well-founded. But once founded, it is a system that has no necessary place and makes no provision for men of the founding kind.

It is clear that not all now regarded as Founding Fathers were thought by the authors of *The Federalist* to belong in that august company. Noting that "it is not a little remarkable" that all previous foundings of regimes were "performed by some individual citizen of pre-eminent wisdom and approved integrity,"[32] *The Federalist* comments on the difficulty that must have been experienced when it was attempted to found a regime by the action of an assembly of men. I think it can be shown that *The Federalist* views that assembly, the Federal Convention, as having been subject to all the weaknesses of multitudes of men. The real founders, then, were very few in number, men learned in the new science of politics who seized upon a uniquely propitious moment when their plans were consented to first by a body of respectable men and subsequently, by equally great good fortune, by the body of citizens. As it were, America provided a rare moment when "the prejudices of the community"[33] were on the side of wisdom. Not unnaturally, then, *The Federalist* is extremely reluctant to countenance any re-opening of fundamental questions or delay in ratifying the Constitution.

This circumstance—wisdom meeting with consent—is so rare that "it is impossible for the man of pious reflection not to perceive in it a finger of that Almighty hand."[34] But once consent has been given to the new wisdom, when the government has been properly founded, it will be a durable regime whose perpetuation requires nothing like the wisdom and virtue necessary for its creation. The Founding Fathers' belief that they had created a system of institutions and an arrangement of the passions and interests, that would be durable and self-perpetuating, helps explain their failure to make provision for men of their own kind to come after them. Apparently, it was thought that such men would not be needed.

But does not the intensity and kind of our modern problems seem to require of us a greater degree of reflection and public-spiritedness than the Founders thought sufficient for the men who came after them? One good way to begin that reflection would be to return to their level of thought-

---

[30] *Federalist*, No. 49, p. 329.
[31] *Ibid.*, p. 328.
[32] *Federalist*, No. 38, p. 233.
[33] *Federalist*, No. 49, p. 329.
[34] *Federalist*, No. 38, p. 231.

fulness about fundamental political alternatives, so that we may judge for ourselves wisely regarding the profound issues that face us. I know of no better beginning for that thoughtfulness than a full and serious contemplation of the political theory that informed the origin of the Republic, of the thought and intention of those few men who fully grasped what the "assembly of demi-gods" was doing.

A Portico Facing the Wilderenss

MERRILL D. PETERSON

When John Adams died on the fiftieth anniversary of the Declaration of Indepence, he said "Thomas Jefferson still survives." Jefferson, who died that same day, is still one of the most eloquent voices of the American Enlightenment. His *Notes on the State of Virginia,* published in 1785 in Paris, where its author had gone as commissioner to negotiate treaties, was written to explain his country to the French. Moving from a meticulous description of geography, climate, and resources, it develops into an expression of belief in the New World as the place where the Enlightenment has its best chance of fulfillment. Convinced that Americans were blessed by an ocean which kept them from "contamination" by the "people of the Old World," he was, nevertheless, fascinated by European achievements in music, scholarship, manners, and the visual arts. Jefferson's aristocratically tempered republicanism, his culturally enlightened nationalism, and his blend of practical caution and idealistic rhetoric have made him an elusive figure for historians. Merrill D. Peterson has caught the range and quality of Jefferson's mind.

MONTICELLO CLEANLY EXPOSED JEFFERSON'S FUNDAMENTAL AMBIguity. "He was of the old order and he was not." The mind fluctuated between its antithetical meanings, those that were past and reminiscent of the Old World, those that were new in the American vernacular. Jefferson inherited a double tradition, Lewis Mumford said, that of the Renaissance man who sought to transcend provinciality through the universal forms of the ancients, and that of the American pioneer whose bent was mechanical and utilitarian. He did not in Monticello, could not in his own mind, Mumford thought, harmonize his formal tastes with his love of vital American things. The locale, the gadgets, the American curiosities that hung from the walls had no organic relation to the build-

Merrill D. Peterson, *The Jeffersonian Image in the American Mind,* 1960, pp. 394–417. Reprinted with deletions by permission of Oxford University Press. Copyright © 1960 by Oxford University Press.

ing itself. Monticello suggested, even in Jefferson's time, the museum of Americana it has indubitably become.

Because it made these ambiguous impressions on the mind, no uniform Monticello image of Jefferson emerged. Monticello predicated culture, but in what precise sense it was difficult to say. The dominant recognition, however, was the one which shocked political preconceptions the most. The poetry of Monticello, in landscape, architecture, and interior decor, was more persuasive than its practical mechanism; the sense of the archaic more powerful than the sense of the modern; the impression of Old World order and refinement more compelling than the impression of New World life. But the portico, after all, faced the wilderness. There was the riddle.

· · ·

Monticello graphically presented Jefferson's prodigious genius. Here were his music stand and his architect's table, the furniture and gardens of his own design, the numerous mementoes of his work in science and invention. The library, the dining room, the old man's lookout over the rising University, the stables and the nailery—the imagination could hardly keep up. Was Jefferson the American Leonardo?

> The big hands clever
> With pen and fiddle
> And ready, ever,
> For any riddle.
>
> From buying empires
> To planting 'taters,
> From Declarations
> To dumb-waiters.

The recognition, which Stephen Vincent Benét thus caught up in rhyme, was first clearly foreshadowed in James Parton's famous description of "a gentleman of thirty-two." "Posterity," the *Springfield* (Mass.) *Republican* correctly observed in 1902, "is apt to remember Jefferson only as a statesman and politician." The appreciation of "how much else he was" besides "the father of democracy" came gradually, first in education, next in law and religion and science, then in the arts and letters. Finally, by 1943, in almost everything from "planting 'taters . . . to dumb-waiters." The varied tributaries of this research fed into the conception of "the civilized man."

Although Jefferson was the recognized architect of Monticello, the importance of that achievement and of his architectural work generally, both from a professional and an artistic standpoint, went comparatively unnoticed until the second decade of this century. For a century or more, practicing architects in this country worked in a tradition of classical design, especially in public buildings, without realizing Jefferson's seminal role. That he had some connection with such eminent architects in this tradition as Robert Mills was noted by William Dunlap in his pioneer history of American art in 1834. That he conceived the Capitol at Richmond from the Maison Carée, the Roman temple at Nîmes on which he had gazed whole hours, as he said, "like a lover at his mistress," was known because of his autobiographical account of this enterprise. That he was the architectural, as well as the educational, father of the University of Virginia was usually taken for granted. All of this vaguely suggested Jefferson's importance without fixing his architectural responsibility.

The architects remained, for the most part, ignorant to Jefferson's pretension in their domain for years to come. In the few instances where they did not ignore, they were skeptical and inclined to attribute the buildings to practicing architects with whom Jefferson consulted. Thus a member of the firm that restored the Virginia Capitol spoke of "Jefferson and his architect," the Frenchman Clerisseau; and Montgomery Schuyler voiced the same opinion even more strongly in an article which traced the classical revival in America to Benjamin H. Latrobe. Glenn Brown, who had earlier associated Mills with Monticello, argued in 1913 that William Thornton was the true architect of the University. Comparing Thornton's drawings for the United States Capitol with unsigned drawings for the University, a number of which Herbert Baxter Adams had published in his 1888 monograph, Brown concluded that they came from the same hand and that hand was Thornton's. Jefferson thus acted, architectural historian Norman M. Isham wrote, "with Thornton's sketches in his hands and Thornton's advice in his mind." These deprecatory opinions were not surprising in view of prevalent ideas about Jefferson. It seemed reasonable to pass off the political hero as a dilettante or dabbler in other fields, one associated with household gadgets, serpentine walls, and impractical plows. Moreover, in the absence of respectable evidence bearing on Jefferson's architectural work, incredulity seemed warranted.

The corner was turned in 1913 with the publication of *Thomas Jefferson as an Architect and Designer of Landscape,* the collaboration of two professionals, William A. Lambeth and Warren H. Manning. The part by Manning on landscape was superficial. The major part, by Lambeth, though far from comprehensive or definitive, anticipated the later canonization of Jefferson as "the father [Lambeth was satisfied with "godfather"] of American architecture." He found no evidence that Thornton contributed anything but possibly a few rough suggestions to Jefferson's plans for the University. Unquestionably, Jefferson was "the real and only

achitect of Monticello." Lambeth called attention to the crucial influence
of the sixteenth-century Italian, Palladio. In England and elsewhere in
America, the Palladian became Georgian. Jefferson, on the other hand,
worked back from Palladio to the pure Roman types, such as the Pantheon.
Every form by Jefferson, Lambeth said, "became increasingly refined and
classical." But he made daring innovations, especially at Monticello, neither
degrading the classic form nor forgetting, in his buildings, "the abiding
integrity" that resides in harmony with time, setting, and function. Lambeth observed the influence of Monticello on other famous Virginia mansions, but he was unable to assign them to Jefferson.

Jefferson's twentieth-century reputation as an architect is very largely
due to the talent and energy of one man, the architect, art historian, museum director, and restorer of historic buildings, Fiske Kimball. The
richest unsearched treasure of Jefferson manuscripts then in existence
opened to Kimball just before the World War, when he was a student at
Harvard and the University of Michigan. This was the collection of over
three hundred sheets of drawings in the possession of Mrs. Thomas Jefferson Coolidge, Jr.[1] In 1915 Kimball published with the appropriate drawings his initial study, *Thomas Jefferson and the First Monument of the
Classical Revival in America.* The Virginia Capitol, mentioned only in
passing by Lambeth and generally attributed to Clerisseau, was not only
Jefferson's work but also the beginning of the classical revival, Kimball
argued. The implications of this position were truly startling. The reign
of the classical in the public architecture of the United States, and by virtue of association in American taste generally, was inaugurated by Jefferson. Indeed, the more Kimball, along with Talbot Hamlin and others,
studied the matter, the more convinced they became that Jefferson's Capitol
prefigured the classical revival everywhere. And since this adaptation of
ancient forms to the service of the new nation's republican ideals represented the first departure from the mindless copybook carpentry of early
American building, Jefferson was "the father of our national architecture."

Kimball reached this conclusion in the text he wrote to accompany the
magnificent folio volume of Jefferson's drawings, *Thomas Jefferson Architect,* which Mrs. Coolidge published as a memorial to her husband in

[1] The Coolidge branch of the family was especially interested in Monticello.
Young Archibald Cary Coolidge attempted to buy his great-great-grandfather's
estate in 1889, and he later opposed the successive efforts to make Monticello
a national shrine. His cousin, Thomas Jefferson Coolidge, Jr., built a near replica
of Monticello as his home on Boston's fashionable North Shore. Collecting in the
Jefferson neighborhood in 1911, he and his wife came upon a great number of
well-nigh forgotten architectural drawings in the keeping of two descendants
in the Randolph line. These formed the bulk of the collection to which Kimball,
with the help of Worthington C. Ford, gained access.

1916. Here for the first time was massive documentation of Jefferson's architectural work from as early as 1769. He must have got his ideas and skills almost entirely from books, chiefly Palladio's, Kimball thought. But no explanation in terms of intellectual influence really sufficed. Why Palladio? Kimball asked. Because Jefferson saw in Palladio's codification of the laws and proportions of classical design the architectural statement of his own philosophy. It confirmed his Newtonian faith in a rational and ordered universe. Palladio appealed to his scientific precision of mind, and also to his love of the ancients. "Jefferson's art was the art of retrospection and of science." His influence, as Kimball showed, was not limited to a few model buildings. Quietly, almost imperceptibly, he worked to encourage a profession of architecture with schools of instruction, and public appreciation and patronage of this most useful of the fine arts.

Many students, lay and professional, followed in Kimball's track; but, as Talbot Hamlin said in his authoritative study, *The Greek Revival in American Architecture* (1944), Kimball had so accurately appraised Jefferson's position "that any further statement is unnecessary." Hamlin, it is worth noting, did not discount Jefferson's importance because his Roman style was soon superseded by the Grecian. The decisive fact was Jefferson's innovation of the distinctive American style, classic but modern in the circumstances of the time, from which the history and profession of architecture in this country took their rise. On the trail of Jefferson's influence, students discovered his contribution to the National Capitol and to numerous Southern mansions. And his name came to be so closely identified with the monumental style in public architecture that it seemed only fitting to enthusiasts like Kimball that a Roman temple should be his memorial in Washington.

The architectural inquiry gradually opened into other branches of the fine arts. The documentary record, illustrated with a few monuments, was most abundant in the instance of landscape gardening. He planned his gardens as carefully as he planned his buildings, yet in a radically different style. One was classical, the other rococo; one straight and purely proportioned, the other serpentine and ornamental to excess. One evoked the humanist, the other the romantic naturalist. None of the explanations advanced for this mingling of styles proved satisfactory. The personality which the architect revealed to Kimball was contradicted by the personality of the landscape gardener. A revealing instance was Jefferson's serpentine garden wall on the grounds of the University. The philosopher Horace Kallen thought the idea must have come from William Hogarth, the English champion of the serpentine line, the line of nature, as he thought, against the artificial lines of the regnant Palladian style. But there was no record of Jefferson's knowledge of Hogarth; Kimball and other scholars explained the design of the famous wall on practical and economical grounds. Then, in 1943, a Jefferson memorandum of 1771 came to light: he was familiar with Hogarth after all. Jefferson's artistic originality, the overjoyed Kallen wrote, lay precisely in his orchestration of the two styles, the austere formalism of the Palladian and the lambent freedom of the Hogarthian. Kallen's student, Eleanor D. Berman, in her *Thomas Jefferson Among the Arts,* flatly stated that Jefferson's serpentine wall was "harmonious with the spirit of American democracy," "a directive toward liberty," because it "goes with both the wilderness and the simple virtuous life of the American countryside." Here again, then, the search for plausible answers to new riddles tempted the student to focus Jefferson's role in providing aesthetic forms agreeable to the native culture.

Of the other arts, only music seriously engaged Jefferson. Stories of Jefferson and his violin were commonplace in the nineteenth century. Their intent was not so much to show his musical forte as it was to illustrate certain personal habits and add amusing or rustic touches to the image. In these stories it was not a violin but a "fiddle"; Jefferson was a "fiddler," and whether the best or the worst in Virginia did not really matter. Then, as Jefferson acquired titles of firstness in so many areas of talent, his reputation in music grew until he was called "America's first great amateur violinist." Jefferson bought a good violin in 1775 (there was an amusing story about this too), generally believed to have been a Cremona by Amati. If so, it was one of the finest in the colonies. Albert Hildebrandt, a cellist and collector of rare violins, while in Charlottesville to play a concert in 1899, asked his barber if he knew of any old violins in the vicinity. The barber sent him to a ninety-three year old Negro who claimed to own a violin bequeathed to his father by Jefferson. Although its authenticity has never been established, the violin Hildebrandt thus bought for a farthing has since been valued at a price that silences doubt.

Beginning with the legend of the violin, students explored the range of Jefferson's musical interests: the music he knew, the compositions he owned and played in Virginia; the operas and concerts he attended in Paris and, while there, his romantic affair with the talented painter and musician, Maria Cosway; his alertness to technical improvements in musical instruments; and his concern for American musical production. The gift of Jefferson's music library to the Thomas Jefferson Memorial Foundation by Fanny Maury Burke, a descendant, led two scholars, Carlton Sprague Smith and Helen Duprey Bullock, to commence a study of his musical life. Although the project never matured, an important by-product was the latter's editing of the Jefferson-Cosway correspondence. During the

Bicentennial, Jefferson's love of music—"the favorite passion of my soul" —was commemorated in concerts devoted to the music he knew.

Jefferson embraced in some fashion all the arts; but how should his aesthetic ideas and interests be characterized? Some thought he was, at heart, an "artistic spirit," perhaps "the father of the arts in America" as well. No contemporary ranged as widely or with more proficiency and enthusiasm. He sought with some success to break down provincialism, to elevate tastes, and to inspire the young nation with ideals of beauty the world could respect. But despite porticoes, opera, and cuisine, some scholars denied that Jefferson was really so far removed from the commonplace life of Americans. A memorandum of 1788, "Traveling Notes for Mr. Rutledge and Mr. Shippen," which Gilbert Chinard uncovered and labeled "a most damning document," seemed to anticipate Mark Twain in the Philistinism and Puritanism it displayed toward European civilization. Jefferson advised the touring Americans to fix their minds on agriculture, the mechanical arts, and politics. Painting and statuary were "worth seeing, but not studying." Two arts were recommended as *useful* to the Americans: gardening, because the noblest gardens might be made at least expense in America; and architecture, because the Americans had to have houses and, besides, "it is desirable to introduce taste into an art which shows so much." Enraptured by the simple virtues of his own country, Jefferson could not surrender to the aesthetic charms of Europe. From this it might be concluded that he, like the bourgeois gentleman, found art amusing but unworthy of serious pursuit. And yet, there was Monticello. Perhaps, as Albert J. Nock thought, it was necessary to distinguish between the *contemplation* of art, which never touched Jefferson deeply, and the *cultivation* of those arts in which he and the mass of practical-minded Americans could participate. Even in music, Kallen observed, Jefferson was "much more articulate about the processes of musical production than about the enjoyment of the musical product; his delight was more in the how than in the what of music."

The marked dualities of Jefferson's aesthetic could not be organized into a uniform pattern, such as would authorize sweeping generalizations about his mind and thought. But like the dualities of Monticello, they tended to fall naturally into the categories of the dual heritage. Thus, Kallen said, Jefferson united in his person Virginia's divided culture: the elegance of the Cavalier and the workmanship of the Pioneer. "Fundamentally Jefferson's aesthetic involved a dissolution of classical attitudes in spontaneously pioneer sentiments and practices." In this dissolution, it would seem, the classical ideals of order and decorum acquired a distinctive American practicality, spaciousness, and freedom. Puzzled by the apparent dichotomies in Jefferson's artistic life, students might make sense of them in the generalized image of one who synthesized two contrasting cultural ideals.

The earlier and continuing appreciation of Jefferson the Scientist helped to check the exaggeration of his "artistic spirit." The scientific side had been evident ever since the publication of the *Notes on Virginia*, called by a leading scientist one hundred years later the most influential scientific work published in America up to that time. One of its purposes was to refute the theory of certain European savants on the degeneration of animal species in the New World. An often repeated story concerned the trouble and expense Jefferson incurred to have the bones of a great moose shipped to Paris in order to vindicate American nature. Jefferson was President of the American Philosophical Society for many years. He sent Lewis and Clark into the Northern wilderness partly with a view to satisfying the scientific curiosity of the world. He even laid the foundations of the Republican party, some would believe, while on a "botanizing excursion" in New York. Because his scientific ideas and activities had a broad public character, they entered into the image of the political man. Satirists worked them into their portrait of the impractical visionary, while admirers eulogized him for uniting in his life "the retired love of science with the practical energy of the world."

Well known as something of a scientist (or natural philosopher) during his lifetime, Jefferson was pretty much forgotten by working scientists for several generations after his death. In the general literature, his scientific aspect was, at best, a subsidiary aid in the characterization of the political leader. It helped Henry S. Randall, for instance, to refute the idea of the visionary. Jefferson's experiments in agriculture, which most interested Randall, showed the same bent toward discovery, the same traits of practicality, he displayed in politics. Henry Adams, on the other hand, though bewildered by the clash between Jefferson's scientific temperament and doctrinaire politics, finally left the impression of "a theorist, prepared to risk the fate of mankind on the chance of reasoning far from certain of its details." Emphasis on one side led to the idea of the gadgeteer, with the American's vaunted practicality. Emphasis on the other side continued the legend of the speculator, with the eighteenth-century philosopher's love of abstraction and treacherous omniscience. On either side, it was hard to take Jefferson seriously as a scientist.

The faint beginnings of the scientists' appreciation appeared in the eighteen-eighties. Frederic N. Luther's article on "Jefferson as a Naturalist," in 1885, first illuminated the subject. The following year, G. Brown Goode of the Smithsonian Institution bracketed Jefferson with Louis Agassiz as the two men who had done most for the advancement of science in America, "not so much by their direct contributions to knowledge, as by the immense weight which they gave to scientific interests by their advocacy." At about the same time the earliest special studies appeared, for example, Henry A. Martin's paper, "Jefferson as a Vaccinator," in the *North Carolina Medical Journal*. Studies of this type, however, would not appear in number for another thirty or forty years. Curious about the American beginnings of their work, scientists were to find Jefferson's writings suggestive and sometimes instructive. By 1943 a sizable literature, ranging from horticulture to astronomy, from entomology to mathematics, had accumulated on Jefferson the Scientist. To his many titles of renown, the scientists added "Pioneer Soil Conservationist," "Pioneer Botanist," "Pioneer Student of American Geography," "Father of American Paleontology," and so on.

While some of this literature added to the stock of the "wild and visionary" conception, the preponderant weight of it fell into the practical scale. Jefferson always sought to turn his investigations to tangible use, it was commonly said. His scientific spirit, as some thought his artistic spirit, looked toward clearly defined social and moral purposes. Especially significant in this connection was his devotion to agriculture: the moldboard of the plow, crop rotation, animal breeding, control of pests, improvement of seeds, and so on. "It was Jefferson more than any other man of his time who foresaw the fruitfulness of the application of science to agriculture." Just as he was more interested in personal and public health than in the science of medicine, he was particularly interested in the economic branches of entomology, botany, chemistry, and geology. He was the kind of man who in the later years of his life, as Albert J. Nock recalled, could seriously ask himself, "Whether my country is the better for my having lived at all"; then seriously name among his best services the removal of obstructions to navigation on the Rivanna River, the importation of olive trees from France and of heavy upland rice from Africa.

Paleontology was Jefferson's one passion in pure science. Frederic A. Lucas named him "the Father of Paleontology" in 1926; such eminent authorities as Henry Fairfield Osborn concurred. Jefferson laid the foundations of the science, it was said, with his systematic refutation of Buffon's degeneracy theory, and with his subsequent work on the "Great Claw," an extinct species which he named Megalonyx and which became known as *Megalonyx jeffersoni*. He constantly interested himself in paleontology. Specimens that passed through his hands are still exhibited in American museums. After Jefferson, according to Osborn, the science slept for several decades in the United States. Jefferson's reputation became well established among paleontologists. How well, and upon what slight basis, is suggested by the statement of George G. Simpson, of the American Museum of Natural History, in his paper on "The Beginnings of Vertebrate Paleontology in the United States," read before the American Philosophical Society in 1942:

> Thomas Jefferson has become a fabulous figure to palentologists, few of whom know what he really did but most of whom consider him as the father or founder of vertebrate paleontology in America. . . . It should not be considered iconoclastic (although I have already learned that it seems so to my colleagues) to state that he was not a vertebrate paleontologist in any reasonable sense of the words, that he never collected a fossil or gave one a technical name, and that his scientific contributions were negligible or retrogressive.

Jefferson's only importance, Simpson said, was in helping to make paleontology respectable and to bring together the materials necessary for its advancement. The entire basis of his natural philosophy was retrogressive, since he denied that animal species could ever become extinct. The science of paleontology could not begin until exactly the opposite premise was established. Having no claim to scientific eminence in the field, Jefferson would have been the first, Simpson thought, to repudiate the legend of the paleontologists.

The true understanding of Jefferson's scientific work could begin only after the investigators realized that Jefferson, and the intellectual species Jeffersoni, was extinct. Too many of his scientific interpreters had interpolated his ideas into their own worlds of thought. The result was distortion of Jefferson's natural philosophy and exaggeration of his importance as the common father, midwife, and nurse, along with Benjamin Franklin, of the American sciences. The first significant study to go on the assumption of an extinct species of thinkers, of which Jefferson was the pre-eminent type, was Daniel J. Boorstin's *The Lost World of Thomas Jefferson* in 1948. The Jeffersonian world of ideas was lost, in science as well as in morals and politics.

Boorstin's book emphasized as never before the activistic and utilitarian bent of Jefferson's mind. While this was the major impression left by the study of Jefferson's science, it could not be forgotten that he cultivated the sensible and useful with a transcendental aim. Just as he believed the useful in architecture would beautify the American landscape and elevate the American character, he regarded science as an instrument in the pursuit of humanitarian goals. Science with the technology derived from it, rather than institutions of government, some came to feel, was the engine of his faith. "It was always his opinion that whoever could make two ears of corn, or even two blades of grass grow upon a plot of ground where only one grew before would deserve better of mankind, and do more essential service to his country than the whole race of politicians put together."

The praise of Jefferson by the votaries of science was not mistaken, though it was often given for the wrong reasons. More important than anything or everything Jefferson did as a scientist was his creation as a statesman of a favorable climate for scientific progress. The connection he made between knowledge and humanitarian purpose, the freedom of inquiry gained by his works for freedom, the encouragement and prestige he gave to scientific endeavor as a private citizen (the American Philosophical Society), public official (the Patents Office, the Coastal Survey, the Naval Observatory), and educator (the curriculum of the University of Virginia)—this statesmanship of science addressed the distant future and assured his fame, if not as a scientist, then as the sciences' best servant and advocate.

Still another side of Jefferson, the Man of Letters, came increasingly into view in the twentieth century. "As a political leader, he was literally a man of letters; and his letters are masterpieces, if viewed as illustrations of the arts by which political leadership may be attained," the critic Edwin P. Whipple wrote in a centennial essay on the nation's literature. He thought Jefferson "the greatest, or, at least the most generally known, of American authors." The view was eccentric, though shared in part by Moses Coit Tyler and a few others. The American people had felt "the magic persuasiveness" of Jefferson's pen in documents (the Declaration of Independence, the Kentucky Resolutions) and in the private letters by which he built and still inspired the Democratic party. But this, of course, was a masterful literary talent in the service of politics. Except for the Declaration, little if anything in the Jefferson canon commended his admission to the world of letters, and he certainly never asked entrance. He was a superb rhetorician, in the ancient usage of that term, interested in the communication of ideas rather than in the beauties of expression. He never wrote a book in the literary sense. Even the *Notes on Virginia* showed scarcely a trace of literary effort. "It is a book of statistics, without pretense of being anything else, and," A. J. Nock added, "it is probably the most interesting statistical work ever produced." Although the response to Jefferson's artistic side led to numerous appreciations of his writings as literature, his growing reputation in the world of letters hinged more securely on two things: his devotion to literature, especially the classics, and his scholarly interest in language.

The attention of philologists was first pointedly drawn to Jefferson in 1882. Henry E. Shepherd, writing in the *American Journal of Philol-*

ogy, scrutinized Jefferson's advocacy of neologism, his belief in the dynamic growth of language from everyday usage, and his detection of the historical process of dialectic regeneration of languages. In these things, Shepherd said, he anticipated the work of the most eminent English philologists. Jefferson's *Essay on Anglo-Saxon Grammar,* though published for instructional use at the University of Virginia in 1851, was first made generally accessible in the Memorial Edition, as were several other literary curios. Before 1920 the scholars were calling Jefferson a "linguistic liberal," "an astute scientific philologist," and "the real pioneer in historical English work in America."

In this field, as in others, Jefferson swept a wide arc. Classicists applied his methods to the analysis of ancient verse, and found them fruitful. Anthropologists discovered in his speculations on language anticipations of the importance of linguistics for the study of primitive cultures. And students of the *American* language hailed him as a pioneer.

One of the major tasks of recent Jefferson scholarship has been the establishment of his literary calendar. The knowledge of the books he owned, and more than likely read, at various intervals of his life gradually came to be regarded as the desideratum of authentic study of his thought. The definitive reconstruction of Jefferson's mind as revealed through his books was manifestly impossible, chiefly because, as Randolph G. Adams observed, "it almost seems as though some ghostly pyromaniac had pursued Mr. Jefferson all of his days." Still there were fragmentary sources: the internal evidence of his letters, the account books where he often enumerated his acquisitions, book lists he prepared at the invitation of friends, the commonplace books into which he copied favorite passages, and, most of all, the more than two thousand volumes saved from the Library of Congress fire of 1851, supplemented by the Library's catalogue of 1815 and subsequent years. The Library, conscious of the scholars' need and eager to repay its debt to Jefferson (not only did his collection become the nucleus of one of the great libraries of the world, but the Library also employed his classification system for the better part of a century), engaged the British scholar and bibliophile, E. Millicent Sowerby, to compile an annotated catalogue of every item in the original Jefferson collection. The project was announced on April 13, 1943.

The calendar, painstakingly assembled, documented a mind too prodigious in its learning and too varied in its wellsprings to permit easy classification. One of the dominant impressions was that of Jefferson's "constant commerce with the ancients." Of course, every educated man in the eighteenth century was a classical scholar of sorts. But Jefferson's knowledge of the histories and languages, the schools of science, ethics, and aesthetics, of the ancient world gave him claim to a higher order of accomplishment, and invited reconsideration of the man's personal style and ideal of civilization. The ideal, like its vivid presentment Monticello, was seen to involve the transplantation of the humanistic heritage from its fountainhead in the ancient world to the western vastnesses of America. An uncompromising innovator, a radical and defiant foe of mere tradition, Jefferson nevertheless, Thomas Fitzhugh warned, "recognized the original and primal leadership of Greece and Rome in human civilization, and saw that the continuity of human ideals and achievement depended upon a continuous maintenance of touch between the ancient and modern leaders of our race."

Jefferson's likes and dislikes in belles-lettres furnished another clue to his well-guarded inner life. Ranging from Homer to Ossian, Jefferson's taste was not markedly different from the taste of his time. He matured in the neo-classic age, but felt the pull of the romantic age, fully arrived when he died. A Virginia scholar, John W. Wayland, argued in 1910 "that Jefferson had the poetical spirit and feeling in considerable measure, and that his poetical tastes were not only keen but also in some degree cultivated." But the evidence was not convincing. Several poems were attributed to him from time to time, but with one or two exceptions all of these have since been traced to other writers, from whom Jefferson copied them. Gilbert Chinard, in the introduction he wrote to *The Literary Bible of Thomas Jefferson,* the commonplace book of philosophers and poets kept by the young Jefferson, came to the opposite conclusion from Wayland's. "In spite of the quotations from ancient and modern poets his was not a poetical mind." Jefferson, it seemed, had at one time the moralist's taste *in* poetry, but never an aesthetic taste *for* poetry. He also had, as *Thoughts on English Prosody* showed, the technician's interest in verse. How a poem was constructed engaged his mind; what a poem was did not seriously engage his emotions.

Of Jefferson as a Man of Letters, Max Herzberg wrote in 1914, he "had in him two powerful tendencies: one that of the idealist and dreamer, one that of the practical man of affairs." Here again, then, was the fundamental duality: Jefferson magnetically gathering to himself the poles of human experience. Wherever in any particular field the revolving needle of his mind turned, as in this field it turned chiefly to the "profit" aspect, it was never possible to forget that it compassed the "pleasure" aspect as well.

The Arts, the Sciences, and Letters: most of the talents of the cultivated man—the Culture Hero—are embraced in these categories, though not every one has been noticed. Jefferson the Lawyer, for example. "It is the fate of great men to devour themselves; the earlier man is swallowed up in the later." Such had been the fate, John W. Davis thought, of "Thomas Jefferson: Attorney at Law." William Wirt's famous eulogy had reminded Americans of the brilliance of Jefferson's early career at the bar and of its influence on the later statesman. But this was quickly forgotten. He could not have been a successful advocate, many believed, because of a temperament indisposed to personal combat and a voice that seldom rose above a whisper. Randall, in 1858, found it necessary to reestablish Jefferson's reputation as a lawyer; lawyers and scholars half a century later took up the task again. By 1943 there could be no question of Jefferson's success at the bar. (He was employed in as many as four hundred and thirty cases in a single year.) His lawyer's knowledge, moreover, was by then widely regarded as the foundation of his political philosophy.

Perhaps the most amazing curiosity gathered from the profusion of talents was *Thomas Jefferson's Cook Book*. Marie Kimball, wife of Fiske Kimball and Curator of Monticello, published this volume of recipes, with an account of Jefferson's Lucullan appetite and culinary arts, in 1941. The recipes were taken from the cookbook kept by a granddaughter at Monticello, Virginia Randolph Trist, and presented to the Memorial Foundation by a descendant. With the help of this book it was at last possible to have a real Jeffersonian dinner! It would be anything but simple. The French cuisine predominated. Jefferson, as Patrick Henry had said, "abjured his native vittels." Although Mrs. Kimball hesitated to acclaim him "Father of Cooking," she pointed out that he introduced Americans to such foods as vanilla and macaroni, and wrote in his own hand the first American recipe for ice cream. "He penned a rule for *Nouilly a macaroni* with the gravity that he signed a treaty." The *Cook Book* belonged to Monticello along with the gardens, the wedgewood, the gilt mirrors, and the wine cellar—relics of the epicure whose great art was "the art of living."

In his life and in his vision, Jefferson transcended politics. He stood for a cultural heritage Americans could admire, cherish, perhaps be elevated by, but could not hope to possess in its fullness. Its remnants lay everywhere—in what Americans thought, in how they were educated and governed, in the way they worshipped, in the sciences they professed, in the houses they built, the words they used, the foods they ate. Jefferson stood for a life planned and executed in full human scale, for thought down to the last detail, for a mind that related every fact to every other fact in the universe, for a life "not split into bits," as Ezra Pound said, but given "wholeness and mental order." Being part of a culture so painfully "split into bits," compartmentalized and intellectually dis-ordered, this century's American has been astounded by the full felicitous sweep of Jefferson's genius. Generously exposed to view, Jefferson's attainments were naturally exaggerated. Men tended to forget that it was not just Jefferson who was different but also the age in which he lived, an age populated with versatile gentlemen, although none, unless the older Franklin, as eminent and brilliant as he.

. . .

More crucial for the new scholarship, which he as much as anyone shaped, was the ripe fruit of Chinard's labors in 1929. This French scholar, teaching at Johns Hopkins, had given many years to the study of the intellectual relations between the United States and France in the eighteenth century. It had led him into Jefferson's correspondence with Volney, Destutt de Tracy, Lafayette, and other Frenchmen, some of which he edited, and finally into the center of Jefferson's thought. By the time he came to write his major book on Jefferson, Chinard had thus shown two dominant concerns. One, in respect to subject, the concern for Jefferson's ideas, particularly in their formative stage about which little was known and later in relation to French thinkers about which there was only a legend. Two, in respect to method, the determination to discover Jefferson afresh in the mass of unpublished papers few scholars had ever troubled themselves to explore.

Tracing the unifying design in the varied carpet of Jefferson's mind, Chinard could find no better word to describe it than Americanism. The point had been made before, most notably by Parton; and Americans had often used Jefferson as a mirror of national character. At the same time, however, and especially in academic circles, there was "the legend of a denationalized Jefferson": a Frenchman in his ideas, a Virginian in his party leadership, a universalist in his ultimate vision. Chinard's own investigation had begun in the shadow of this legend. But having set out to determine the French influence on Jefferson, having then experienced the cultural shock incident to the transplantation from Europe to America, and, as his fascination led him more deeply into Jefferson's papers, having found the same cultural contrasts in the eighteenth century, Chinard came to realize that Jefferson was "the most integrally and truly American among his contemporaries."

The gradual mergence of Jefferson's personality in a philosophy which ought, in Chinard's judgment, to be known as Americanism instead of Jeffersonian Democracy, began with his education in English law. "His was eminently the mind of the lawyer." Converted by his youthful legal studies to the Anglo-Saxon conception of English history, this became the true foundation of his political system. (John Fiske had broached the key idea decades before: that Jefferson was "simply the earnest but cool-headed representative of the rural English freeholders that won Magna Charta and overthrew the usurpations of the Stuarts.") Jefferson's position was racial not philosophical, historical and legal not abstract, conservative not radical. The two faces he proposed in 1776 for the shield of the new nation—the children of Israel in the Wilderness and the Saxon chiefs Hengist and Horsa—expressed his conviction the Americans were a people chosen to reclaim the Saxon birthright. "The Jeffersonian Democracy was born under the sign of Hengist and Horsa, not the Goddess of Reason." Viewed in this light, Jefferson's radicalism was, like so much of American radicalism, retrospective. He ruled, as Henry Adams had said, with a Golden Age in view; but it was set in the past. Chinard made his point with the extravagance of a discoverer.

"We are led to a very unexpected conclusion," Chinard said of Jefferson's years abroad, 1785–90. "There is little doubt that Jefferson's democratic theories were confirmed and clarified by this prolonged stay in Europe. But this was not due to the lessons he received from the French philosophers." Recent historians of the French influence (the American, Charles Hazen, and Chinard's French contemporary, Bernard Fay, for example) had not really changed the underlying idea of the European experience as a form of intellectual expatriation for Jefferson, who thus became, upon his return, the advance agent of radical democracy in the United States. Chinard thought the effect of Jefferson's immersion in European, particularly French, civilization just the reverse. His mental horizon and his manner of life were unchanged. But Europe strengthened his sense of nationality. As an American minister abroad, Jefferson was compelled to subordinate his provincial attachment to Virginia and to think of the United States as "one nation." Europe swelled Jefferson's pride in the simple virtues of American life and the superiority of American character. At first dazzled by the splendors of the Old World, he soon concluded "that the game was not worth the candle." In letters to American friends, he warned against the aesthetic temptations of Europe; and he denounced the moral corruptions of European civilization, Chinard said, "as vehemently as any Puritan preacher and with the same frankness of expression." His political principles, which laws and social conditions made practicable in America, merely beat the air in Europe. Seeing this, Jefferson, reluctantly but decisively, curtailed the universal references of his political philosophy and made it into the creed of Americanism.

Europe, the world, being what they were, Chinard went on, isolation seemed to Jefferson the wisest policy for the United States. His ideal did indeed transcend the limits of nationality—he dreamed of "a family of nations." But since, as Jefferson learned, the European powers were not prepared for his liberal system, and since no real co-operation appeared possible except among free nations, he advocated a realistic foreign policy while at the same time holding intact his ideal of a universe of freedom. Here, Chinard thought, was perhaps the most striking instance of Jefferson's happy faculty of maintaining his ideals apart from, but in constant tension with, political realities. "Far from being a single-track mind, his was decidedly a double-track intellect with two lines of thought running parallel without any apparent contradiction, for theory never seemed to have interfered with his practice." Much of the confusion about Jefferson centered in this trait. So often condemned either as a visionary philosopher or as a hardheaded politician, even as both at once and therefore a hypocrite and deceiver, Jefferson in fact, Chinard said, combined idealism and practicality in a creative outlook all the world has since taken to be the characteristically American outlook of "Practical Idealism." Its expression in American foreign policy was "an equal balance between national selfishness and philosophical idealism," the maintenance of which was beset with the greatest difficulties in Jefferson's time and was now unworkable.

Jefferson, like American civilization itself, could not be reduced to formula. Such polarities as idealism and practicality, universalism and isolationism, the agrarian dream and scientific progress, which observers found in American life, Chinard found in Jefferson. The roots of his thought spread into many traditions, chiefly the classical, the Christian, and English law. But Jefferson took from these only the ingredients America needed, synthesized them, and thus helped to make America the heir of all without being the heir of any one. The political creed he espoused in 1800 owed nothing to Europe. It was a national, not a partisan, creed: the first complete definition of Americanism in government, Chinard thought. Contrary to Bowers, Jefferson had not been a party leader during the previous decade of party warfare, and the little "Quarrel with Hamilton" had no significant influence on the destiny of the nation. Contrary to Beard, Jefferson never conceived of his party as agrarian, his faith as a class faith, or sought to favor agriculture at the expense of industry. Contrary to Henry Adams, he no longer (if he ever had) regarded himself as "a world prophet of the democratic faith"; and thus most of Adams's arraignment of Jefferson fell to the ground.

Coming to the study of Jefferson from outside the provincial setting of American scholarship, Chinard broke the molds of partisan interpretation and comprehended what others had only vaguely glimpsed—the Americanism of Jefferson.

The Shadowy Grandeurs of the Past: Irving and Longfellow

CUSHING STROUT

For its hopeful citizens America was from its national beginning a New World. Here would flourish a new society, more free and equal than anything known in the Old World. American innocence and simplicity were held to be the moral virtues of a society defined in polar contrast to European corruption and complexity. Reinforced by the fascination with the American West, this theme would provide support for the diplomatic policy of nonentanglement with what Washington called in his Farewell Address "the ordinary vicissitudes" of European affairs. Jefferson in 1820 had argued the need for a formal "meridian of partition through the ocean which separates the two hemispheres, on the hither side of which no European gun shall ever be heard, nor an American on the other." The Monroe Doctrine of 1823 boldly warned the Old World to keep its hands off the New.

This invidious contrast was, however, at the same time counterpointed by a continuing fascination with European culture. Writers, scholars, and artists went to school to Europe out of necessity. The romantic cultivation of the medieval past, however, added a new dimension to this American interest in the Old World. American voyagers to Europe were inevitably vulnerable to ambivalent feelings. How could this European world with all its cultural advantages for Americans be reconciled with the patriotic polar imagery of the contrast between the New World and the Old? How did the early nineteenth-century American discoverers of Europe come to terms with the values of both worlds?

FOR THE AMERICAN LITERARY MIND OF THE EIGHTEENTH CENTURY THE feudal darkness of the Old World had only a menacing political meaning.

Cushing Strout, "The Shadowy Grandeurs of the Past," *The American Image of the New World,* 1963, chapter 5, pp. 74–85. Reprinted by permission of Harper & Row, Publishers, Inc. Copyright © 1963 by Cushing Strout.

It stood for the iniquities of kings, nobles, and clergy who ruled by tyranny and superstition. The exciting prospects of the future opened up by the American Revolution were gloriously enthralling to the most ardent literary spirits of the age of Enlightenment. Philip Freneau, the new nation's first important poet, celebrated the New World against the Old as early as early as 1771 in a commencement ode delivered at Princeton on "The Rising Glory of America." By its happy emancipation from European evils America was destined, he prophesied, to become "a new Jerusalem" by "no second Adam lost" with no "dangerous tree" of "deathful fruit" or "tempting serpent to allure the soul" into a fatal loss of "native innocence."[1] Freneau was to become the poet laureate of Jeffersonian Republicanism, and his rhetoric chanted with mythological force the theme of New World innocence, happiness, and liberty in contrast to Old World vice, misery, and despotism. He was seized with a passionate vision of the apotheosis of America through westward expansion. Nature and Reason would collaborate in the Western wilds to perfect the development of free man. In this way the eighteenth-century cult of Reason mingled with the agrarian cult of the soil to bolster the myth of a world geographically separated into the children of light and the children of darkness. By definition, history-laden Europe with its pomp and ceremony could never nurture that innocence peculiar to the American wilds where it was always "the morning of the world."

The hostile version of the American-European contrast, the literary analogue of political isolationism, was especially appropriate to the early days of the Republic. While the delegates were sitting in Constitution Hall at Philadelphia, New Yorkers were witnessing Royall Tyler's *The Contrast*, America's first professionally produced comedy with its vivid creation of the "true-born Yankee American son of liberty." Tyler's Jonathan, a rube from Bangor, and his master, Manley, a Revolutionary officer, were posed in virtuous contrast as honest provincials to the wily foppishness of Dimple and his slavish servant, who had been abroad to acquire "the polish of Europe." Tyler's comic Yankee later became widely popularized by the monologues of George Handel Hill and the newspaper sketches of the humorist Seba Smith, while the play spawned a swarm of imitations. One of the most popular successes of the nineteenth-century American stage, Anna Cora Mowatt's *Fashion*, which in 1845 did much to make theater-going socially respectable, was unabashedly derived from Tyler's formula. Mocking the fashionable aping of

---

[1] Frederick Lewis Pattee, ed., *The Poems of Philip Freneau, Poet of the American Revolution, I* (Princeton, Princeton University Library, 1902), pp. 80–81.

French manners, the play celebrated the triumph of Nature's Noblemen over foreign follies and bogus counts.[2]

At the same time, on a higher level of culture, a more sophisticated, if equally mythological, view of the American-European contrast developed in the nineteenth century. Influenced by the new sympathy for the medieval historical past and the fascination with folklore and ancient customs, which had been stimulated by the Romantic movement, the American literary imagination turned to Europe as a symbol of romance, hallowed by the charm of ivied ruins, picturesque scenes, and quaint customs. On these terms the contrast between the Old World and the New could be accented without tension. The Past became attractive by virtue of its very opposition to the Present. The New World remained unquestioned as the land of the free, the home of virtue, and the hope of the future, but its undecorated simplicity and bustling practicality stifled conventional romantic impulses.

This new attitude towards Europe was accentuated by a literary sense of cultural dependency on an older and richer civilization. Even Tyler, for all his pride in displaying his muse on native themes, had cleverly imitated the mannered style of English wits like Sheridan. While Americans were inspired by the outcome of the War of 1812 to redouble their energies in a patriotic crusade for an American literature redolent of the New World, their real literary pioneers went overseas to spend fruitful years in Europe, their minds deeply responsive to the authority and appeal of an officially alien culture.

Washington Irving began his literary career as a New York wit who collaborated in 1807 with James K. Paulding on the satirical sketches known as *Salmagundi*. Paulding alone produced the second series; Irving had left for Europe. While Paulding continued to exploit the vein of caustic, belligerent criticism of Europe, Irving moved on to discover a romantic Europe warmly appealing to the American mind. Sailing to Sicily on his first tour in 1805, "accustomed to our *honest* American hills and dales where *stubborn fact* presides and checks the imagination in its wanderings," he was full of enthusiasm for "that Island of fable and Romance" where "fiction has shed its charms o'er every scene."[3] Setting out again in 1815 for England on a matter of business, sick of his life

---

[2] The image of the Yankee is explored in Constance Rourke, *American Humor: A Study of the National Character* (New York, Harcourt, Brace, 1931), Chap. 1.

[3] Letter to "Quoz," January 1, 1805, quoted by Stanley T. Williams, *The Life of Washington Irving,* I (New York, Oxford, 1935), 59. For Paulding's republican critiques of Europe see, for example, "A Trip to Paris," *The New York Mirror,* 8 (January 15, 1831), 220–221 and "Want of Excitement or a Trip to London," *ibid.,* 8 (January 22, 1831), 228–229.

as a literary man-about-town in New York, he became a seventeen-year expatriate and won a vast public for his graceful vignettes of the pictursque in English, Spanish, and German life and legend. Later, when he had become America's most prominent man of letters, Irving sometimes longed for the life that he had enjoyed in his wandering years. After a day spent with businessmen in Honesdale, New York, where they had named a cliff in his honor, he wrote to his niece in Paris that he had spent a commonplace day among commonplace people: "Good lord deliver me from the all pervading commonplace which is the curse of our country."[4]

Longfellow, whose own pilgrimage to Europe had been inspired by Irving's, piously joined the cry for a national literature. If it was not necessary that "the war-whoop should ring in every line," at least American poets should break away from bookish imitative poetry and remember that for Americans skylarks and nightingales "only warble in books." But for all this genuflection before the national creed he really believed that the torch of culture was "lighted at the old domestic fireside of England," and that English "solid sense" needed to be lightened by German tenderness, Spanish passion, and French vivacity.[5] He had himself gone to school not in "the forest primeval" or "by the shores of Gitchie Gumee," but at the University of Heidelberg.

If in America life was real and life was earnest, that was just the trouble for a romantic poet. "In truth it must be spoken and recorded," he noted in his journal in 1846, ". . . this is a dreadful country for a poet to live in. Lethal deadly influences hang over him, the very 'Deadly Nightshade' of song. Many poetic souls there are here, and many lovers of song; but life and its ways and ends are prosaic in this country to the last degree."[6] As America's most popular poet, he was the singer of the pleasures of home and hearth, and as a good republican he once refused a decoration from King Emmanuel of Italy. "Please don't get expatriated," he could counsel others, reminding them that "life is not all cathedrals or ruined castles, and other theatrical properties of the Old World."[7] Yet it was just these theatrical properties that for long had fascinated him. From his house in Portland young Longfellow could see

---

[4] Letter to Mrs. Sarah Storrow, July 31, 1841; Williams, op. cit., II, 97.

[5] Cf. his "Defense of Poetry," North American Review, 34 (January, 1832), 69, 75, with "Mr. Churchill's" opinion in Kavanagh, The Prose Works of Henry Wadsworth Longfellow, Riverside Edition, vol. 2 (Boston, Houghton Mifflin, 1899), 368.

[6] Quoted by Lawrance Thompson, Young Longfellow (1807–43) (New York, Macmillan, 1938), p. 317.

[7] Quoted by Edward Wagenknecht, Longfellow: A Full-Length Portrait (New York, Longmans, Green, 1955), p. 195.

the Atlantic he longed to cross, and he was overjoyed when first Bowdoin College in 1826, then Harvard in 1835, sent him abroad to prepare for his professional duties. He later almost resigned his professorship at Harvard, where he had succeeded Ticknor, to go to Europe as a tutor to a young son of the Astor family, and he often dreamed of wrangling a post as secretary of the legation at Madrid. Like Irving, whose life and work he partly imitated, Longfellow was spellbound by the Old World.

The Europe that enthralled Irving and Longfellow was not quite the same Europe that had inspired Ticknor, Everett, Bancroft, and other scholars. It was not scholarship, but romance that these poetic voyagers were looking for, and they did not much cultivate that Spartan devotion to intellectual labor that characterized those other pioneers. If Irving doggedly toiled at a biography of Columbus in Madrid, and Longfellow took Ticknor's advice and settled down in Heidelberg to learn German literature before taking up the Smith Professorship at Harvard, these were episodes. Both men were essentially romantic artists, not students. For them the European past shimmered, as Irving put it, with "all the charms of storied and poetical association." For all the "youthful promise" of America, Europe offered "masterpieces of art, the refinements of highly cultivated society, the quaint pecularities of ancient and local customs" in which one could indulge the desire to lose himself "among the shadowy grandeurs of the past."[8] "I, too, in a certain sense," wrote Longfellow in *Outre-Mer,* which paid Irving the compliment of imitating his famous *Sketch Book* in both form and format, "have been a pilgrim of *Outre-Mer;* for to my youthful imagination the Old World was a kind of Holy Land, lying afar off beyond the blue horizon of the ocean," which made the heart grow "swelled with the deep emotions of the pilgrim."[9]

Through the eyes of Irving and Longfellow the Old World became enchanted, in a compensating irony, by the very intensity of America's official commitment to the future. A new nation, composed of immigrants, was inevitably vulnerable to the impulse to take a wistful backward glance at the life left behind. The new image of Europe, saturated as it was with romantic nostalgia and drained of nearly all contemporary social significance, did not challenge native pieties, but complemented them. Through a dialectic generated by their position Americans could, in this romanticized Old World, vicariously enjoy the forbidden fruits of the past. To dream of a feudal past existing in America was not only

---

[8] *Sketch Book, The Complete Works of Washington Irving,* vol. 1 (Paris, Baudry's, 1834), 226.

[9] *Outre-Mer, The Prose Works,* vol. 1, 20.

impossible, but treasonable. It would have turned a splendid vision of man's republican destiny into a nightmare of reaction. To find that wistful dream incarnated in Europe was to appease American nostalgia for values alien to the national mythology without violating it.

The enormous popularity of both Irving and Longfellow owed much to their instinctive recognition and exploitation of this situation. Without the slightest compromise of his Americanism, Irving could describe for his avid readers a merry England, dominated by the rural gentry who lived with their estates and tenants in the ruddy afterglow of medievalism amid scenery "associated in the mind with ideas of order, of quiet, of sober well-established principles, of hoary usage, and revered custom."[10] As a diplomat, attached to the London legation and compelled to negotiate with these genial English squires over the West Indian trade, Irving was an adequate defender of the American cause, while in his role as the American romantic traveler he could deeply wish that John Bull's splendid mansion would not be meddled with by agitating "levellers" devoted to democratic progress.[11] Old England would lose its usefulness as an American symbol if it lost its antithetical charm. Its age was for Americans its novelty. To English eyes Irving, with his evident apprenticeship to the romanticism of Byron, Scott, and Moore, and his stylistic indebtedness to the felicity of the English essayists of the eighteenth century, was a pious traditionalist, "a bit of home," as Fanny Kemble exclaimed when she embraced him on her travels in America. To Americans he seemed fresh and original, creating a Europe peculiarly available to the native imagination.

With equal success Longfellow made the continent an American dream. The public responded eagerly to his pleasure in the color and traditionalism of French rural sports, fairs, dances, festivals, and ceremonies; his poetic reveries before the ruined temples and moldering aqueducts of Rome; his Irvingesque rhapsodies over the famed castle of Alhambra in Spain, like "the memory of a gorgeous dream," which was "a fortress, a palace, an earthly paradise, . . . a ruin, wonderful in its fallen greatness!"[12] A true son of the Romantic movement, he found delight in every vestige of the Middle Ages. At Rouen the ancient cathedral gave him such a vivid sensation of being "transported back to the Dark Ages" that he refused to visit it again for fear of losing his first impression of its "awful sublimity."[13] At the château of Chambord his imagination heard the clang of arms and sounds of revelry and

[10] *Sketch Book*, p. 245.
[11] *Ibid.*, p. 325.
[12] *Outre-Mer, The Prose Works*, vol. 1, 226–227.
[13] *Ibid.*, p. 30.

wassail, while the epics and lyrics of the troubadour poets from the age of Charlemagne aroused his warmest poetic sympathies.

In his *Hyperion* (1839), which reflected the influence of Goethe and Richter and was widely used as a guidebook for travelers in Germany, he continued the account of his adventures abroad in the guise of fiction. Paul Flemming's unrequited love for an English girl provides a sentimental framework for a romantic conflict between the charms of the past and the duties of the present, a theme especially significant for Americans. The heroine (recognizable as the American girl Longfellow later made his second wife) possesses a tender sense of the past; she has written sketches on the pageantry of the Middle Ages, with its ladies, knights, jousts, and minnesingers, so angularly pictured in illuminated manuscripts, and on the glory of the artist's life in Rome. Flemming's own nostalgia for the past is troubled by a consciousness of the claims of the present. A German Baron tells him, "It seems to me like falling in love with one's grandmother. Give me the Present, . . . warm, glowing, palpitating with life."[14] But for Paul the warm, glowing, palpitations of romanticized history are more appealing than the present. His crisis comes when he meets in a village church a tablet with an inscription urging man to forget the mournful past and "wisely improve the Present." The advice, symbolically, turns his thoughts "to his distant home beyond the sea." Renouncing his life as "a dreamer among shadows," he resolves to return to America to pursue "a life of action and reality."[15] But he leaves behind, along with the glories of the past, his beloved "Dark Lady," and so the book ends, in approved romantic fashion, on a note of melancholy.

Like his hero, Longfellow returned to America, but his dream of Europe remained as vivid as his professorial life was a burden. How could Portland, Cambridge, or even Boston compare with Nuremberg, lovingly described in his poem as "quaint old town of toil and traffic, quaint old town of art and song," with its "memories of the Middle Ages" when emperors lived in castles "time-defying, centuries old" while all around rose "the wondrous world of Art"? His conflict was not severe; he signed his peace gracefully. With characteristic mellowness his poetry dealt easily with either European or American themes. As Henry James, whose European experience was to be longer and deeper, wonderingly remarked, if Longfellow's life seemed "a piece of the old world smoothly fitted into the new, so it might quite as well have been a piece of the new fitted, just as intimately, into the old."[16]

---

[14] *The Prose Works,* II, 139.

[15] *Ibid.,* p. 277.

[16] *William Wetmore Story and His Friends from Letters, Diaries, and Recollections,* I (Boston, Houghton Mifflin, 1903), 311–312.

Washington Irving also came back from Europe to grow up with the country, throwing himself into the American life of his time with all the zest of an immigrant. He wrote an admiring biography of Washington, "roughed it" on a tour of the Western prairies, played the role of glorifying publicist for John Jacob Astor's fur trade, speculated on the stock market, lectured his nephews on the importance of sacrificing their fashionable life to the business of getting on in the world, and basked in the honor of having his name given to mountains, hotels, steamboats, public squares, and even cigars. He was, because of his European success, a literary Horatio Alger in the United States. He had not forgotten the national vision of the special destiny of the Republic and the hostile image of Europe it entailed. "I come from gloomier climes to one of brilliant sunshine and inspiring purity," he piously proclaimed at the welcoming dinner held for him in New York in 1832.

I come from countries lowering with doubt and danger, where the rich man trembles and the poor man frowns . . . where all repine at the present and dread the future. I come from these to a country where all is life and animation; where I hear on every side the sound of exultation; where every one speaks of the past with triumph, the present with delight, the future with glowing and confident anticipation.[17]

In a gesture to live up to his rhetoric he pledged himself, in the heat of the moment, to stay in America as long as he lived. Ten years later, when his friend Daniel Webster recommended him for Minister to Madrid, America's "Ambassador of Letters from the New World to the Old" once again gratefully set sail for Spain, where he had earlier occupied for a delightful month the royal apartments of the Alhambra castle, so rich in the romantic past of Moorish Spain.

If Irving's and Longfellow's reconciliation of the American myth of the New World with their affection for the Old World was achieved with few evident signs of personal strain, it was largely because their own vision of Europe was such a very complementary one. Only a society that had defined itself as a fresh start in history could have produced such nostalgic hungers for a Europe made enchanted by the traces of an ancient past. In their poetic image the traditional antithesis between the two worlds, far from being abandoned, was restated by being rediscovered in a romantic light.

This same romantic image of Europe was created for less sophisticated Americans by Nathaniel Parker Willis. Reared in Boston by narrowly pious parents, Willis left his local church, became a popular journalist in New York, and was sent to Europe in 1831 as a correspondent. For

[17] Quoted by Williams, *op. cit.*, II, 334, n. 2.

him it was a delightful liberation, and his widely copied letters to *The New York Mirror* bubbled over with his pleasure in the stimulation of the European scene. Snubbed at home by the guardian of the girl he had hoped to marry, he found abroad that he could swim in the most frothy currents of European social life, thanks to the quasi-diplomatic privileges he had secured from the American minister in Paris and the letters of introduction to Italian society he received from the editor of an English journal. The thought of returning to "naked America" from this fabulous world where there was "so much to fill one's mind and eye" depressed him. "I love my country," he explained, "but the *ornamental* is my vocation, and of this she has none."[18] In London he became, through the kindness of Walter Savage Landor, a member of Lady Blessington's *salon*. Willis was overwhelmed at his good fortune. "All the best society of London exclusives," he naively wrote his sister, "is now open to me—me! a sometime apprentice at setting type—me! without a sou in the world beyond what my pen brings one, and with not only no influence from friends at home, but a world of envy and slander at my back."[19] Lionized by fashionable society, admitted to the Athanaeum, given a pass to the opera, and presented at court, he seriously thought of becoming an expatriate. When attacked by some prominent English literateurs as a name-dropping snob who invaded the privacy of the aristocracy to write up "high-life" in his columns, Willis was undaunted. He returned to America five years later with the hand of an English girl, daughter of a General. It was a provincial triumph, rather incomprehensible to a present generation that sees more charm in his good looks than in his slight literary works.

His American success was quite understandable. Willis was a shrewd journalist who reported on his travels with the spontaneous colorfulness his public craved. Instinctively, he grasped and reported the forbidden charm of aristocratic life for republican America. "The Americans are queen-mad," noted the *Mirror* in 1838. "We have Victoria bonnets, Victoria shawls, Victoria songs, Victoria marches, Victoria mint-juleps, and somebody has just opened a shop in Broadway which he calls 'The Victoria Hair-Dressing Establishment.' "[20] It was this easily titillated public that took Willis to its heart when he confided to his readers that at Dalhousie Castle in Scotland "you may fatigue yourself in a scene that is formed in every feature from the gentle-born and the refined.

---

[18] Quoted by Henry A. Beers, *Nathaniel Parker Willis, American Men of Letters* (Boston, Houghton Mifflin, 1885), pp. 122–123.

[19] *Ibid.*, p. 140.

[20] Quoted by Frank Luther Mott, *A History of American Magazines 1741–1850* (New York, Appleton, 1930), p. 397.

The labor and the taste of successive generations can alone create such an Eden. Primogeniture! I half forgive thee."[21]

In his fiction half-forgiven primogeniture struggles seductively with manly republicanism until the issue, despite the author's intention, is dubious. The young American artist in Willis's novel *Paul Fane* returns from "the perfumed atmosphere of Europe," where by "arts of inhalation not elsewhere to be learned" his lungs have been given "their full trial of expansibility," to marry his childhood sweetheart.[22] The plot, however, is largely taken up with demonstrating Paul's success in bringing to his feet every European woman he meets whose beauty is hallowed by aristocratic lineage. As in cheap, popular fiction thereafter, Willis's literary image of Europe was a racy mixture of the vulgarized fascinations of art, sex, and high birth, crudely mixed in a casserole of genteel romanticism and low comedy.

It was the function of Willis, the traveler, as a reviewer remarked in 1855, to express "in the most apt and airy manner, the average natural sentiment of an intelligent American in Europe, just as Byron hits the general tone of romance in Venice and Rome." If it was true that "the eyes which see are set in a *tête exaltée* by early success, and the hands which record tremble a little with the pressure of the hands of famous wits, and noble lords, and lovely ladies," these were weaknesses which the public could more than half forgive. His success was natural, the explanation simple, as his reviewer said: "With desires and aspirations for the reverend and historically beautiful, forever unsatisfied at home, fed for years upon the splendid literature of all time, and the pompous history of the nations that have occupied and moulded the earth," yet separated "by the essential spirit of society around him" from them, "the American mind is solicited by Europe with unimagined fascination."[23] More perceptive writers, like Cooper, Hawthorne, and James, recognized that the romantic posture was superficial, but their concern with it as an American problem was tacit acknowledgment of its importance for the nineteenth century. It was a characteristic American way of sympathetically relating oneself to a Europe which by national self-definition was regarded as the alien opposite of the New World.

---

[21] *Pencillings by the Way, The Complete Works of Nathaniel Parker Willis* (New York, J. S. Redfield, 1846), p. 196.

[22] *Paul Fane, or Parts of a Life Else Untold* (New York, Scribner's, 1857), p. 395. Christof Wegelin sees Willis's fiction as countering the snobbish tone of his newspaper reports, but there is ambiguity in both. See Wegelin, "Social Criticism of Europe in the Fiction of N. P. Willis," *American Literature*, 20 (November, 1948), 313–322. Willis does anticipate the "international theme" which Henry James exploits so much more seriously.

[23] "American Travellers," *Putnam's Monthly*, 5 (June, 1855), 570, 563–564.

A Decaying Church
and a Wasting Unbelief

CONRAD WRIGHT

Perry Miller demonstrated in 1950 that transcendentalism emerged out of the complex religious history of New England as "an expression of religious radicalism in revolt against a rational conservatism" and found abroad new forms of expression in literary patterns suggested by Cousin, Wordsworth, Coleridge, and Carlyle. Seen in this context, the movement was wider than Emerson and Thoreau and composed mainly of Unitarian reformers. William Ellery Channing had given the major exposition of Unitarian religion in his Baltimore Sermon (1819), and in the following year the Massachusetts Supreme Court (itself Unitarian) gave the majority of the parishioners, rather than the members, of the First Church in Dedham the right to choose their minister. By this decision, Unitarians acquired control of many Congregational Churches. The personal and intellectual context of Emerson's famous Divinity School Address (1838) provides a clear window on the issues which made his speech a focal point of bitter controversy.

IN MAY, 1819, RALPH WALDO EMERSON WAS STILL A STUDENT AT Harvard College. His own minister was Channing, since his mother had taken up going to the Federal Street Church after the death of Emerson's father in 1811. Presumably he read Channing's sermon when it was fresh from the press; but we do not know what his reaction was, or the extent to which he shared in the excited discussions of the Baltimore expedition.[1]

Conrad Wright, *Three Prophets of Religious Liberalism: Channing, Emerson, Parker*, part III, 1961, pp. 19–32. Reprinted by permission of the Beacon Press. Copyright © 1961 by Conrad Wright.
[1 Dr. William Ellery Channing.]

There was another occasion, however, when an address by Channing made a very deep impression on him. In March, 1821, Channing was the Dudleian Lecturer at Harvard, taking as his assigned topic "The Evidences of Revealed Religion." Emerson recalled the address vividly two years afterwards, when Channing dealt with the same subject in a Sunday sermon. "I heard Dr. Channing deliver a discourse upon Revelation as standing in comparison with Nature," he wrote. "I have heard no sermon approaching in excellence to this, since the Dudleian Lecture. . . . He considered God's word to be the only expounder of his works, and that Nature had always been found insufficient to teach men the great doctrines which Revelation inculcated." In April, 1824, when Emerson took account of himself, his talents and his failings, preparatory to beginning the professional study of theology, Channing's lecture came back to his mind as an example of the sort of reasoning he hoped to pursue. "Dr. Channing's Dudleian Lecture is the model of what I mean, and the faculty which produced this is akin to the higher flights of the fancy."[2]

Emerson's praise of this lecture serves as a reminder that at the beginning of his career he accepted without reservation the system of rational theology that prevailed among the Unitarians of that day. The Divinity School Address, in 1838, revealed the extent to which he had departed from that system; and the vigor of the response on the part of men like Andrews Norton indicated how much seemed to be at stake. Channing's Dudleian Lecture helps us to measure the distance Emerson moved in a decade and a half, as well as to appreciate the growing divergence between the generations for which the two men spoke.

Channing's concern in the Dudleian Lecture was to vindicate the miracles of Christ as confirmation of the supernatural basis of Christianity. "Christianity is not only confirmed by miracles," he declared, "but is in itself, in its very essence, a miraculous religion." He recognized a prevailing tendency, fostered by the discoveries of science, to deny that the uniform order of nature will ever by interrupted by supernatural agency, and he acknowledged that all claims for miracles must be more carefully sifted than would be necessary for reports of common facts. But one who believes in God, the author of the uniformity of nature, must admit that he has the power to suspend the laws he has himself ordained, if the great purposes of the universe are thereby promoted. The great end of God in establishing the order of nature is "to form and advance the mind"; and if his purpose can best be achieved by departing from this

[2] *The Journals of Ralph Waldo Emerson* (Boston, 1909–14), I, 290, 361.

order, "then the great purpose of the creation, the great end of its laws and regularity, would demand such departure; and miracles, instead of warring against, would concur with nature."[3]

Admittedly, God will not suspend the order of nature for trivial ends. But in extraordinary circumstances, for extraordinary purposes, miracles may reasonably be expected. Such was the situation when Jesus Christ came into the world. Pagan superstition had so obscured the doctrine of one God and Father, which is the basis for all piety, and pagan philosophy had so shaken the doctrine of immortality, which is the foundation of morality, that a miraculous manifestation of God's power was required. Jesus Christ was therefore divinely commissioned to recover mankind from its darkness and folly, and to disclose the way to eternal life. The miracles were vivid confirmation of his unique authority.

Channing did not rest the argument for Christianity solely on the historical miracles of Christ. He was familiar with the other evidences commonly adduced by Christian apologists: the fulfillment of prophecy; the fitness of Christian truths to meet the needs of sinful men; the marvelous spread of Christianity, despite its appearance among obscure and humble people; the confirmation of the gospel history to be found in pagan writers; and so on. But in his Dudleian Lecture, he devoted more attention to the argument for miracles than to any of the other internal or external evidences; for there was a tendency among the liberal Christians to insist on the historicity of the miracles as the cornerstone of the whole structure of Christian apologetics.

The temper of Emerson's mind, as he himself realized, was more poetic or imaginative than strictly rational; and so Channing's lecture appealed to him because he detected in it a certain quality of "moral imagination" which set it apart from routine treatments of the same theme. Locke and Samuel Clarke, by comparison, he regarded as "reasoning machines." Yet in his early preaching, as minister of the Second Church in Boston, Emerson remained within the rationalistic tradition for which Locke and Clarke were spokesmen. In a sermon preached in 1831, he declared that "a miracle is the only means by which God can make a communication to men, that shall be known to be from God," and that the New Testament miracles have a "peculiar credibility." To be sure, he was more inclined to prove the credibility of the miracles from the truth of the doctrines of the gospels than the other way around; and to this extent he was moving in the direction of the Divinity School Address. But in 1831, he believed that "the truth and the miracle mutually confirm each other," and he had as yet no other basis for religious truth than rational argument founded on the experience of the senses, together with special revelation attested by miracles.[4]

By 1834, Emerson had broken away from the old patterns of thought and had moved into a new intellectual climate in which the familiar arguments for miracles could be casually dismissed as irrelevant. In May of that year, in a letter to his brother, he used Coleridge's distinction between the "Reason" and the "Understanding," which seemed to him to be "a philosophy itself." Reason, he said—using the word in a way peculiar to the Transcendentalists—is "the highest faculty of the soul"; it is the power by which we apprehend truth immediately, without calculation or proof. The Understanding, on the other hand, "toils all the time, compares, contrives, adds, argues, near-sighted but strong-sighted, dwelling in the present the expedient the customary." On the level of the Understanding, men have varying degrees of intellectual capacity; but "Reason is potentially perfect in every man." Our everyday life may be lived on the level of the Understanding; but our deepest insights into timeless truths are intuitions of the Reason, and religion and poetry belong in its domain.[5]

The emergence of this intuitional philosophy led inevitably to conflict and crisis within the Unitarian community. For more than a century, the accepted philosophy in New England had been based either on the sensational psychology of John Locke or on the modified Lockeanism of the Scotch Realists. True ideas, said Locke, are based on the evidence of the senses, as ordered and organized by the ability of the mind to reflect on the ideas derived from sensations. But now Emerson's generation was beginning to assert that the truths of religion and morality are not founded on the experience of the senses but are immediate intuitions of the divine. What this meant to Unitarianism was sensed with especial clarity by Convers Francis, minister of the church in Watertown. "I have long seen," he wrote in 1836, "that the Unitarians must break into two schools,—the Old one, or English school, belonging to the sensual and empiric philosophy,—and the New one, or the German school (perhaps it may be called), belonging to the spiritual philosophy."[6] But if the spiritual or "transcendentalist" school should prevail and the truths of Christianity be regarded as valid only so far as they correspond to direct intuitions of absolute truth, Jesus would lose his function as the unique

---

[4] A. C. McGiffert, Jr. (ed.), *Young Emerson Speaks* (Boston, 1938), pp. 120, 123.

[5] Ralph L. Rusk (ed.), *The Letters of Ralph Waldo Emerson* (New York, 1939), I, 412–13.

[6] John Weiss, *Discourse Occasioned by the Death of Convers Francis, D.D.* (Cambridge, 1863), pp. 28–29.

channel of divine revelation, and the miracles wrought in confirmation of his authority would shrink into triviality.

Despite Channing's impatience with the tendency of Unitarianism to settle down into a new orthodoxy, and his generous tolerance of the views of younger men, his theological allegiance remained with the old school. Emerson's altered attitude toward him is a measure of the growing gulf between the generations. "Once Dr. Channing filled our sky," he wrote in 1837. "Now we become so conscious of his limits and of the difficulty attending any effort to show him our point of view that we doubt if it be worth while. Best amputate."[7]

If the Divinity School address was an event in the intellectual life of New England, it was also an event in the spiritual biography of its author. In his discussion of the role of the minister, addressed to young men about to enter the ministry, Emerson was struggling with his own vocational conflicts and doubts; and it may even be argued that he was indirectly justifying his own withdrawal from the calling to which he had been solemnly consecrated.

Emerson had once sought the "prized gown and band" because of his "passionate love for the strains of eloquence." Public preaching, he had decided, would give him an opportunity for the inspired utterance of which he felt himself capable. But he found much of drudgery in the minister's tasks, and the routine of parish calling in particular was uncongenial. Even before he resigned as minister of the Second Church, he had become restive, and critical of his own profession: "It is the best part of a man, I sometimes think, that revolts most against his being a minister." The difficulty was that ministers must accommodate themselves to institutions already formed, and each such accommodation is "a loss of so much integrity and, of course, of so much power."[8]

Emerson's resignation was directly occasioned by a disagreement over the administration of the Lord's Supper; but his growing dissatisfaction with the ministry would doubtless have led to his withdrawal sooner or later. Yet he did not break completely with that profession. Following his return from Europe in 1833, he continued to do occasional preaching, and for about three years he served as "stated supply" at the church in East Lexington. He was gradually finding his way into a new career as lecturer, and it was only when he achieved some degree of public acceptance that he finally gave up the East Lexington pulpit. "But henceforth perhaps I shall live by lecturing which promises to be good bread," he wrote to his mother in March, 1838. "I have relinquished my ec-

7 Emerson, *Journals*, IV, 239.
8 *Ibid.*, I, 363; II, 448–49.

clesiastical charge at E Lexington & shall not preach more except from the Lyceum."[9]

This decision was not an easy one for him to make. It involved the abandonment of the clerical tradition he had inherited; more painful, it amounted to an admission that the profession of the ministry made demands on him that he was unwilling or unable to meet. But he could not handle the situation in such a frank and undisguised form. Instead, he sought to justify himself by arguing that the church was tottering to its fall, almost all life extinct. In short, the blame for his failure as a minister lay not with himself but with the institutions of organized religion, which he declared could no longer command respect.

On the Sundays when Emerson was not preaching at East Lexington, or elsewhere on exchange, he ordinarily attended church in Concord. There, in the preaching of the Rev. Barzillai Frost, Emerson found ample confirmation of what, for his own peace of mind, he had to believe. Frost was a graduate of the Divinity School in Cambridge and a firm believer in the historical argument for Christianity, based on the miracles. He was also a faithful parish minister, regularly discharging his pastoral duties and making the rounds of his three hundred families. But he was a mediocre preacher, as even his best friend had to acknowledge. "Doubtless you all early felt," declared Henry A. Miles in a eulogy following Frost's death, "that there was neither flexibility of voice, nor play of imagination, nor gush of emotion to give him, as a preacher, that power to which other endowments fairly entitled him."[10] He wholly lacked the gift of eloquence, the power to change men's lives in an instant by the spoken word, that Emerson looked for in the true preacher. In short, he was a living example of all that Emerson thought was wrong with the clergy of his day.

Emerson's reaction to Frost's preaching, as the *Journals* reveal, was almost uniformly unfavorable. Time and again, he returned from church on Sunday morning to record his dissatisfaction. It is significant that the intensity of his criticism of Frost seems to have been greatest in March, 1838, just at the time that he was finally arranging to relinquish the East Lexington pulpit. After the decision had been made, and Emerson had solved the problem of his relationship to the profession for which Frost served as the symbol, the intensity of his condemnation perceptibly diminished.

The clustering of events is significant. It was on March 14 that Emerson wrote to his mother of his decision to quit his ecclesiastical charge.

[9] *Letters,* II, 120.

[10] Henry A. Miles, *A Sermon Preached . . . at the Burial of Rev. Barzillai Frost* (Cambridge, 1859), p. 9.

Sunday, the eighteenth, in a lengthy entry in the *Journal,* he condemned Frost as a sincere person based on sham; and he declared: "I ought to sit and think, and then write a discourse to the American Clergy, showing them the ugliness and unprofitableness of theology and churches at this day. . . ."[11] That same week, by a strange coincidence, he received a letter from a committee of the senior class of the Harvard Divinity School. Dated March 21, it invited him "to deliver before them, in the Divinity Chapel, on Sunday evening the 15th of July next, the customary discourse, on occasion of their entering upon the active Christian ministry."[12] The last Sunday at East Lexington was March 25. The following Tuesday, Emerson wrote to the committee to accept their invitation.

The address he carried with him to Cambridge, four months later, seemed to be an objective and impersonal report of the universal decay of faith, and a protest against the triumph of formalism in the pulpit. The text gave no hint of the fact that crucial passages condemning the clergy of the day had been drawn from Emerson's *Journals,* where in their original context they were references to the minister in Concord. Indeed, as the day for the delivery of the address drew near, Emerson was able to persuade himself that he was speaking "simple truth without any bias, any foreign interest in the matter."[13] But we are now able to discern what the audience of that day could not know, and Emerson himself could not admit: that there is a hidden meaning in the Divinity School Address, the clue to which lies in Emerson's relationship to his own minister and in the vocational crisis with which he was struggling.

The little chapel in Divinity Hall seats less than one hundred; and on the evening of July 15, all the places were taken. Edward Everett Hale, who arrived late, had to be content with a chair in the entry. We can list the names of perhaps a score of those present. Presumably six of the seven members of the graduating class were there; one of them, we know, was preaching in East Bridgewater. The members of the faculty were on hand, as well as a number of recent graduates of the School, such as Convers Francis, Caleb Stetson, Cyrus Bartol, William Henry Channing, John Sullivan Dwight, and Theodore Parker. Finally, there were young men, like Joseph Henry Allen, Rufus Ellis, and James H. Perkins, who were to enter the ministry in due course; and young ladies, like Elizabeth Peabody and Sarah Hale, who may have been there because the young men were.

No detailed description of the order of exercises has come down to

---

11 *Journals,* IV, 413.
12 *Letters,* II, 147 n.
13 *Journals,* V, 7.

us. We do know that Emerson prefaced his remarks with a brief invocation, which Cyrus Bartol long afterwards recalled as follows: "We desire of the Infinite Wisdom and Goodness to be led into the Truth. So may it be by our lowliness and seeking! This we ask of the Infinite Wisdom and Goodness."[14] The burden of the address that followed was simple. It was a reminder that the life of religion must be re-created anew in the souls of each successive generation of men, and a declaration that it is the responsibility of the minister to "acquaint men at first hand with Deity." But Emerson was not content to state his position positively and let the matter rest. The corollary was explicitly stated, that the "great and perpetual office of the preacher" was not being discharged, and that there prevailed generally "a decaying church and a wasting unbelief."

The young transcendentalists in the audience were delighted by the performance. It is reported that Elizabeth Peabody was "enraptured." But many of those present were sharply critical, partly because of the ideas expressed, but also because they felt that Emerson had shown exceedingly poor taste in criticizing the clergy on such an occasion. They could hardly have been aware of the inner compulsion that had made him speak as he did. "I did not like it at all," wrote Edward Everett Hale. "Mr. E. held that the Christianity of the present day is little better than none; . . . that churchgoing was less popular than formerly, owing to the bad preaching of the ministers of the day, whom he rated severely as not putting enough of self into their sermons."[15] Hale's complaint that Emerson's strictures on the clergy were an insult to the Divinity School teachers who had trained them was echoed by his brother Nathan. "I didn't hear Emerson's lecture," he wrote, "& was very glad that I didn't, when I was told what it was. . . . It seems there were two divisions; the first asserting that *no* ministers of the present day (he made *no exceptions*) did their duty or did anything; doing away all the good the poor Divinity teachers hoped they had been doing for three years— the second was an express denial of *all* the divine claims of our Savior. . . ."[16]

After the exercises were over, the congregation broke up into small groups. Some of them walked over to Dr. Palfrey's house, where they lingered to talk. Henry Ware, Jr., invited Mr. and Mrs. Emerson to spend the night; but they preferred to drive back to Concord through the soft summer night, illuminated by a brilliant aurora. Before they left, however, Ware expressed to Emerson some of his uneasiness about

[14] Cyrus A. Bartol, *Ralph Waldo Emerson* (Boston, 1882), p. 9.

[15] Jean Holloway, *Edward Everett Hale* (Austin, Texas, 1956), p. 40.

[16] Nathan Hale, Jr., to James Russell Lowell, July 24, 1838. MS., Harvard College Library.

the doctrines preached that evening; and Emerson seems to have reassured him by qualifying in conversation some of his bolder statements. The next day, however, Ware sought to make his position clear in a friendly letter. "It has occurred to me," he wrote, "that, since I said to you last night, I should probably assent to your unqualified statements, if I could take your qualifications with them, I am bound in fairness to add, that this applies only to a portion, and not to all. With regard to some, I must confess, that they appear to me more than doubtful, and that their prevalence would tend to overthrow the authority and influence of Christianity. On this account, I look with anxiety and no little sorrow to the course which your mind has been taking."[17]

The storm that blew up over the address seems to have come as a surprise to Emerson. This was no Baltimore Sermon, carefully calculated in advance to arouse controversy and to advance the principles of a party. And so, for a time, Emerson wondered whether the text should be revised before publication—or, indeed, whether it should be made available for general circulation at all. He finally concluded that he would have to stand or fall by what he had actually said, and so the Address appeared without significant revision late in August.

Inevitably it became a subject for public controversy as well as private conversation. From the point of view of the Divinity School authorities, the immediate problem was to make it plain that Emerson's views were his own and were not in any sense sanctioned by the School. The faculty felt that Emerson had placed them in a false light in the eyes of the public by choosing that particular platform and occasion for his remarks; and some of them wondered whether, in future years, the students should have complete freedom when it came to extending invitations to speak under the auspices of the School. Andrews Norton could not contain himself; he wrote an intemperate letter to a Boston newspaper to emphasize "the disgust and strong disapprobation" felt by the authorities. The members of the graduating class, he declared, "have become accessories, perhaps innocent accessories, to the commission of a great offence"; and he called upon them for whatever exculpation or excuse they could give.[18]

The more persistent issues, however, were doctrinal. One of them was posed by Henry Ware, Jr., in a sermon entitled "The Personality of the Deity," preached at the Divinity School on September 23, 1838. Although not a direct attack on Emerson, it was prepared with the Divinity School Address in mind. Ware was troubled by a prevailing tendency, of which Emerson's Address was but one instance, to think of

---

17 John Ware, *Memoir of the Life of Henry Ware, Jr.* (Boston, 1846), p. 395.
18 Perry Miller, *The Transcendentalists* (Cambridge, 1950), p. 195.

God in terms of "divine laws" instead of as a Being who is at once the Creator, the Governor, and the Father of Man. Emerson's assertion that "the soul knows no persons" seemed to him to be both theologically unsound and psychologically untrue. It is our concern for human personality that is the mainspring of progress in human affairs; and it is our response to a divine personality that is at the heart of worship. Ware was at least as much concerned as Emerson about the prevalence of moral and religious deadness; but, for him, the surest way to lose the sense of the presence of the Living God is to define religion as "a reverence and delight in the presence of certain divine laws." A relationship to an inanimate abstraction is not enough to satisfy the religious sentiments. Only as men "come more to realize the presence and the authority of the living Father" is there any grounds to hope for a "wider prevalence of elevated piety or of happy devotion to duty."[19]

The other doctrinal issue was the familiar one of the miracles. Emerson had long since made up his mind that converts to genuine Christianity are made by "the reception of beautiful sentiments, never by miracle."[20] And so he casually dismissed a doctrine that was regarded, by both Unitarians and orthodox, as essential to the acceptance of Christianity as a revealed religion. Jesus spoke of miracles, Emerson declared— playing on the word—"for he felt that man's life was a miracle, and all that man doth. . . . But the word Miracle, as pronounced by Christian churches, gives a false impression; it is Monster. It is not one with the blowing clover and the falling rain." Or, more pointedly: "To aim to convert a man by miracles is a profanation of the soul."

This heresy was not peculiar to Emerson. In 1836, George Ripley had bluntly declared in the *Christian Examiner* that "the design of the miracles, in the Old and New Testament, was not to confirm a revelation of spiritual truth, but to accomplish quite a different purpose."[21] Andrews Norton had reacted promptly by withdrawing as a sponsor of the magazine. That same year, William Henry Furness had argued that the so-called miracles of Jesus "were not departures from the laws of nature, but new facts in nature"; they were not performed "merely for the sake of the influence they might have on the understandings of others," but were "the simple, natural, irrepressible manifestations of that mighty spiritual force which was the inmost God-inspired life of Jesus."[22]

But Emerson's fault was that he had spoken on a public occasion under

[19] *The Works of Henry Ware, Jr.* (Boston, 1847), III, 39.
[20] Emerson, *Journals*, IV, 429.
[21] George Ripley, "Martineau's *Rationale of Religious Enquiry*," *Christian Examiner*, XXI (1836), 251.
[22] William Henry Furness, *Remarks on the Four Gospels* (Philadelphia, 1836), pp. 187, 199.

the auspices of the Divinity School. To Norton it seemed that a correspondingly important occasion was required for reply. The opportunity came a year later, at a meeting of the alumni of the School. Norton made no mention of Emerson in his "Discourse on the Latest Form of Infidelity" but attacked rather the tendency of certain German theologians to discount the evidential value of miracles. "The latest form of infidelity," he declared, "strikes directly at the root of faith in Christianity, and indirectly of all religion, by denying the miracles attesting the divine mission of Christ." No one had any doubt that Norton regarded Emerson as the leading local spokesman for this position, or that he was addressing himself to Emerson when he insisted that "for any one to pretend to be a Christian teacher, who disbelieves the divine origin and authority of Christianity, and would undermine the belief of others, is treachery towards God and man."[23]

Emerson made public reply neither to Henry Ware, Jr., whom he held in the most affectionate regard, nor to Andrews Norton, whose dogmatic pronouncements he found thoroughly distasteful. The defense of the transcendentalist point of view was left to others, George Ripley and Theodore Parker in particular. But despite his aloofness from the controversy, Emerson was emotionally much more deeply involved in the whole episode than he was perhaps willing to admit. The Address, according to a recent scholar, "came as close to the irresistible truth he felt called upon to announce to his generation as any of his utterances. . . . He was correspondingly affected by its hostile reception." He was reminded that eloquence and poetic insight do not necessarily carry all before them. It was "an angular intrusion of fact into the smooth world of his thoughts" which permanently affected his philosophical outlook, at least to the extent that it forced him thereafter to be more cautious in his proclamation of the identity of the ideal and the real.[24]

In time, the Unitarians abandoned the traditional theory of miracles, as well as much of the theological structure built upon it. Emerson and Ripley doubtless contributed to this outcome. But even more important was the spread of a scientific and critical attitude which was, in a somewhat different way, as destructive of the older theology as was Transcendentalism. The Divinity School Address remains, therefore, a perennially fresh solvent of dogmatic orthodoxies, especially Unitarian orthodoxies, rather than an indication of the permanent philosophic bent of Unitarianism in this country.

[23] Andrews Norton, *A Discourse on the Latest Form of Infidelity* (Cambridge, 1839), pp. 11, 37.

[24] Stephen E. Whicher, *Freedom and Fate* (Philadelphia, 1953), p. 73.

The Romance of History in America

WILBUR R. JACOBS

The writing of history was itself a part of literature in the nineteenth century. The great historians, Prescott, Motley, Bancroft, and Parkman, were part of the Boston Unitarian community of men of letters, whose sense of history derived from Puritan roots and from the contemporary interest in historical criticism of the Bible. These historians were also trained in the classics and familiar with the romantic literature of Scott, Cooper, Wordsworth, Coleridge, and Byron. They consciously conceived their histories in terms of drama, painting, and scenery. "Their histories," as David Levin points out in *History as Romantic Art,* "provide a foundation in documented fact for the tension between form and essence, head and heart, civilization and Nature, that preoccupied so many of their contemporaries."

The greatest of the romantic historians in America was Francis Parkman whose many volumes on the struggle between the English and the French for control of North America memorably dramatized his feeling for the wilderness and his skill in using romantic conventions. Wilbur R. Jacobs shows how Parkman's commencement oration at Harvard in 1844 provides insight into the sources of his later work and the romantic conception of history.

ON AUGUST 28, 1844,[1] THE TWENTY-ONE-YEAR-OLD FRANCIS PARKMAN delivered a commencement oration on the occasion of his graduation from Harvard. The original manuscript, lodged among his papers in the

Wilbur R. Jacobs, "Francis Parkman's Oration 'Romance in America,'" *American Historical Review,* 68 (April, 1963), pp. 692–697. Reprinted by permission of the author and the publisher.

Mr. Jacobs edited this unpublished essay of Parkman's. The essay is published through the courtesy of the Harvard College Library.

[1] The folder containing the MS gives the date of the oration. (Harvard Archives, HUC 6843.55.)

Harvard College Library and unknown to present-day historians, is in Parkman's handwriting, signed "F. Parkman, August '44."

"Romance in America," as Parkman called the oration, reveals for us the springs from which his later work flowed, providing us with new insight into the romantic concept of history held by one of our greatest historians. Indeed, Parkman's later multivolumed masterpiece *France and England in North America* is, in many respects, a projection of the ideas that so fascinated Parkman in these early undergraduate days. Certainly Parkman's interests crystallized remarkably early in his career, so that the reading of his college days was of real value to him in his literary work. As he himself noted, in a letter written many years later, a literary career early suggested itself as combining his two boyhood loves: love of the forest and of books.[2]

What is known of Parkman's academic career supports his own contention that he was a lover of books. For his scholastic record at Harvard, which was excellent though not brilliant,[3] masks the fact that the prescribed curriculum was only a minor part of his program of study.[4] From his early reading lists and correspondence it is apparent that he carried on a secondary program of reading in literature, ethnology, and history, with particular emphasis on the romantic themes of François René de Chateaubriand, Jules Michelet, Sir Walter Scott, and James Fenimore Cooper, all of which readied him for his own literary work.[5]

But though his readings were valuable in preparing him for the oration and his later writings, a six months' grand tour of Europe, taken because of an apparent breakdown in his health, supplied him with the immediate framework for his oration, a comparison of nature in Europe and nature in America. In the early summer of 1844, after returning from Europe, before writing his oration and before his graduation from Harvard in August 1844 (a graduation which seems to have been delayed from the

[2] Parkman to Pierre Margry, Dec. 6, 1878, *Letters of Francis Parkman,* ed. Wilbur R. Jacobs (2 vols., Norman, Okla., 1960), II, 124.

[3] Term Books, Harvard Archives.

[4] *Letters of Francis Parkman,* ed. Jacobs, I, xxxiv ff.

[5] Parkman's letter of April 29 [1842] to Jared Sparks, written during his Sophomore year in college, indicates that he was busily engaged in reading on military campaigns at Lake George during the "Old French War." In his autobiographical letter of 1886 to Martin Brimmer, Parkman wrote: "Before the end of the sophomore year my various schemes had crystallized into a plan of writing the story of what was known as the 'Old French War'. . . ." (*Ibid.,* 9, 184 n.) Additional evidence of Parkman's youthful interest in early French American history is in the Library Charge Lists, Harvard Archives, and in the notes accompanying Mason Wade's excellent edition of *The Journals of Francis Parkman* (2 vols., New York, 1947).

early summer because of his temporary absence from college), he gave evidence of his state of mind with these random jottings in his journal:

> The traveller in Europe.
> Art, nature history combine.
> In America Art has done her best to destroy nature, association nothing.[6]

The quiet beauty of the English countryside had impressed the youthful tourist; in Scotland he was captivated by the "heathery" hills closely associated with the life and writings of Scott. Here were art, legend, nature, and history. America, by contrast, had failed to appreciate the romance of its wilderness heritage, and it was this failure that Parkman hoped to rectify by writing a good—perhaps a great—book on a North American theme, a book that would be recognized as a product of the New World.

It was the sheer grandeur of nature in the wilderness that provided the most impelling motive for Parkman's literary activity. His feeling for this theme is exhibited by the comments of Vassall Morton, the hero of his novel. "Here in America," declares Vassall, "we ought to make the most of this feeling for nature; for we have very little else . . . savageness and solitude have a character of their own; and so has the polished landscape with associations of art, poetry, legend and history."[7] The polished landscape of Europe held little enchantment for Parkman. Rather he turned to the mountains and the virgin forests for his New World symphony. Parkman's fascination with the history of the American forest, stimulated by Cooper's "Leatherstocking Tales," is described in one of his autobiographical letters. In recalling his youth, Parkman (writing in the third person) said: "his thoughts were always in the forests, whose features not unmixed with softer images, possessed his waking and sleeping dreams, filling him with vague cravings impossible to satisfy."[8]

Parkman's treatment of the Indians, unlike his treatment of nature, was far from romantic. He rejected completely the idea of the noble savage, depicting the Indian warrior as a barbarian of the Stone Age. Yet, in spite of this unromantic attitude, his enthusiasm for the Indian was a lifelong affair. Friends of Parkman's college days said that he exhibited symptoms of " 'Injuns' on the brain" and entertained them with wild tales of Indian scalps, birchbark canoes, and wampum, tales that surpassed anything in Cooper's stories, though they were clearly influenced by them.[9]

---

[6] *Journals of Francis Parkman,* ed. Wade, I, 277.

[7] Francis Parkman, *Vassall Morton, A Novel* (Boston, 1856), 112.

[8] An autobiographical letter to George E. Ellis [1864], *Letters of Francis Parkman,* ed. Jacobs, I, 177.

[9] Charles Haight Farnham, *A Life of Francis Parkman* (Boston, 1904), 78, in Frontenac ed. of *Francis Parkman's Works* (16 vols., Boston, 1899–1907).

His *Oregon Trail* of 1849 was a personal narrative of his youthful expedition on the Great Plains and his life with the Sioux, as well as a record of preparation for the historical books that followed, especially the *Conspiracy of Pontiac*. Parkman eventually decided that the story of the French and English in North America would provide the same opportunities for an exciting theme and would be of more interest to civilized readers than his originally planned history of the North American Indians, with the Six Nations of the Iroquois as a focal point.[10]

Parkman's early fascination with Indian history blended with the interest he developed in studying the heroic figures of Canadian history. The age of the black-robed missionary, the adventurous *gentilhomme* of the forest, and the chivalrous Field Marshal Montcalm held peculiar attraction for him. Painted with splendor on the natural canvas of the primeval wilderness was the history of the soldier in plumed helmet, Indian warriors with barbarous trophies, and the great Jesuit martyrs.

Parkman imagined the past as a kind of theater. The forest was his stage, and historic figures like Robert de La Salle, the Comte de Frontenac, James Wolfe, and Montcalm were "actors" in his drama.[11] Take from his pages in the *History* the backdrop of the woods with its hum of insects, its smell of pine, and its roar of cataracts, and the image dims. Remove the fighting, sweating, and shouting actors, and the interest vanishes, for Parkman did not see his works as a dry chronicle of events, but as drama dependent on people and places. Parkman aspired to create a romantic but authentic image of another age with characters that had the passions of living men and women. His self-assumed task, a half century of gathering manuscripts, touring historic sites, and writing, was the culmination of a college dream to capture the romance of America's past and make it come to life for others.

That Parkman as a graduating college senior had learned his art is evident from his oration. His prose is made vivid by its appeal to the senses of sight, hearing, and smell. At Lake George a "gentle girl . . . gazes .·. . down the Lake"; the sound of a "gun reverberates down the long vista of mountains, and the sullen murmurings dwell for many moments on the ear"; and a raven appears which "once gorged on the dead." The language of the oration reflects also Parkman's youthful affection for poetry, particularly his admiration for the Byronic hero and the forest hymns of William Cullen Bryant. The excellent vocabulary, the graceful

---

[10] Parkman to Abbé Henri-Raymond Casgrain, Oct. 23, 1887, *Letters of Francis Parkman*, ed. Jacobs, II, 213.

[11] In his correspondence published in the *Letters of Francis Parkman*, Parkman uses the word "actors" in referring to the chief characters of his narrative. The word "drama," or the phrase "dramatic interest," also appears in the letters in which he discusses plans for the organization of his works.

sentences merging into smoothly molded paragraphs and transitions, the skillful characterization of the slatternly log hut pioneer occupied with reading newspapers or cultivating potatoes suggest literary sophistication. But perhaps Parkman is most eloquent when his emotions are aroused, as in praising the unspoiled woods, a subject that was always close to his heart.[12] Yet his style does not violate the beauty of simplicity; it lacks the pedantries and pompous language that punctuated much nineteenth-century prose.

That Parkman gave serious thought to the American Revolution as a historic theme is apparent in his college oration, but he turned away from his subject because it contained, as he wrote, "no display of chivalry or of headlong passion, but a deliberate effort in favor of an abstract principle." What romance was there in a war resulting from a meeting that calmly deliberated and then "voted resistance"?

For him the epochs of the Anglo-French struggle in North America were recalled, as he says in his oration, by the "wild scenery" of Lake George. This glistening jewel in the wilderness, with its rugged shore line escarpments, pine and hemlock forests, was the "holy lake" christened Lac St. Sacrement by Father Isaac Jogues before he was tormented by the Mohawks. It was the scene of Sir William Johnson's bloody victory over the French and of the massacre of captives following Montcalm's capture of Fort William Henry. Afterward it was the silent witness of the escapades of one of Parkman's favorite heroes, Major Robert Rogers, the colonial ranger.[13] In many respects Lake George was a focus of history for Parkman, a kind of geographical center for his narrative of *France and England in North America*. Even forty years after his college oration Parkman included descriptions of this lake in his *Montcalm and Wolfe*.[14]

Parkman's *History* was recognized in his lifetime as it is today as a gem of historical writing. His books have long been held as models for style and honest research by those historians who aspire to write readable narrative history that has appeal for both the general reader and the specialist. Parkman's college oration reveals in early form the romantic image of history that inspired his later and well-known volumes.

[12] "For my part, I would gladly destroy all his works [the *nouveau riche*] and restore Lake George to its native savagery—which shows plainly that you are a better American than I am." (Parkman to Casgrain, Oct. 5, 1892, *Letters of Francis Parkman,* ed. Jacobs, II, 265.)

[13] One of Parkman's treasured possessions was an engraving of Rogers (reproduced in *The Conspiracy of Pontiac and the Indian War after the Conquest of Canada* [Boston, 1906], Frontenac ed., I, 266), which he hung in his study at 50 Chestnut Street, Boston. The study was recently dismantled and reconstructed in a similar room at the headquarters of the Colonial Society of Massachusetts, 87 Mount Vernon Street, Boston.

[14] See, e.g., *Montcalm and Wolfe* (Boston, 1907), Frontenac ed., II, 181.

ROMANCE IN AMERICA

The tourist in Europe finds the scenes of Nature polished by the hand of art, and invested with a thousand associations by the fancies and the deeds of ages. The American traveller is less fortunate. Art has not been idle here for the last two centuries, but she has done her best to ruin, not to adorn, the face of Nature. She has torn down the forests, and blasted the mountains into fragments; dammed up the streams, and drained the lakes, and threatens to leave the whole continent bare and raw. Perhaps the time will come when she will plant gardens and rear palaces, but the tendency of her present efforts forbids us to be too sanguine.

When Columbus first saw land, America was the sublimest object in the world. Here was the domain of Nature. For ages her forest-trees had risen, flourished, and fallen. In the autumn, the vast continent glowed at once with red, and yellow, and green; and when winter came, the ice of her waters creaked and groaned to the solitude; and in the spring her savage streams burst their fetters, and swept down the refuse of the wilderness. It was half the world a theatre for the operations of Nature! But the charm is broken now. The stern and solemn poetry that breathed from her endless wilderness is gone; and the dullest plainest prose has fixed its home in America.

Once Spain, Italy, England was also a wilderness. The haunts of Nature were *there* in like manner invaded, and her charm broken; but since that remote day, the deeds of many a generation of wise and gallant men have flung around that land the halo of romance and poetry. Its streams and mountains are hallowed by associations that ours have not, and may never have; and the hand of art has polished the rough features of Nature. The warfare of fierce and brave men, seen through the obscure veil of centuries, has given a charm to the Cheviot Hills that will never belong to ours, though our forests have seen struggles more savage and bloody.

The fanciful child, as he journeys through the passes of our northern mountains, looks with awe into the black depths of the woods, and listening to the plunge of the hidden torrent, he recalls the stories of his nursery of Indian wars and massacres. A fearful romance invests all around him, for he associates it with those scenes of horror. And surely the early days of no nation could afford truer elements of romance. They need but to be magnified by superstition and obscured by time. But we live in an enlightened age. History has recorded the minutest circumstance of our fathers' wars; and when we look at the actors, we find the same cool-blooded, reasoning, unyielding men who dwell among us this day—the very antipodes of the hero of romance.

The traveller may pause over the battle-fields of Saratoga or Bennington, and moralize, if he pleases, or give vent to his patriotic ardor. But they have none of the romantic charm, so hateful to the Peace-society. He will not feel the inspiration of Flodden or Otterburn. Here, on these American fields, was no display of chivalry or of headlong passion, but a deliberate effort in favor of an abstract principle. Cool reason, not passion, or the love of war, sent the American to the battlefield. When Napoleon placed his brother on the throne of Spain, the Spanish peasant sprang to the gun and the dagger and leaped on the invader with the blind fury of a tiger. The men of New England heard that they were taxed, called a meeting, and voted resistance. Philanthropists may rejoice over the calm deliberation of such proceedings, but the poet has deep reason to lament.

The soldier of the Revolution has handed down to his grandchildren his own cool reasoning temper, so that the traveller finds even fewer elements of the picturesque in the character of the men, than in the aspect of the country. But, perhaps, being young and inexperienced, and having heard that wild men still linger in the recesses of the Scottish Highlands and the mountains of Wales, he imagines that the depths of the yet unwasted forest may contain some form of human nature more strange and wonderful to his American eye. So, with infinite toil, he penetrates to a narrow gap in the woods on the outskirts of civilization;—a small square space hewn out of the forest, and full of the black and smoking carcases of the murdered trees, while the still living forest palisades the place around. Here dwells the pioneer, in his log-hut. The disappointed traveller finds him like other people, with no trace of primitive ignorance or romantic barbarism. He reads the newspapers; supports Polk and Dallas with fiery zeal; knows the latest improvements in agriculture, and keeps a watchful eye on all that is going on in the great world. Though quite confident in his power to match the whole earth in combat, he has no warlike ardor, preferring to watch his saw-mill and hoe his potatoes, since these seem to him the more rational and profitable occupations. In short, the enthusiast can make nothing of him, and abandoning the thought of finding anything romantic on his native continent, he sighs for Italy, where there are castles and convents, stupid priests, and lazy monks, and dresses of red and green; where people are stabbed with stilettos, instead of being slashed with bowie-knives, and all is picturesquely languid, and romantically useless.

Yet beauties enough to be on the northern traveller's path; beauties scarce surpassed on earth, and one spot, at least, whose wild scenery has gained a deeper interest from the early history of his country. A lake which Romish priests, charmed by its matchless beauty, consecrated to the Prince of Peace when that country was an untrodden wilderness, yet which has seen a thousand death-struggles, and been dyed with the blood of legions. To the eye, Lake George seems the home of tranquility and mild repose. The gentle girl sits on the green mound of the ruined fort, and gazes in quiet happiness down the Lake. All is calm and peaceful, yet lovely and wild, by the red light of evening; waters as deep and pure as the eyes of the gazer; mountains whose sternness is softened into a wild beauty. The evening gun reverberates down the long vista of mountains, and the sullen murmurings dwell for many moments on the ear.—There was a time when other sounds awoke those echoes,—the batteries of Montcalm; the yells of a savage multitude, and the screams of a butchered army. Blood has been poured out like water over that soil! By day and by night, in summer and in winter, hosts of men have struggled and died upon it. It is sown thick with bullets and human bones, the relics of many a battle and slaughter. The raven that plucks the farmer's corn once gorged on the dead of France, of England, and a score of forgotten savage tribes.

But the Holy Lake is alone. There are other scenes of grandeur and beauty, yet none where associations throng so thick and fast; and as they seem doomed to rest undistinguished in song, we must hope for them the colder honors of prose, and look forward [to] the day when the arts of peace shall have made them illustrious.

The Great Descent:
Cooper's Home as Found

MARVIN MEYERS

In the legendary figure of Natty Bumppo, raised by Moravian missionaries
and the Delaware Indians to become one of Nature's noblemen, James Fenimore Cooper created a romantic symbol which made him internationally
famous. Cooper himself was a very self-conscious member of the New
York gentry and had spent seven years in Europe. In his less well-known
essays and fiction Cooper displayed his talent for social analysis and criticism. While he cannot be rated as an American Tocqueville, whose *Democracy
in America* remains a relevant masterpiece, Cooper does illuminate the ambivalence towards past and future which recent scholars have found in
Jacksonian America. In Cooper's *Notions of the Americans,* a gentleman-
democrat from New York (Cadwallader) introduces a travelling Bachelor
from Europe to a favorable view of the United States. In 1838 Cooper's
Effinghams of *Home as Found* return from Europe with much more critical
views. Cooper's complex relationship to Jacksonian America provides a
valuable focus for the historian sensitive to cultural tensions.

COOPER DID NOT SHOW THE BACHELOR MIRAGES. HE NEVER SUGGESTS
that great, strange forces invaded America between the stranger's departure
and the Effinghams' (and his own) return. How then did the land of
common sense and progress, decency and order, become a place good men
cursed, lamented, or abandoned? A change in Cooper's private outlook,
only tenuously related to general social trends, is one source of answers:
the *Notions* were an antidote for vitriolic British travel notes, like Captain

Marvin Meyers, *The Jacksonian Persuasion: Politics and Belief,* 1957, chapter
4, pp. 55–75. Reprinted by permission of the publishers, Stanford University Press.
Copyright © 1957 by the Board of Trustees of the Leland Stanford Junior University.

Hall's; harsh personal experiences with unruly neighbors and rude press critics soured Cooper; an extended stay in Europe suggested nobler standards of culture. Perhaps the very existence of Jacksonian Democracy as an embattled political force, disputing the possession of American loyalties, gave a sharper polemical cast to the visible world. All these have some plausibility; and yet I find an essential consistency in outlook.

The ordinary at its best, for all its pleasant aspect, was never taken for the ideal order by Cooper's standards: at best, the sacrifices were real, the achievements limited. More important, society organized by the middling standard was a precarious creation: its mobility could run wild, its naturalness give way to oafishness, its prudence turn to greed, its pragmatism become mere craftiness, its decency decay into an arrant philistinism, its subtly graded order sink into a false equality. The Bachelor of the *Notions* was amazed to see American society functioning so well because he was a European; still he was a European of Cooper's making and his wonder was, in some part, Cooper's warning that a nation self-made in the image of common sense was a most delicate balance of forces. Cooper's line between the good in the middling standard and the evil in the "social bivouac"[1] of the 1830's is thin: a little excess in the parts, a shift in center of gravity, and the ordinary reveals its mangy underside.

I suspect that Cooper's deepest shock came with the conviction that the 5 per cent leaven of natural gentility would never be; that the Effingham-Hawker-Caverly-Cadwallader set—the established families of wealth, breeding, taste, political virtue—was a tiny coterie, locked out of American society; that the rising middle class was fatally anchored to the mass and would rise no higher, or that it would settle, where it could, for a cheap brand of snobbery. In Cooper's explicit analysis the great descent occurs in three main areas: where the rising tempo of mobility disintegrates communal centers of order and decorum; where the related quest for gain turns feverish, despoiling real values in a speculative riot; where false democracy usurps control of opinion and taste, reducing all to a vile cant of equality. Dodge and Bragg are the dominant types of the new order; the Effinghams its vestigial elite; Captain Truck a relic of strong character in the commons, preserved by salt water; and the Leatherstocking its legend of presocial virtue.

"The whole country," John Effingham remarks, "is in such a constant state of mutation, that I can only liken it to the game of children, in which, as one quits his corner another runs into it, and he that finds no corner to get into, is the laughing-stock of the others."[2] Social flux is so far the essence of American life in the 1830's, as Cooper finds it, that he

[1] *Homeward Bound*, p. 289.
[2] *Home as Found*, p. 118.

taunts his readers thus: "The author has endeavored to interest his readers in occurrences of a date as antiquated as two years can make them, when he is quite aware, that, in order to keep pace with a state of society in which there was no yesterday, it would have been much safer to anticipate things, by laying his scene two years in advance."[3] What appeared in the *Notions* as a wholesome sign of national vigor must be reviewed in terms of the deepest skepticism.

In a penetrating sociological history of Templeton—the upstate New York seat of the Effinghams, virtually of the Coopers—the writer outlines the pattern of American settlement and its social consequences. Entering a "new country," Americans pass through three standard stages of development. At first society is characterized by strong community feeling and interest. The hazards of settling a wilderness make mutual effort necessary and greatly reduce the social "distance" between men of different habits, manners, education. The gentleman in the first stage of settlement maintains his character and station, but with "that species of goodfellowship and familiarity, that marks the intercourse between the officer and the soldier in an arduous campaign." The classes mingle: men—"even women"—break bread together in a way that would be unthinkable in settled circumstances,

the hardy adventures and rough living of the forest apparently lowering the pretensions of the man of cultivation and mere mental resources, to something very near the level of those of the man of physical energy and manual skill. In this rude intercourse, the parties meet, as it might be, on a sort of neutral ground, one yielding some of his superiority, and the other laying claims to an outward show of equality, that he secretly knows, however, is the result of the peculiar circumstances in which he is placed.[4]

This primary stage of "mere animal force" is the happiest period in the first century of settlement. Great cares drive out small, good will abounds, neighbors are helpful, and life has the "childhood" qualities of "reckless gayety, careless association, and buoyant merriment." After this era of "fun, toil, neighborly feeling, and adventure" comes the second major phase of settlement: "society begins to marshal itself, and the ordinary passions have sway."

Now it is that we see the struggles for place, the heartburnings and jealousies of contending families, and the influence of mere money. Circumstances have probably established the local superiority of a few beyond all question, and the condition of these serves as a goal for the rest to aim at.

The learned professions take natural precedence—"next to wealth, how-

---

[3] *Homeward Bound,* Preface, p. iv.
[4] *Home as Found,* p. 162.

ever, when wealth is at all supported by appearances." At this point, "gradations of social station" multiply and crystallize, in defiance of equalitarian ideas and institutions.[5]

The least inviting condition of society in a free country above the state of barbarism is met in this transitional phase of settlement. Tastes too crude to accept regulation impose themselves with all the pretension and forced effort of "infant knowledge." Because of "the late *pele-mele*" in the "community" stage, the status struggle is particularly sharp: men aspire above their reach, as that reach would be understood in older communities. Manners are at their worst, exposed to the influence of "the coarse-minded and vulgar." Finally, with the arrival of the third stage, "the marshalling of time quietly regulates what is here the subject of strife." Settlement has reached maturity and "men and things come within the control of more general and regular laws." The essential trait of the third phase is not a particular form of civilization but a general settling down: the community assimilates a stable culture conforming to the regional pattern; class distinctions are more or less rigidly established.[6]

In America the first stage of settlement is highly variable in length; often it is quite short. But the second is almost always long, "the migratory habits of the people keeping society more unsettled than might otherwise prove to be the case." Maturity comes only when a great majority of the living generation are regional natives, bred to one culture standard. Yet: "Even when this is the case, there is commonly so large an infusion of the birds of passage, men who are adventurers in quest of advancement, and who live without the charities of a neighborhood, as they may be said almost to live without a home, that there is to be found for a long time a middle state of society [between the second stage and the third]. . . ." Templeton remains in this ambiguous condition, divided almost equally between the third-generation descendants of the pioneers and a flock of "migratory birds" whose influence "nearly neutralized that of time and natural order of things." An emerging sense of loyalty to place and tradition among the natives provides the sole restraint upon a "nameless multitude" who briefly occupy real estate and live entirely in the flat dimension of present interest.[7]

Templeton is by no means an extreme example of the social flux which is shaking the foundations of American society. It requires the delicate sensibilities of an Effingham or a Cooper to find the signs of social upheaval in the history of a quiet country village—not one of the boom towns of the period—which has grown at a moderate pace and appears

[5] *Ibid.*, pp. 162–63.
[6] *Ibid.*, pp. 163–64.
[7] *Ibid.*, pp. 164–66.

already to be leveling off. New York is the ultimate case: "a social bivouac, a place in which families encamp instead of troops." New York or Templeton, to Cooper and the Effinghams the principle is the same. The gentle Ned Effingham—a natural aristocrat of sound heart and fair but dull mind—does his best to understand and pardon the strange creatures who challenge the proprieties, and the proprietors, of Templeton. He supposes that the unprecedented prosperity of the masses must worsen manners and morals, "by introducing suddenly large bodies of uninstructed and untrained men and women into society"—"a body of strangers, birds of passage, creatures of an hour."[8]

But cousin John Effingham, Cooper's angry prophet of the Yorker gentry and a man whose sharp blade always goes to the heart of matters in the novels, excuses nothing. The "vagrants" of Templeton "fancy everything reduced to the legal six months required to vote." John asks his kindly relative to look about him, "and you will see adventurers uppermost everywhere; in the government, in the towns, in your villages, in the country, even. We are a nation of changes." At first this is the expected response of a people engaged in settling an immense forest.

But this necessity has infected the entire national character, and men get to be impatient of any sameness, even though it be useful. Everything goes to confirm this feeling. . . . The constant recurrences of the elections accustom men to changes in their public functionaries; the great increase in the population brings new faces; and the sudden accumulations of property place new men in conspicuous stations. The architecture of the country is barely becoming sufficiently respectable to render it desirable to preserve the buildings, without which we shall have no monuments to revere.

To all this Ned can only mumble something about exaggeration, and patience, and taking the bad with the good.[9]

While the flux sometimes appears a vast dirty trick of history upon the Effinghams, it is more than that to Cooper because the Effinghams are more than private worthies, ornaments. Without the saving remnant of the quality, middling society turns into its ugliest form. The flux turns America loose, brashly to satisfy its natural promptings at the level of its common nature. Above all, that delicate articulation of formal equals according to natural distinctions is lost. Abandoning the Effinghams, society sacrifices itself. The reign of Dodge and Bragg begins.[10]

---

[8] *Homeward Bound*, p. 289; *Home as Found*, pp. 117–18, 224. For a later view of New York, see Cooper, *New York*.

[9] *Home as Found*, pp. 225–26.

[10] Evidence of the damage to tastes, manners, and values is considered in *Homeward Bound*, p. 38; *Home as Found*, pp. iv–v, 15, 42–97, 113–17, 120, 150, 156–57, 160, 186, 312–13, 335–37, 375–77. See also *The American Democrat*.

In the pathology of the great descent, violent economic fevers accompany the social flux. Where nothing is fixed, money is everything. Acquisition becomes the urgent, continuous preoccupation of society, until even useful enterprise is forgotten in the universal frenzy of speculation. Although this is not exclusively an urban phenomenon, Cooper finds his richest material in the business district of New York.

Cooper as usual employs the Effinghams as cicerones, this time to introduce their titled English visitor to the improbable wonders of Wall Street in the thirties. The tour begins at the office of one of the greater auctioneers, lately become the genius of the "town trade." Here one can buy villas, farms, streets, and towns of assorted types. As they enter, the auctioneer is presenting a choice offering: the old Van Brunt farm, which had given comfortable support to the family for over a century. It was first sold to "Feeler" for $5,000, resold the next spring to "Search" for $25,-000; sold again the next week to "Rise" for $50,000, who unloaded to a company, before his own purchase had been completed, for $112,000. The fifty acres then were divided into lots, which were sold at auction for the gross sum of $300,000. The auctioneer explains that he has many such properties; some have risen 3,000 per cent in five years, some a mere few hundred per cent. These speculative properties are miles beyond town. If the same land were called a farm, it would bring only a farm price, but once surveyed and detail-mapped it reaches what the auctioneer calls its "just value." Well mapped, even ocean bottom sells high. In the auction salesroom a crowd is bidding wildly for rocks, bogs, all on the credit of maps, and all "in the fearful delusion of growing rich by pushing a fancied value to a point still higher."[11]

Such weird affairs are beyond the grasp of Squire Ned—of course he knows that they are wrong—and John Effingham is obliged to interpret the experience. Land mania is but a special instance, for John, of the unlimited extravagance pervading the whole community.

Extravagant issues of paper money, inconsiderate credits that commence in Europe and extend throughout the land, and false notions as to the value of their possessions, in men who five years since had nothing, has [sic] completely destroyed the usual balance of things, and money has got to be so completely the end of life, that few think of it as a means. . . . All principles are swallowed up in the absorbing desire for gain—national honor, permanent security, the ordinary rules of society, law, the constitution . . . are forgotten, or are perverted. . . .

The entire community is in the situation of a man who is in the incipient stages of an exhilarating intoxication, and who keeps pouring down glass after glass, in the idle notion that he is merely sustaining nature in her ordi-

11 *Home as Found*, pp. 100–103.

nary functions. This wide-spread infatuation extends from the coast to the extremest frontiers of the West; for, while there is a justifiable foundation for a good deal of this fancied prosperity, the true is so interwoven with the false, that none but the most observant can draw the distinction, and, as usual, the false predominates.[12]

As the tour continues through the warehouse district, John describes the further ravages of the economic fever, when it passes from the extremities of land speculation to the ordinary business of the country.

The man who sells his inland lots at a profit, secured by credit, fancies himself enriched, and he extends his manner of living in proportion. The boy from the country becomes a merchant—or what is here called a merchant—and obtains a credit in Europe a hundred times exceeding his means, and caters to these fancied wants; and thus is every avenue of society thronged with adventurers, the ephemera of the same widespread spirit of reckless folly. Millions in value pass out of these streets, that go to feed the vanity of those who fancy themselves wealthy, because they hold some ideal pledges for the payment of advances in price like those mentioned by the [land] auctioneer, and which have some such security for the eventual payment, as one can find in calling a thing that is really worth a dollar, worth a hundred.[13]

John's hope for the country lies only in the prospect that a disease so violent cannot last. Possibly the inevitable season of repentance will restore a decent economic balance. But one cannot be too confident: not even the great fire in New York's business district, a flagrant providential warning, had been sufficient for a moral awakening.[14]

Cooper's clumsy satire, *The Autobiography of a Pocket-Hankerchief,* contains possibly his most bitter and thorough commentary on the economic derangements of the 1830's. Among a lot of gougers, parasites, confidence men, and touts—the new economic men—the type figure is one Henry Halfacre, land speculator and paper millionaire. He has come from nowhere and built a paper fortune out of town-lot speculations in New York and the newly settled regions of the West. Halfacre's empire rests upon a flimsy pyramid of interlocking credits: he buys and sells on paper promises; manages to make his assets appear in liquid condition by discounting a fraction of the paper he receives, enough to show a five-figure bank account and meet his current demands. As one of those "who shoot up like rockets, in two or three years," Halfacre supports the illusion of his affluence by maintaining a mortgaged home on Broadway—an address which gives "a sort of patent of nobility"—and a showy style of life,

[12] *Ibid.,* p. 103.
[13] *Ibid.,* p. 105.
[14] *Ibid.,* pp. 105–9.

symbolized by the hundred-dollar handkerchief his daughter Eudosia flaunts.[15]

Jackson's removal of the government deposits from the Bank of the United States gives a momentary jolt to the Halfacre career: money becomes scarce, "more especially with those who had none," and Halfacre breaks down in the effort to cover his commitments. "His energy had overreached itself," Cooper writes, "like the tumbler who breaks his neck in throwing seventeen hundred somersets backwards." Temporarily, the Halfacres are crushed, and curse the author of their downfall, "that tiger, Jackson"—"the old wretch." Soon enough the nimble Henry recovers his senses and plots a course for riding out his bankruptcy. The kernel of his plan is to create an illusion of honest character which will divert attention from the lots still in his possession. The family ostentatiously abandon their house, auction the furniture, and—the dramatic climax—return the costly handkerchief, all to the loud applause of the New York press: here is an honest man sacrificing his goods to raise funds for the creditors. In the meantime Halfacre shrewdly liquidates his holdings, paying creditors in much overvalued lots, and reserving his little cash for the few recalcitrants who would otherwise start suit. Finally, he has balanced his books, pocketed half the real value of his holdings, and maintained the reputation of an honorable man.[16]

Thus is common sense in economic life diverted from utility and decency. Enterprise is reduced to a bag of tricks, a fantastic juggling act.

To attempt an interesting *roman de société* with American materials was, in Cooper's mind, a desperate venture which justified all sorts of literary devices to create diversion or entertainment in a drab subject: "more ship" for the Effingham plot, curious characters anywhere. (Indeed, Cooper's long attachment to Natty Bumppo and his Indian comrades stems at least partly from the literary conviction that fictional interest could be sustained only at the wild margins of American life.)[17] Steadfast Dodge and Aristabulus Bragg cannot be taken for accidents of fiction, however; their appearance in the Effingham novels is determined by grim social reality. Cooper's only literary concession is to do the portraits in the style of caricature. Both Dodge and Bragg are village figures, self-made quasi-gentlemen risen from the mass just high enough to sense its mind and take it where it wants to go. One is a brash Yankee editor, serving his ambition by confirming the provincial mind in all its worst

[15] *Pocket-Handkerchief*, pp. 126–28, 158–60, 128–31.

[16] *Ibid.*, pp. 155, 158–60, 161–67. Another dimension of the tale is the record of the cold exploitation of a poor seamstress by the merchants who cater to the vulgar demands of the newly rich.

[17] *Homeward Bound*, Preface, p. iii; *Home as Found*, Preface, pp. ii–v.

tendencies; the other an adroit upstate New York lawyer, a virtuoso player of all the economic and political angles in the new social pell-mell. Their careers are enmeshed with the critical changes in American life; their character makes them unmistakably new men; even their village situation is typical in a nation still—despite its rising commercial towns—predominantly rural, settled in dispersed clusters.[18]

Steadfast Dodge is without doubt the lowest character in all Cooper's gallery of American defectives. He has not a single good moment in two longish novels, is granted not even the credit for downright villainy: Dodge is a shapeless mass of ignorance, arrogance, cowardice, avarice, envy, vanity, and servility, mixed with a certain low cunning—a subhuman absurdity. Cooper no doubt saw in him the Weeds and Webbs and all that rancorous tribe of Whig editors; the editors at any rate seemed to see themselves and struck back in a long campaign of vilification against the author.[19]

Dodge is the pure product of Yankee community and conformity. In a region where individuality was smothered in conventions, caucuses, public meetings, and associations of all sorts, Dodge "from his tenth year up to his twenty-fifth . . . [had] been either a president, vice-president, manager, or committee-man of some philosophical, political, or religious expedient to fortify human wisdom, make men better, and resist error and despotism." He was a master of "the language of association" and could match any American in his control of such terms as " 'taking up'— 'excitement'—'unqualified hostility'—'public opinion'—'spreading before the public,' or any other of those generic phrases that imply the privileges of all, and the rights of none." (The root phrase of this vocabulary, Cooper remarks in another book, is "they say." "No one asks 'who says it,' so long as it is believed that *'they* say it.' ")[20]

A habit of speech is in Dodge an element of character. His miserable physical cowardice is compounded always by concealment behind a fabricated committee, or alleged public opinion. He perceives the world entirely in the terms of popular majorities and minorities, of "streaks of public opinion" identified by party labels. "So much and so long had Mr. Dodge respired a moral atmosphere of this community-character, and gregarious propensity, that he had, in many things, lost all sense of his individuality; as much so, in fact, as if he breathed with a pair of county lungs, ate with a common mouth, drank from the town-pump, and slept in the open air." The image is deceptive, however, if it suggests some deep organic bond between Dodge and his fellows. He shares their limi-

---

[18] *Homeward Bound*, pp. 290–91.
[19] Waples, *Whig Myth*, pp. 208–21, stresses the Whig identity.
[20] *Homeward Bound*, pp. 38–39; *American Democrat*, p. 175.

tations of mind and spirit, to be sure; but he communicates with them only in a mechanical, manipulative way, seeking favor and fearing rejection. Dodge never took a step "without first weighing its probable effect in the neighborhood." The great question in any public gesture is always "whether it would be likely to elevate him or depress him in the public mind." In political relations, Dodge is an "Asiatic slave" to the majority and a "lion" in defying the minority.[21]

Only in the protective environment of "party-drill," however, has Dodge the nerve to defy anyone; "in all other things he dutifully consulted every public opinion of the neighborhood." Self-distrust bred a "rabid desire" for universal approval, especially for the sanction of his natural superiors; for Dodge did vaguely sense his own deficiencies. His jealous detraction of superior qualities, concealed under "an intense regard for popular rights," expresses just this grudging respect "for everything that was beyond his reach." He would like nothing better than acceptance by the Effinghams; he approaches them full of the "distrust and uneasiness" of the "vulgar and pretending" when faced with "the simplicity and natural ease of the refined." The Effingham set amuse themselves briefly with this windbag, and then dismiss him firmly and without further thought.[22]

Steadfast Dodge is, as I have said, terribly real to Cooper, and so important that he has not a private gesture, a scrap of dress, an act or word, which is merely for the story: everything goes for evidence in the case against the false democrat. Cooper forgives Dodge nothing, though he pardons America a little for creating him. It is natural that a young and scattered population should be provincial. The moral foundation in America is broad, and supports "a moral superstructure so narrow," because "popular sentiment" rules over domains where it has only "limited and superficial attainments." The Dodges are the inevitable punishment of the people for their vain pretense to omni-competence. Vapidity, folly, malice, envy, bigotry, arrogance, hypocrisy, ignorance, poured out through the popular press, are the fate of America until maturity—if it ever comes—effects "a greater concentration of taste, liberality, and knowledge."[23]

Eve Effingham, Cooper's candied vision of the good in American civilization, offers a further explanation of "the animal," Steadfast Dodge. Perhaps the prevalence of the Franklin legend is to blame for making every green printer fancy himself a sage and prophet. American boys are taught that they can achieve anything by merit; they conclude that they

[21] *Homeward Bound,* pp. 88–89.

[22] *Ibid.,* pp. 89, 92–100, 195–99.

[23] *Home as Found,* pp. 317–18. Some of Dodge's glaring deficiencies are shown in *Homeward Bound,* pp. 183–84, 231–32, 268–69, 367–68.

are in fact fit for everything; and thus the teaching causes "pretenders to start up in all directions." The male Effinghams draw out the consequences: Dodge's type dominates the American press, doing vast damage by shaping the minds of helpless readers. Liberty is confounded with personal envy and "the jealousies of station"; self-interest is installed in place of public duty. The gravity of the Dodge menace is obvious in the United States, where government has become a gross *"press-ocracy."*[24]

Dodge is sheer cant done up into a man; Aristabulus Bragg is a different and better issue of the same social stock. Where Dodge is wholly absorbed in the mirror world of opinion manipulation, Bragg touches the world of real affairs at various points, in a bold, breezy, often skillful way. Bragg is a "plastic character," in Cooper's estimate, "bold, morally and physically, aspiring, self-possessed, shrewd, singularly adapted to succeed in his schemes where he knew the parties, intelligent after his tastes, and apt." If Bragg had had better luck in his early influences, his native gifts could have made him a gentleman and a valuable social servant. It was his misfortune, not his fault, that he was shaped by the common standard of village democracy.[25]

Bragg was a native of western Massachusetts who migrated to upstate New York at nineteen. In two years he had been admitted to the local bar and founded a successful practice. The Effinghams had employed him as agent for their Templeton properties during their long absence, at once a mark of trust and, in John's hard phrase, a calculation "on the principle that one practiced in tricks is the best qualified to detect and expose them." Where Bragg meets Dodge, in the realm of false democracy, he is unequivocally a bad actor. In his general role as a plastic, versatile village careerist Bragg represents an ambiguous quality. He stands at the margin of the middling standard. Cooper calls him the epitome of the good and evil in a very large class of Americans.[26]

Bragg is quick-witted, prompt in action, enterprising when he has no stake and wary when he does. He is ready to turn hand, heart, and principles to anything that offers an advantage. Nothing is above his aspiration, nothing too menial to do. Expert in legal and business affairs, Bragg is also a smooth talker, in accents uncouth and provincial; a deliberate self-improver with his smattering of classics, dancing, medicine, and divinity. One Effingham sees in him "an amusing mixture of strut, humility, roguery, and cleverness"; another finds

a compound of shrewdness, impudence, common-sense, pretension, humility, cleverness, vulgarity, kind-heartedness, duplicity, selfishness, law-honesty,

[24] *Homeward Bound*, pp. 202–4.
[25] *Home as Found*, pp. 222–23.
[26] *Ibid.*, pp. 9–10.

moral fraud, and mother-wit, mixed up with a smattering of learning and much penetration in practical things. . . . Mr. Bragg, in short, is purely a creature of circumstances, his qualities pointing him out for either a member of Congress, or a deputy sheriff, offices that he is equally ready to fill.[27]

Any thought that Bragg deserves to be taken in as apprentice to the real quality, in the old hope of recruiting aristocracy from the middle ranks, is quickly scotched by Cooper and the Effinghams. John Effingham, the most candid of the lot, classes Bragg with "a valuable house-dog." Edward, without insults, maintains a wide distance between client and lawyer. And the perfect Eve involuntarily prolongs Bragg's cautious suit through the length of a novel simply because she cannot recognize that such a creature could hope for her hand. Whenever Bragg comes too close, he acts the clumsy oaf, to the annoyance or amusement or indifference of the Effinghams. Typically, they "detect" but do not "notice" his *faux pas*. Cooper calls Bragg a gentleman, with an apology, "for we suppose Aristabulus must be included in the category by courtesy, if not of right."[28]

Through Bragg, Cooper collects the attitudes and opinions of the country. He serves as a kind of native informant for his lofty and remote employers, bringing especially the news of ordinary life. Thus Bragg tells of the village lawyers in New York, men like himself, who mix professional business with horse dealing or—the current rage—"dealing in Western cities" and "other expectations." His conversation is burdened with references to good business prospects in milk or sweet potatoes. When John Effingham tries to make him see that these latter at least are "honester and better occupations," Bragg is puzzled, for "with him everything was eligible that returned a good profit, and all things honest that the law did not actually punish."[29]

This conversion of all values into cash equivalents does not exempt the values of home and neighborhood. Poor Sir George, the English visitor, is astounded at Bragg's innocent report of "the Western fever" carrying many New Yorkers away from home, especially the "regular movers." And Bragg in turn is a little touched by Sir George's picture of stationary Old England: "Very poetical. . . . It must be a great check to business operations." He explains that history is no "incumbrance" to mobility in America: one "may do very much as interest dictates." "A nation," Bragg concludes, "is much to be pitied that is weighed down by the past . . . since its industry and enterprise are constantly impeded by obstacles that grow out of its recollections." Bragg assures the company that he and his

[27] *Ibid.*, pp. 9–11.
[28] *Ibid.*, pp. 11, 16–19, 138, 299–302.
[29] *Ibid.*, pp. 20–22.

fellows feel no attachment to a home, a tree, or a churchyard which they would not readily abandon for a price.[30]

What Cooper sees in Bragg, then, is the new man of pell-mell, the perfect adaptive organism for a situation without rules or bounds. Physical and economic mobility make "love of change" the exclusive principle. As Bragg informs Powis (Eve's eligible suitor and, as it happily turns out, her cousin): "Rotation in feelings, sir, . . . is human nature, as rotation in office is natural justice." Some of his friends suggest it would be healthy if "the whole society be made periodically to change places." Are they all agrarians, then? Powis is quickly reassured on this score by the canny lawyer: "As far from it as possible; nor do I believe you will find such an animal in this country. Where property is concerned, we are a people that never let go so long as we can hold on, sir; but beyond this, we like lively changes."[31]

A last view of Aristabulus Bragg, as he juggles his dual role of Effingham agent and popular favorite in the Point affair, must emphasize his most doubtful qualities. (Cooper drags Dodge back upon the scene quite artificially to make the lesson perfectly obvious.) The episode in the novel is the parallel to Cooper's famous wrangle with his neighbors, which opened a bitter history of legal suits and newspaper polemics. The importance of the incident does not lie in a conflict of substantial economic interests; on the contrary, the case suits Cooper's purpose precisely because the stake is a small piece of scenic property, and the principle alone counts. The "all-powerful, omnipotent, overruling, law-making, law-breaking public" insists upon converting its picnic privileges on Effingham property (the Point) into a legal right. Even the gentle, tolerant Ned Effingham is made to lose his temper over such presumption.[32]

The unfortunate Bragg is caught in the middle of the affair. As lawyer to the Effinghams he must press the case against the invading villagers. As village leader, with some responsibility for instigating the incursion, he must carefully sustain his popularity. As product of his age, he cannot conceive the motives of the Effinghams in defying public opinion on so trivial a matter. When "they say" they own the Point, it must be so: "for it is impossible that everybody should be mistaken." Finally, the Effinghams condescend to show him legal proof for their claim—their word alone should have been enough—but Bragg is no less "aghast" at the "unheard-of temerity" of the family in ignoring organized public protest and even threatening suit against the authors of an insulting public resolution. The sole outright virtue in Bragg, through the entire controversy, is

[30] *Ibid.,* pp. 22–25.
[31] *Ibid.,* pp. 323, 145–48.
[32] *Ibid.,* pp. 202–22, 205.

his "profound deference for the principles, character, and station of Mr. Effingham, that no sophistry, or self-encouragement in the practices of social confusion could overcome." Bragg respects, at least, what he cannot understand or be.[33]

Cooper winds up the Effingham tale with a series of matches, joining like to like: Dodge gets none; Sir George takes Grace, the imperfect American heiress (about right for a mere English baronet); Paul Powis, John Effingham's lost son, alone is worthy of Eve—the perfect match of quality. Bragg wins Eve's French maid, who will be taken for a lady by most Americans, and goes West, where he will practice law, or keep school, or go to Congress, or saw lumber, or do whatever comes to hand, while his new wife will set up as dressmaker and French teacher. In the end, Bragg is perhaps as much a mystery to the Effinghams as they are to him. They know certainly what he is not: one of them. His origin in social pell-mell is clear; his characteristics as a fluid careerist can be described. But what he *is,* and how to come to terms with him, remain a puzzle. As Eve, always so sure in her judgment, confesses: "He seems so much in, and yet so much out of his place; is both so rusé and so unpracticed; so unfit for what he is, and so ready at everything, that I scarcely know how to apply terms in any matter with which he has the smallest connection."[34]

The perspective of the Effingham books is bounded in one side by Ned, on the other by John, with Powis, Eve, and the author comfortably between. Bragg, Dodge, Truck, and the others are just what Effinghams see when, reluctantly, they look out upon America. Each general fault is the contrary of an Effingham virtue. In short, we know the best people from all the previous discussion, and only a little more remains to be said of their traits and of their function.

The Effinghams are everything that the elect of the twenties aspired to, with the added perfection of a cosmopolitan polish. Everything about them—their possessions, their appearance, their style of life, their manners—is a beautiful blend of Continental grace and republican simplicity; everything is keyed to quiet elegance, impeccable dignity, pure refinement. It would be as shocking to discover an Effingham acting in bad taste as it would be to catch Natty Bumppo losing an Indian trail.[35]

The Effingham men, each in his way, define the possibilities of gentility in America. Knowledge, independence, manners, noble bearing, elevated principles, wealth, habits of refinement, gentle extraction, liberal attainments in every direction, place Edward and John in the first rank of inter-

33 *Ibid.,* pp. 208–11, 220, 222, 219.
34 *Ibid.,* pp. 429–30, 142.
35 *Ibid.,* pp. 1–8, 12, 17–19, 183–85.

national society. Both are tall, handsome Yorkers of commanding presence. Edward lives on the income of a large hereditary landed estate. He has succeeded to his property at an early age, and so for many years has lived in an "intellectual retirement." In this fortunate situation, he has achieved a notable freedom from prejudice, an even temper, and a just mind. He makes little pretension to greatness; his strength is in his goodness. Almost by instinct he manages to "hit the line of truth" in all questions; and he is never thrown off by excitement or interest: "Independence of situation had induced independence of thought." Toward America, Ned is loyal, just, tolerant: he neither betrays his country abroad, in the fashion of the touring *arriviste,* nor gives it mawkish flattery at home. "He loved his native land, while he saw and regretted its weaknesses."[36]

Ned's cousin, friend, and traveling companion, John Effingham, is a gamier dish of gentility. Dorothy Waples, in her effort to identify strict party lines in Cooper's work, has placed John in the enemy camp: a gentleman conceded to the Whigs. Yet on every important count—principles, manners, taste, position—John belongs with the family. If John votes Whig—a dim possibility, though I doubt whether he troubles to vote at all—he would despise his party, in no wise represent them, and remain in mind and character solely Effingham. He is severe and cynical where his cousin is winning and kindly; but then he is acute and knowing, and his judgments of America express the Effingham mind in hard, clear truths, explaining often what Ned can only vaguely sense. By the end of the Point affair, there is little difference in the views of Ned and John.[37]

James Grossman has appraised the Effingham function brilliantly. They are perfect, passive, almost disused ornaments of the republic. They hold their example before a society which is at least envious, at most awed, but on no account inspired to imitation. They will enforce the laws and remind the presumptuous that the power of the "re-public" is still more awful than the power of the public. But no substantial force in American life runs in their direction. Nor do they entertain ambitions for entering the life of their time. The Effinghams exist in retirement, live on income, and cultivate graces and virtues in privacy. Indeed, a good deal of their positive effort is expanded precisely to maintain privacy. The mating of Effingham cousins is Cooper's final stroke, to isolate the vestige of American quality in purity, and concede the active world to the rising Braggs.[38]

It is true that the Effinghams win their Point battle and prove that some common sense, common honesty, and prudence remain in the public

---

[36] *Ibid.,* pp. 181–83; *Homeward Bound,* pp. 53–56.

[37] *Ibid.,* pp. 53–56.

[38] *Home as Found,* p. 219; Grossman, *Cooper,* pp. 114–24.

when it can break loose from the demagogues of false democracy; and yet it is hard to find a hopeful figure anywhere beneath the Effinghams. The best in the commons is Captain Truck, and he is as much a relic as the Effinghams: a bluff original of an obsolete breed, raised on catechism and piety, deeply respectful to his betters, whose virtue has been preserved by ship's discipline. Significantly, Truck and a still crustier remain, the old "commodore" of Lake Otsego, are the only links Cooper provides to the one social hero deemed worthy of the republican succession, Andrew Jackson. The antique captain agrees with the superannuated Commodore that Old Hickory is a man's man: "Tough, sir; tough as a day in February on this lake. All fins, and gills, and bones."[39]

Even in the *Notions* of the twenties, Jackson appeared not as the leader of masses but as an impressive personal figure in the Doric style, as the rugged gentleman patriot of simple commanding ways. Jackson's direct appearance in the *Pocket-Handkerchief* satire, although it involves the policies of the Bank War, is made to seem a personal encounter between the champion of the republic and the Halfacre frauds. Of necessity Cooper places Jackson in the midst of life, but only to preserve the old decencies, as an individual figure of authority. Dodge and Bragg may be Whigs, yet essentially they represent the widely prevalent social type, the false democrat, bred by the changing American climate. Against them Cooper masters only two old oddities to vote for Jackson, and the seceded Effinghams to place their veto on the whole mess.

The Effingham element is a frozen vestige; Jackson is a distant individual champion of the Doric republic. Cooper's last resort for a sign of American nobility is the passing echo of a Yorker legend. The gentlefolk of Templeton, taking in the natural beauties of Lake Otsego, come upon the old site of Natty Bumppo's hut. Each in turn reaches out his hand to acknowledge another, long-extinct strain of virtue. To the refined Eve, Natty was "a man who had the simplicity of a woodsman, the heroism of a savage, the faith of a Christian, and the feelings of a poet. A better than he, after his fashion, seldom lived." Sophisticated John Effingham is, in a rare moment, almost tenderly affected by the reminiscence: "Alas! . . . the days of the 'Leather-Stockings' have passed away. He preceded me in life, and I see few remains of his character in a region where speculation is more rife than moralizing, and emigrants are plentier than hunters."[40]

This brief encounter with legend is more, I think, than a quaint interlude in the tale. That it immediately precedes the eruption of the Point affair at least suggests an intention to juxtapose primitive virtue and present degradation; and the Effingham remarks confirm the purpose. In one

[39] *Home as Found*, p. 222; *Homeward Bound*, p. 242; *Home as Found*, p. 285.
[40] *Home as Found*, pp. 196–97.

respect, Natty is the masterpiece of the presocial democracy of the woods: natural experience has trained him to perfection in active competence and moral purity. The democracy of the clearing shows no capacity for shaping his successor. For active duty society must turn to Aristabulus Bragg. As always in his novels, Cooper does not permit the Effingham elite to weigh the merits of its own brand of cultivated excellence, perfected in retirement, against the natural and active virtues of the Leatherstocking.[41] Both are worthy models for America; both have been banished from the settlements, one to the remote prairie, the other behind the walls of privacy.

Long before the Effinghams made their *pro forma* stand against the invasion of their picnic grounds, satisfying their principles and changing nothing, Natty Bumppo had abandoned Lake Otsego. As settlers infested his woods, Natty—according to local legend—would notch a pine for each arrival, until "reaching seventeen, his honest old heart could go no further, and he gave the matter up in despair." The eccentric ancient, the "commodore" of the lake, delivers the final judgment: "They may talk of their Jeffersons and Jacksons, but I set down Washington and Natty Bumppo as the two only really great men of my time."[42]

ON COOPER AS A SOURCE

I have suggested at the outset that Cooper's America is neither a Jacksonian projection nor a transcript of reality, but something between: the product of a probing for the moral strains which Cooper felt, in common with Jacksonian allies, in the changing social environment of the thirties. Cooper demanded more of America (especially a directive role for the quality) and regretted more in the change (including the new modes of democratic politics which Jacksonians had largely developed). Indeed he presents only two eccentrics from the class beneath the Effinghams with the moral sensitivity to feel the great descent and react against it. Nevertheless, he helps us to define the temporary equilibrium of the Old Republic which Jacksonians remembered (with a good deal of selection) as an ideal past; and to feel the painful pressures of flux and fever which predisposed Jacksonians to condemn the agencies of social change. The conservatism of Cooper and the conservatism of the Jacksonians crossed a wide gap to meet in a common resistance; while the Braggs—and Whigs— plunged into action.[43]

[41] Henry Nash Smith has made this point most effectively in his Introduction to Cooper, *The Prairie*, pp. v–xx.

[42] *Home as Found*, pp. 199–201.

[43] How Cooper steeled himself to choose the lesser evil is a subtle biographical question which I cannot resolve here. His dilemma had much in common with that of other intellectuals—men like Hawthorne, Melville, Paulding—who came

Unfortunately, Cooper will take us no further into the political life of his generation. He had given his sympathy, as a citizen, to the measured and modest, the vigorous and decorous, democracy of common sense; and America had betrayed him. Cant democracy, fevered avarice, and blind mobility were everywhere beyond the Effingham gate. Unlike Tocqueville, Cooper neither explored with understanding the feelings of a people so circumstanced, nor looked curiously for a "new science of politics" to fit the new condition of Americans. The American democrat in retreat is more rigid than the resigned French aristocrat, perhaps because he asks more for his country: a share of both the democratic and the aristocratic goods, in just the right proportions.

Nonetheless, Cooper—with his closer vantage point, his briefer perspective, and his more intimate involvement—adds to Tocqueville's findings on Jacksonian society. On fundamental facts there is broad agreement: that equality is the salient public value; that majority opinion rules the state and dominates the minds of its individual citizens; that acquisitiveness is the master motive; that rootlessness and continuous practical improvisation define a way of life. Tocqueville, with his systematic understanding of democracy, unquestionably makes his findings count for much more, yet Cooper does have his points as a historical witness. If America had been drifting from the start on the great tide of the universal democratic revolution—Tocqueville's view—still the events of a decade which could sap Cooper's faith in the republic were peculiarly significant. The outsider took what he saw in 1830 as a matter of course—for the Americans. The insider felt with much of his generation the shock of change from one to another stage of middle-class democracy.

Again, the outsider with a telescopic view, Tocqueville, could not take seriously the limited social stratification which persisted within a radical equality of condition; although he could write brilliantly of the insatiability of the popular equalitarian passion, even in the leveled democratic

---

to a similar Jacksonian choice: men who could not expect Jacksonian Democracy to realize their own essential values. I have been content to find in Cooper a useful intermediary, a cicerone whose inflamed sensibilities reported the climatic changes of an era, and whose intelligence gave some order to the process. From Cooper's enigmatic bond with the Jacksonians I would derive no more than this: to an agrarian conservative of that age the last faint image of the Doric order could be found in the virile old patriot of the Democracy and in the cause of moral restoration. The tenuous connection will not sustain an independent argument either on the nature of Fenimore Cooper's convictions or on the character of Jacksonian Democracy. Interestingly, Cooper's home county in New York, Otsego, was firmly Jacksonian; but this only compounds the difficulty, for the local Democratic leaders had enough of Dodge and Bragg in them, I judge, to discourage Cooper's sympathy.

universe. Cooper, with something of John Adams' nose for the eternal aristocrat in plain dress, flushed the business and financial upstarts, and the self-made opinion manipulators of press and party, who had displaced the Washingtons and Jays and Effinghams and Coopers as notables and leaders of American society. Neither Tocqueville nor Cooper effectively explores the curious alternations of jealousy and envy and esteem which Americans expressed in politics toward those who now took the prizes in the democratic market place. Perhaps the most arresting single insight on this score is still Tocqueville's: in Jacksonian times the new elite would keep their pride and vanity and ambition behind closed curtains, and act the plainest of common men upon the public streets. Much of Cooper's hatred for the *nouveaux* arose precisely here: the offense of their grossness and provincialism was compounded by that cold hypocrisy which let them play their political game through Steadfast Dodge, the mere dirty tail of an American democrat.

The great descent of the common-sense republic meant, for Fenimore Cooper, the turning of democracy from its better to its worse nature. Representative Jacksonians shared neither Cooper's demands for a gentle, decorous democracy nor his fear of an equalitarian society and culture. For this reason, perhaps, they rarely inquired so far as Cooper did into the workings of a democratic social system. Jacksonians did sense a social turning which would bring corruption to the manners and morals of their beloved republic; and, like Cooper, they found a major source of evil in new economic ways. The Bank became their Monster, symbolizing forms and powers hostile to the commonwealth of virtuous producers.

Solitude and Society:
Nathaniel Hawthorne

MARIUS BEWLEY

Modern literary critics have emphasized the fable-like character of classic American literature of the nineteenth century. They have also pointed to the typical polarities which inform it—between America and Europe, democracy and aristocracy, self and society, passion and morality, or agrarianism and industrialism. Characteristically, American writers have not resolved these antitheses so much as they have incorporated the tensions which polar tendencies generate. Lionel Trilling remarked in 1940 that an unusually large proportion of America's notable writers of the nineteenth century were "repositories of the dialectic of their times—they contained both the yes and the no of their culture, and by that token they were prophetic of the future." Marius Bewley, who sees American classic literature in relation to the polarities of America and Europe, democracy and aristocracy, tradition and progress, finds a historical precedent for these antitheses in the differing political values of Jefferson, John Adams, and Hamilton. Bewley illustrates the value of this dialectical approach for the intellectual historian in his discussion of Nathaniel Hawthorne.

IN HIS ESSAY, 'SOCIETY AND SOLITUDE', EMERSON HAS A FINE PASSAGE through which we can enter into a consideration of one of the central problems in Hawthorne's art, his concern with solitude in a democratic society. Emerson writes:

Though the stuff of tragedy and romance is in a moral union of two superior persons whose confidence in each other for long years, out of sight and in sight, and against all appearances, is at last justified by

Marius Bewley, *The Eccentric Design: Form in the Classic American Novel*, 1963, pp. 113–127, 138–139. Reprinted by permission of Columbia University Press. Copyright 1963 by Columbia University Press.

victorious proof of probity to gods and men, causing joyful emotion, tears and glory,—though there be for heroes this *moral union,* yet they too are as far off as ever from an intellectual union, and the moral union is for comparatively low and external purposes, like the co-operation of a ship's company or of a fire-club. But how insular and pathetically solitary are all the people we know! Nor dare they tell what they think of each other when they meet in the street. . . .

Such is the tragic necessity which strict science finds underneath our domestic and neighbourly life, irresistibly driving each adult soul with whips into the desert, and making our warm covenants sentimental and momentary. We must infer that the ends of thought were peremptory, if they were to be secured at such ruinous cost. They are deeper than can be told, and belong to the immensities and eternities. They reach down to that depth where society itself originates and disappears; where the question is, which is first, man or men? where the individual is lost in his source.

And he goes on to emphasize the isolation of men of genius: 'We pray to be conventional. But the wary heaven takes care you shall not be if there is anything good in you. Dante was very bad company . . .' and so on. In these quotations we have the problem of the artist, the exceptional spirit, in a democratic society. It was a problem that preyed on the nineteenth-century American conscience. Was the man of genius worth the special privileges and indulgences he required from society, or was the first duty of all men to sacrifice themselves in the interests of a levelling social fabric to which American political theory had already attached a mystique?

To the nineteenth-century American, such a society as he believed was developing in his own country was indeed one of the preemptory ends of thought, but at the same time the writers whom we are considering were aware, like Emerson, of the ruinous cost; and they were aware of it because it was principally they, as artists, who were called upon to pay. The penalty of genius was isolation, exclusion from the democratic community whose tendency, as Cooper had said, was 'in all things towards mediocrity'. The problem of the artist was, at one level, a political one. We can come at this aspect of it most directly in the early Federalist writers of the Republic such as Joseph Dennie or Fisher Ames. In 1807 an anonymous writer in the *Boston Anthology* had written:

We know that in this land, where the spirit of democracy is everywhere diffused, we are exposed, as it were, to a poisonous atmosphere, which blasts everything beautiful in nature, and corrodes everything elegant in art; we know that with us 'the rose petals fall ungathered' and we believe that there is little to praise and nothing to admire in most of the objects which first present themselves to the view of the stranger.

While something of this attitude was to be preserved later in the genteel tradition, the development of a democratic philosophy in Jeffersonianism, and later in Jacksonianism, attracted the best intelligences away from a programme of mere reaction and finance. Here, then, is a clearly defined split in the consciousness of the American artist of the time. Wasn't it possible that the practice of his art, which by its very nature set him apart from society as an observer and an analyst—wasn't it possible that it somehow constituted a betrayal of his own nature as an American? It often seemed so to Hawthorne's New England conscience. But, with a shift of mood, wasn't it perhaps the artist after all who was betrayed by his political and social traditions? The problem could cut both ways and did. We have already considered the debate, finally un-resolved, between Cooper's European political novels and his Littlepage trilogy. The tension between solitude and democratic community is not identical with that, but it is related.

Had Hawthorne been able to regard the matter from the point of view of the anonymous writer in the *Boston Anthology* it would have been a simple matter to put the case in terms of a black and white contrast in favour of the artist. In stories like *The Devil in Manuscript* Hawthorne's rage at society sometimes broke through, but ultimately he saw the role of the artist as involved in the greater question of his human relationship with his fellow men. And on this score Hawthorne was never secure. One of the most personal passages in Hawthorne's writings occurs in his introduction to *The Scarlet Letter,* 'The Custom House':

Either of these stern and black-browed Puritans would have thought it quite a sufficient retribution for his sins that after so long a lapse of years the old trunk of the family tree, with so much venerable moss upon it, should have borne, at its topmost bough, an idler like myself. No aim that I have ever cherished would they recognize as laudable; no success of mine, if my life, beyond its domestic scope, had ever been brightened by success, would they deem otherwise than worthless, if not positively disgraceful. 'What is he?' murmurs one grey shadow of my forefathers to the other. 'A writer of story books! What kind of business in life, what manner of glorifying God, or being serviceable to mankind in his day and generation may that be? Why, the degenerate fellow might as well have been a fiddler!' Such are the compliments bandied between my great grandsires and myself across the gulf of time! And yet, let them scorn me as they will, strong traits of their nature have intertwined themselves with mine.

There is evidence that throughout his life he suffered an incapacity to adjust himself practically to the society that, as an American, he wished to believe in. He wished to express his solidarity with it, and this became a nervous necessity in that degree in which he found it difficult to cast aside his dissatisfactions with it. To state the case succinctly: Hawthorne's compulsive affirmation of American positives, particularly in the political sense, led to a rejection of the idea of solitude; and solitude as an expression of aristocratic withdrawal seemed to side with Europe rather than with America when the two traditions stated their respective claims. But unfortunately it also seemed to side with the practice of his art.

This ambiguity, which is a very complex one, lies near the centre of all of Hawthorne's art, and it reflects that 'tragic necessity' Emerson described in the passage quoted above. The 'moral union' envisaged by democracy—especially Jacksonian democracy—is for comparatively low and external purposes, and practically speaking it often seems to preclude anything better. Emerson's native optimism achieved a rather too facile resolution of the tension in his short 'Society and Solitude' essay (which reads like a footnote on Hawthorne), but for Hawthorne himself no easy resolution was possible. The tension between solitude and society, particularly as it is focused in the role of the artist, may be examined to advantage in 'Ethan Brand'. Written about 1848, it is not one of his best stories, but it is one of his most famous and most praised ones. The story is ostensibly concerned, as Mr. Mark Van Doren has pointed out, with 'the idea of a man whom an obsessive desire for perfection in knowledge or virtue or art has driven beyond nature, making him an accomplished but cold-hearted monster'. More fundamentally it is concerned with the problem of the creative artist, and particularly the writer. Hawthorne analyses the problem—or tries to—not in terms of the relation of the artist to his art, but in terms of his relation to society.

Before considering 'Ethan Brand' here, I should like to lead into that story by pausing for a moment on the character of Holgrave in *The House of the Seven Gables*. Holgrave is presented as a type of the artist, and although a daguerreotypist may seem a somewhat limited kind of artist to us, Hawthorne's choice of this particular art is significant. Holgrave takes likenesses. That is to say, he freezes personalities, arrests their vital movement in a static posture. His relation to them is not vital and reciprocal, but rather he stands in relation to them as a collector. His art becomes a symbol of his participation in life. A lodger in the house of Hepzibah Pyncheon and her brother Clifford, he has a tendency to stand aside from their human tragedy and merely observe—to take their likenesses, as it were. He speaks of his own role in these terms:

'But you have no conception of what a different kind of heart mine is from your own. It is not my impulse, as regards these two individuals, either to help or hinder; but to look on, to analyse, to explain matters to myself, and to comprehend the drama which, for almost two hundred years has been dragging its slow length over the ground where you and I now tread. If permitted to witness the close, I doubt not to derive a moral satisfaction from it, go matters how they may.'

Obviously young Holgrave, like Henry James, was a 'restless analyst' and Hawthorne's implication clearly is that Holgrave is a type of the novelist or writer. The reader of *The House of the Seven Gables* can scarcely refrain from concluding that Holgrave is meant to be Hawthorne's comment on himself as artist. Holgrave is certainly not presented as a villain in the novel. He is, indeed, the hero. But his description of his own heart in the passage I have quoted cannot be distinguished from the nature of Ethan Brand's 'crime'. When we compare Holgrave and Ethan Brand—one a hero and the other a monster—and when we consider that, despite Hawthorne's conflicting attitudes towards them, their moral reality is almost identical, we see that Hawthorne is faced here with the seeds of an impossible dilemma. This is the consequence of his trying to treat two problems—the problem of art and the problem of social morality—as if they were one and identical. Hawthorne's art is frequently the point at which two conflicting tendencies in him cross. The conditions of American society repel him, just as they had repelled Cooper, and drive him to retreat from society; but his democratic social conscience urges him, on the contrary, to take a role in society. Naturally enough, he finds that his creative and critical impulses inevitably side with the tendency to withdraw that he feels so strongly. This arouses his sense of guilt, and leads him to entertain confused feelings about art itself. And it would be wrong to underestimate Hawthorne's confusion on the subject of his own art. A greater artist than Cooper, and a finer critic of his own production, he lacked Cooper's clarity of vision concerning his own motives and the function he wished to perform as an artist.

I said that 'Ethan Brand' gives us the artist in his social relations. This identification of Ethan Brand as an artist depends in some measure on seeing him in the full context of Hawthorne's work, but even so, Hawthorne's meaning is sufficiently contained in the story to make it possible to come at it without outside references.

Ethan Brand the watcher of the lime kiln, who has started out many years before the opening of the story on a quest to find the Unpardonable Sin, returns to the scene which had been his starting point. Approaching the lime kiln at night, he finds Bartram, his stupid and vulgar successor, keeping the blaze alight with the help of his little son Joe. The news is spread that the legendary wanderer has returned, and the villagers gather at the kiln to see and question Ethan Brand. Confronted with the villagers themselves, a crew of unattractive and more or less decayed human beings, Ethan Brand seems to have all the advantages on his side, and yet the 'monstrous' element in his nature is revealed by his human remoteness from his former neighbours:

The idea that possessed his life had operated as a means of education; it had gone on cultivating his powers to the highest point of which they were susceptible; it had raised him from the level of an unlettered labourer to stand on a star-lit eminence, whither the philosophers of the earth, laden with the lore of universities, might vainly strive to clamber after him. So much for the intellect! But where was the heart? That, indeed, had withered,—had contracted,—had hardened,—had perished! It had ceased to partake of the universal throb. He had lost his hold on the magnetic chain of humanity. He was no longer a brother-man, opening the chambers or the dungeons of our common nature by the key of holy sympathy, which gave him a right to share in all its secrets; he was now a cold observer, looking on mankind as the subject of his experiment, and, at length, converting man and woman to be his puppets, and pulling the wires that moved them to such degrees of crime as were demanded for his study.

Ethan Brand was clearly no Jacksonian democrat, and as the story proceeds we gather that Hawthorne means to present him as a symbol of the artist:

An old German Jew travelling with a diorama on his back, was passing down the mountain-road towards the village just as the party turned aside from it, and, in hopes of eking out the profits of the day, the showman had kept them company to the lime kiln.
'Come, old Dutchman,' cried one of the young men, let me see your pictures, if you can swear they are worth looking at!'
'Oh yes, Captain,' answered the Jew,—whether as a matter of courtesy or craft, he styled everybody Captain,—'I shall show you, indeed, some very superb pictures!'
So placing his box in a proper position, he invited the young men and girls to look through the glass orifices of the machine, and proceeded to exhibit a series of the most outrageous scratchings and daubings, as specimens of the fine arts, that ever an itinerant showman had the face to impose on his circle of spectators. The pictures were worn out, moreover, tattered, full of cracks and wrinkles, dingy with tobacco smoke, and otherwise in a most pitiable condition. Some purported to be cities, public edifices, and ruined castles in Europe; others represented Napoleon's battles and Nelson's sea-fights; and in the midst of these would be seen a gigantic, brown, hairy hand,—which might have been mistaken for the Hand of Destiny, though, in truth, it was only the showman's,—pointing its forefinger to various scenes of the conflict, while its owner gave historical illustrations. When, with much merriment at its abominable deficiency of merit, the exhibition was concluded, the German bade little Joe put his head into the box. Viewed through the magnifying glasses, the boy's round,

rosy visage assumed the strangest imaginable aspect of an immense Titanic child, the mouth grinning broadly, and the eyes and every other feature overflowing with fun at the joke. Suddenly, however, that merry face turned pale, and its expression changed to horror, for this easily impressed and excitable child had become sensible that the eye of Ethan Brand was fixed upon him through the glass.

'You make the little man to be afraid, Captain,' said the German Jew, turning up the dark and strong outline of his visage from his stooping posture. 'But look again, and, by chance, I shall cause you to see something that is very fine, upon my word!'

Ethan Brand gazed into the box for an instant, and then starting back, looked fixedly at the German. What had he seen? Nothing, apparently; for a curious youth, who had peeped in almost at the same moment, beheld only a vacant space of canvas.

'I remember you now,' muttered Ethan Brand to the showman.

'Ah, Captain,' whispered the Jew of Nuremberg, with a dark smile, 'I find it to be a heavy matter in my show-box—this Unpardonable Sin!'

The diorama, like Holgrave's camera in *The House of the Seven Gables,* is a symbol of the way external reality is imprisoned in art, and of the way human beings can be exploited for the purpose of artistic effect by the artist. It will be recalled that before his departure on his quest for the Unpardonable Sin, Ethan Brand had in some way betrayed a young girl, Esther. In the paragraph immediately preceding the diorama passage above, Hawthorne says that Ethan Brand, with cold and remorseless purpose, had made Esther 'the subject of a psychological experiment, and wasted, absorbed, and perhaps annihilated her soul, in the process'. Hawthorne is not explicit about the nature of this betrayal, but the reader is sure that it was nothing along the lines of the usual fictional seduction. It was a matter of the spirit, some kind of violation of the soul. The diorama passage, following immediately on this reference to Esther, is meant to make the nature of the crime explicit, and it associates the crime with the creative process as Hawthorne frequently, if not always, conceived it.

The pictures in the diorama are the usual subject-matter of fiction, as subject-matter was thought of by the nineteenth-century novelist. They remind one of Henry James's famous list of all the American novelist did *not* possess in the way of subjects: cities, public edifices, ruined castles, heroic battles and sea-fights. But here they are all reduced to dioramic scale, looking a little like reality, and yet not reality. Into this box, which inevitably reminds the reader of the framework of an art form, one sees the manipulating hand of the showman, which might be mistaken for the Hand of Destiny. Obviously Hawthorne means to suggest the manipulating intelligence of the artist who exploits reality for the sake of his art. The action suddenly takes on a more sinister tone in the next incident. The German Jew asks little Joe to put his head into the box, which he does with childish joy:

Viewed through the magnifying glasses, the boy's round, rosy visage assumed the strangest imaginable aspect of an immense Titanic child. . . . Suddenly, however, the merry face turned pale and its expression changed to horror, for this easily impressed and excitable child had become sensible that the eye of Ethan Brand was fixed on him through the glass.

At best this is an enigmatic passage, and its interpretation at any level must be a little forced. But it seems most obviously to mean that Joe has been transported from his natural habitat in the world into another and illusory world which possesses only a fake reality. The implication is that in this strange little world of dioramic illusion he is at Ethan Brand's mercy, and the passage is clearly intended as an implicit commentary on the relationship between Brand and Esther in which she had been made the subject of psychological experiment.

After little Joe has withdrawn his head from the box, the Jew says to Brand, apparently with irony:

'But look again, and, by chance I shall cause you to see something that is very fine, upon my word.'
'Ethan Brand gazed into the box for an instant, and then starting back, looked fixedly at the German. What had he seen? Nothing . . . only a vacant space of canvas.'
'I remember you now,' muttered Ethan Brand to the showman.
'Ah, Captain,' whispered the Jew of Nuremberg with a dark smile, 'I find it to be a heavy matter in my show-box,—this Unpardonable Sin!'

What Hawthorne is saying here, somewhat obscurely, is that the reality of art, being a false reality, ends in nothing—only an empty space on canvas. And then the German Jew identifies the diorama with the Unpardonable Sin itself—all of which adds up to no very flattering conception of Hawthorne's own art. The role of the German Jew is not as puzzling as it first appears. Mr. Richard Harter Fogle, with a point that escapes me, says that he is the Wandering Jew who brings with him the fascination of myth and legend. Actually, he represents a daemonic extension of Ethan Brand's personality so that the showman, manipulating the diorama, stands essentially for Ethan Brand as artist.

I do not think that 'Ethan Brand' is a successful story. It is ambiguous in an unsatisfactory way, and at times it seems to totter on the brink of ultimate incoherence. At no time does the imagery and symbolism take over in the way the symbolism of 'My Kinsman, Major Molineux' compels the imagination to unfold, leaving one like its hero Robin, almost trembling with pity and terror. Nevertheless, 'Ethan Brand' does tell us a good deal about Hawthorne's relation to American society, and his inability to conceive an adequate function for the artist in such a society. The conception of art which is developed in this story is unsatisfactory. It sees art, not as a channel of communication and understanding between individuals, but as a field of conflict upon which the artist conducts his nefarious trade of human exploitation. If Emerson's resolution in 'Society and Solitude' seems a little easy to be wholly convincing, Hawthorne as democrat achieves no resolution at all in such a story as this. In effect, he rejects the creatively gifted who cannot or will not be levelled down. But I wish to add at once that when Hawthorne appears in this role it is almost by inadvertence, and because his society offers him no help at all in resolving the tension between the individual and itself.

This tension can be recast in many different forms. In 'Ethan Brand' it is presented in a distorted fashion as the problem of the artist in a democratic society. It is even more obviously capable of a political interpretation, and the psychological variations that can be played on the theme are, of course, nearly unlimited. In any attempt to assess the respective values of the individual and the community when they are deemed to be in conflict, one is, in fact, concerned with the ultimate problem of determining and evaluating the nature of reality itself. 'All literature', Mr. Trilling writes, 'tends to be concerned with the nature of reality—I mean quite simply the old opposition between what really is and what merely seems.' In a society where neither traditional manners nor an orthodoxy exists, the problem is nearly overwhelming, and the serious artist becomes a metaphysician in spite of himself. The sense of intolerable spiritual isolation which is characteristic of so much of Hawthorne's writing, and is perfectly embodied in a figure like Melville's Ahab, would have been impossible had the social and religious traditions of Europe been at Hawthorne's disposal—either for acceptance or rejection. Under the impact of Unitarianism and Transcendentalism, Calvinism had ceased to exist in Hawthorne's New England except as the mantle of respectability worn by Boston merchants, or a nostalgic shadow stripped of sanctions. Without either a mystical Christian community or the living, fluid framework of a traditional social mode, the nineteenth-century American was forced back on the democratic abstraction as the only possible escape for his imprisoned identity.

If Hawthorne felt called upon to press the claims of democracy against the individual and the artist, even to the point of appearing to give the stupid and vulgar Bartram a practical and repulsive triumph over Ethan Brand, it was necessary for him to justify his choice, at least implicitly, by attempting to distinguish between illusion and reality. He had to be able to say that the democratic values were reflections of genuine reality and that aristocratic and artistic values (associated under the rubric of solitude), whenever they conflicted with the claims of the former, were sham. But what traditional criteria did Hawthorne's New England provide him with for making a valid distinction?

We can, I think, uncover a metaphysic concerning the nature of reality that is implicit in Hawthorne's body of fictions. It enters into his stories on two levels. It enters most unpleasantly and unsuccessfully in those stories which reflect Hawthorne's suspicion of the artist, the gifted, creative individual, whom he instinctively sees as the anti-democrat. But on a higher level it becomes the inspiriting life of his art and constitutes the essential form of his stories. On this level it does not reflect the negative conflict between society and solitude, the democrat and the artist, but positively it reflects the community that is sometimes possible between exceptional souls—that 'intellectual' as opposed to 'moral' union which Emerson desired but almost despaired of. Hawthorne is always called a Puritan writer, and before attempting to describe the conception of reality out of which he created his art it will perhaps be advisable to consider very briefly the nature of his religious belief.

Dogmatically speaking, Hawthorne was neither a Calvinist nor a Transcendentalist. Despite his brief association with Brook Farm, his scepticism in regard to the latter is well known. As for the Church, he seems always to have maintained a friendly but unyielding distance. During the years when he was American Consul in Liverpool he took a pew in the American Unitarian church there and sent his son Julian every Sunday, but he himself never appeared. There is a frequently quoted letter of Hawthorne's in which he describes a visit that Melville had made to him during which they went on a long walk together. This letter is always cited as revealing a great deal about Melville, but in fact it reveals as much about Hawthorne himself. Hawthorne says that they

sat down in a hollow among the sand hills (sheltering ourselves from the high, cool wind) and smoked a cigar. Melville, as he always does, began to reason of Providence and futurity, and of everything that lies beyond human ken, and informed me that he had pretty much made up his mind to be annihilated; but still he does not seem to rest in that anticipation; and, I think, will never rest until he gets hold of a definite belief. It is strange how he persists—and has persisted ever since I knew him, and probably long before—in wandering to and fro over these deserts, as dismal and monotonous as the sand hills amid which we were sitting. He can neither believe nor be comfortable in his disbelief; and he is too honest and courageous not to try and do one or the other. If he were a religious man, he would be one of the most truly religious and reverential; he has a very high and noble nature, and better worth immortality than most of us.

The longer one considers the two men the harder it is to resist the conclusion that Melville's was indeed a more religious nature than Hawthorne's. He was tormented by the absence of an acceptable or usable orthodoxy in a way that Hawthorne was not, and at bottom *Moby Dick* is the story of a theological quest which issues, after many years, in the tired disillusionment of *Clarel*. But no better phrase can be devised to describe Hawthorne's temperament than to say that he was a Puritan agnostic. Hawthorne appears to be concerned with religious problems in his art, but on analysis we find that the kind of truth Hawthorne is concerned with is radically different from the kind that Melville seeks, and is, ontologically speaking, on a lower level. Melville's quest is for God, however much he may despair of achieving his end; Hawthorne's, for the fulfilment of the human heart. Despite the frequent suggestion of theological implications in Hawthorne's art, they turn out to be largely illusory. His stories only *seem* religious in their point of view. A representative instance occurs in one of his greatest stories, 'Young Goodman Brown'. Despite its air of Christian propriety, this is one of the most deeply agnostic works of art in existence. The burden of the story is young Goodman Brown's, and hence Hawthorne's, inability to understand either the nature or the *locus* of spiritual reality. If Hawthorne and Melville may ever be said to resemble each other it is on their blackest levels of despair. The ending of 'Young Goodman Brown' reminds one of the last page of *The Confidence Man:*

> Often, waking suddenly at midnight, he shrank from the bosom of Faith; and at morning or eventide, when the family knelt down at prayer, he scowled and muttered to himself, and gazed sternly at his wife, and turned away. And when he had lived long, and was borne to his grave a hoary corpse, followed by Faith, an aged woman, and children and grandchildren, a goodly procession, besides neighbours, not a few, they carved no hopeful verse upon his tombstone, for his dying hour was gloom.

But even here the interests of the two men diverge. Melville has not focused his tragic comedy in terms of the human being at all. The final figure who is betrayed by the masks of illusion in *The Confidence Man* is the old patriarch, symbolizing God, who is led away into darkness on the final page. Melville's darkest book is God's tragedy more than man's. But in 'Young Goodman Brown' the tragedy is fixed squarely in the human heart. 'Young Goodman Brown' can no doubt be read in different ways, but it can hardly be argued in any interpretation that Hawthorne is much concerned with Goodman Brown's theology as such, or with what is likely to happen to him after his burial. The tragedy occurs on the nearer side of the grave, and in man's tormented heart.

Hawthorne tortures moral questions into forms of attenuated subtlety because he cannot bring them to a focus in any perspective of belief. The heir of the Puritan tradition, he inherited the rigid forms of Calvinism, but it was a Calvinism that had already collapsed, and he lived among the remnants of a dead faith while breathing the libertarian air of a New England Transcendentalism that he could not accept. There is, then, a tension in Hawthorne's mind that is peculiarly his. He often seems to pose questions in the old perspective of Calvinist faith, but he approaches the answers to them with an inquisitiveness and curiosity— even with an infidelity—that is the result of the new intellectual freedom of New England. As a result, there sometimes seems to be a discrepancy between Hawthorne's questions and answers if we ponder them for long; or rather let us say that the answers Hawthorne gives often exist in a carefully maintained margin of doubt.

The opening paragraph of Hawthorne's story, 'The New Adam and Eve', is his most complete statement of agnosticism:

We who are born into the world's artificial system can never adequately know how little in our present state and circumstance is natural, and how much is merely the interpolation of the perverted heart and mind of man. Art has become a second and stronger nature; she is a stepmother, whose crafty tenderness has taught us to despise the bountiful and wholesome ministrations of our true parent. It is only through the medium of the imagination that we can lessen those iron fetters which we call truth and reality, and make ourselves even partially sensible of what prisoners we are.

It is interesting to note that this passage is in itself ambiguous. By 'art' does Hawthorne mean the craft of men who have evolved systems of thought that distort reality, or does he mean the art of the creative mind? If the latter, he makes an odd distinction between the art which enslaves and the imagination which frees. Probably Hawthorne was not quite sure what he did mean here, for the ambiguity is typical of Hawthorne whenever he is on the subject of art. What is important in this passage is its complete rejection of any philosophic or theological perspective in which to pose moral questions. All our thought, all our faith, have become an expression of the world's artificial system, and our minds and hearts are so perverted that even our most fundamental concepts of truth and reality are lies. He almost puts the human mind beyond the possibility of knowing truth at all. But Hawthorne does believe in a truth. It is never forthrightly stated in the form of an explicit credo, but when its scattered parts are gathered together it becomes the only confession of faith that we ever really get from him. A suggestive statement occurs in this same story, 'The New Adam and Eve'. In this story, which is not among Hawthorne's best ones, he imagines that all the people in the world have suddenly died, and life begins anew with the creation of a second Adam and Eve, who awaken to find themselves in the midst of a modern but completely empty city:

Just when the earliest sunshine gilds the mountain tops, two beings have come into life, not in such an Eden as bloomed to welcome our first parents, but in the heart of a modern city. They find themselves in existence, and gazing into one another's eyes. Their emotion is not astonishment. Nor do they perplex themselves with efforts to discover what, and whence, and why they are. Each is satisfied to be, because the other exists likewise; and their first consciousness is of calm and mutual enjoyment, which seems not to have been the birth of that very moment, but prolonged from a past eternity. Thus content with an inner sphere which they inhabit together, it is not immediately that the outward world can obtrude itself upon their notice.

Hawthorne's reality is not concerned with the great metaphysical questions that became a creative motive in Melville's art—questions of what, and whence, and why. The domain of Hawthorne's reality is the inner sphere of reciprocal love and affection which he describes here. It is not the sphere only of love between the sexes. The magnetic chain of humanity which poor Ethan Brand is supposed to have violated is a current of sympathy among these inner spheres. It is this inner sphere of feeling and sympathy which is the psychological and moral world that Hawthorne as an artist regularly inhabits, but it is an extremely rarefied country, and Hawthorne has created some of his best art through his uncertainties as to what the right relationship is between this inner sphere and external reality, which he describes as the world's artificial system. He has created some of his best art on this theme, and, in quantity, a good deal more of his inferior art, art that leaves one with a sense of confusion and frustration.

. . .

It is obvious that the magnetic chain of humanity, which exists at the level of doctrine in Hawthorne's mind, is a democratic concept as he uses it; but it also transcends those limits and raises Hawthorne to the contemplation of the imprisoned identity, with which our age is so tragically familiar.

Reform in the Romantic Era

JOHN L. THOMAS

Mid-nineteenth-century America was an age of reform. It led Emerson to conclude: "There are always two parties, the party of the Past and the party of the Future; the Establishment and the Movement." The schism appeared, he added, "in Literature, Philosophy, Church, State, and social customs." Asylums for the deaf and dumb, mass revivals in town and country, suffragettes and abolitionists, Zions in the wilderness, and sages in Concord—these were the signs of new times. All these currents of change were part of the romantic age. "A yearning toward social reconstruction," wrote John Humphrey Noyes, a divinity student during the influence of "the Revival afflatus" and founder of the Oneida Community, "has become a part of the continuous, permanent, inner experience of the American people."

If there was a Movement, a party of the Future, it was a sprawling one— "a Puritan carnival" in Henry James's phrase. How can the historian understand this upsurge of reform so as to link together philanthropy, revivals, transcendentalists, and utopians? By looking for the perfectionist religious impulse at the bottom of these movements, John L. Thomas finds a unity which marks this period off from the Enlightenment which preceded it and the Civil War which ended it.

CONFRONTED BY THE BEWILDERING VARIETY OF PROJECTS FOR REGEN-erating American society, Emerson concluded his survey of humanitarian reform in 1844 with the observation that "the Church, or religious party, is falling away from the Church nominal, and . . . appearing in temperance and nonresistance societies; in movements of abolitionists and of socialists . . . of seekers, of all the soul of the soldiery of dissent." Common to all these planners and prophets, he noted, was the conviction

John L. Thomas, "Romantic Reform in America, 1815–1865," *American Quarterly*, 17 (Winter, 1965), pp. 656–681. Reprinted by permission of the author and the publisher.

of an "infinite worthiness" in man and the belief that reform simply meant removing "impediments" to natural perfection.[1]

Emerson was defining, both as participant and observer, a romantic revolution which T. E. Hulme once described as "spilt religion."[2] A romantic faith in perfectibility, originally confined by religious institutions, overflows these barriers and spreads across the surface of society, seeping into politics and culture. Perfectibility—the essentially religious notion of the individual as a "reservoir" of possibilities—fosters a revolutionary assurance "that if you can so rearrange society by the destruction of oppressive order then these possibilities will have a chance and you will get Progress." Hulme had in mind the destructive forces of the French Revolution, but his phrase is also a particularly accurate description of the surge of social reform which swept across Emerson's America in the three decades before the Civil War. Out of a seemingly conservative religious revival there flowed a spate of perfectionist ideas for the improvement and rearrangement of American society. Rising rapidly in the years after 1830, the flood of social reform reached its crest at midcentury only to be checked by political crisis and the counterforces of the Civil War. Reform after the Civil War, though still concerned with individual perfectibility, proceeded from new and different assumptions as to the nature of individualism and its preservation in an urban industrial society. Romantic reform ended with the Civil War and an intellectual counterrevolution which discredited the concept of the irreducible self and eventually redirected reform energies.

Romantic reform in America traced its origins to a religious impulse which was both politically and socially conservative. With the consolidation of independence and the arrival of democratic politics the new nineteenth-century generation of American churchmen faced a seeming crisis. Egalitarianism and rising demands for church disestablishment suddenly appeared to threaten an inherited Christian order and along with it the preferred status of the clergy. Lyman Beecher spoke the fears of more than one of the clerical party when he warned that Americans were fast becoming "another people." When the attempted alliance between sound religion and correct politics failed to prevent disestablishment or improve waning Federalist fortunes at the polls, the evangelicals, assuming a defensive posture, organized voluntary benevolent associations to strengthen the Christian character of Americans and save the country

[1] Ralph Waldo Emerson, "The New England Reformers," *Works* (Centenary ed.), III, 251; "Man the Reformer," *Works*, I, 248–49.

[2] T. E. Hulme, "Romanticism and Classicism," *Speculations: Essays on Humanism and the Philosophy of Art,* ed. Herbert Read (London, 1924), reprinted in *Critiques and Essays in Criticism, 1920–1948,* ed. Robert Wooster Stallman (New York, 1949), pp. 3–16.

from infidelity and ruin. Between 1815 and 1830 nearly a dozen moral reform societies were established to counter the threats to social equilibrium posed by irreligious democrats. Their intense religious concern could be read in the titles of the benevolent societies which the evangelicals founded: the American Bible Society, the American Sunday School Union, the American Home Missionary Society, the American Tract Society. By the time of the election of Andrew Jackson the benevolent associations formed a vast if loosely coordinated network of conservative reform enterprises staffed with clergy and wealthy laymen who served as self-appointed guardians of American morals.[3]

The clerical diagnosticians had little difficulty in identifying the symptoms of democratic disease. Infidelity flourished on the frontier and licentiousness bred openly in seaboard cities; intemperance sapped the strength of American workingmen and the saving word was denied their children. Soon atheism would destroy the vital organs of the republic unless drastic moral therapy prevented. The evangelicals' prescription followed logically from their diagnosis: large doses of morality injected into the body politic under the supervision of Christian stewards. No more Sunday mails or pleasure excursions, no more grog-shops or profane pleasures, no family without a Bible and no community without a minister of the gospel. Accepting for the moment their political liabilities, the moral reformers relied on the homeopathic strategy of fighting democratic excess with democratic remedies. The Tract Society set up three separate printing presses which cranked out hundreds of thousands of pamphlets for mass distribution. The Home Missionary Society subsidized seminarians in carrying religion into the backcountry. The Temperance Union staged popular conventions; the Peace Society sponsored public debates; the Bible Society hired hundreds of agents to spread its propaganda.

The initial thrust of religious reform, then, was moral rather than social, preventive rather than curative. Nominally rejecting politics and parties, the evangelicals looked to a general reformation of the American character achieved through a revival of piety and morals in the individual. By probing his conscience, by convincing him of his sinful ways and converting him to right conduct they hoped to engineer a Christian revolution which would leave the foundations of the social order undisturbed. The realization of their dream of a nonpolitical "Christian party" in America would ensure a one-party system open to moral talent and the natural superiority of Christian leadership. Until their work was

---

[3] For discussions of evangelical reform see John R. Bodo, *The Protestant Clergy and Public Issues, 1812–1848* (Princeton, 1954) and Clifford S. Griffin, *Their Brothers' Keepers* (New Brunswick, N. J., 1960).

completed, the evangelicals stood ready as servants of the Lord to manage their huge reformational apparatus in behalf of order and sobriety.

But the moral reformers inherited a theological revolution which in undermining their conservative defenses completely reversed their expectations for a Christian America. The transformation of American theology in the first quarter of the nineteenth century released the very forces of romantic perfectionism that conservatives most feared. This religious revolution advanced along three major fronts: first, the concentrated anti-theocratic assault of Robert Owen and his secular utopian followers, attacks purportedly atheistic and environmentalist but in reality Christian in spirit and perfectionist in method; second, the revolt of liberal theology beginning with Unitarianism and culminating in transcendentalism; third, the containment operation of the "new divinity" in adapting orthodoxy to the criticism of liberal dissent. The central fact in the romantic reorientation of American theology was the rejection of determinism. Salvation, however variously defined, lay open to everyone. Sin was voluntary: men were not helpless and depraved by nature but free agents and potential powers for good. Sin could be reduced to the selfish preferences of individuals, and social evils, in turn, to collective sins which, once acknowledged, could be rooted out. Perfectionism spread rapidly across the whole spectrum of American Protestantism as different denominations and sects elaborated their own versions of salvation. If man was a truly free agent, then his improvement became a matter of immediate consequence. The progress of the country suddenly seemed to depend upon the regeneration of the individual and the contagion of example.

As it spread, perfectionism swept across denominational barriers and penetrated even secular thought. Perfection was presented as Christian striving for holiness in the "new heart" sermons of Charles Grandison Finney and as an immediately attainable goal in the come-outer prophecies of John Humphrey Noyes. It was described as an escape from outworn dogma by Robert Owen and as the final union of the soul with nature by Emerson. The important fact for most Americans in the first half of the nineteenth century was that it was readily available. A romantic religious faith had changed an Enlightenment doctrine of progress into a dynamic principle of reform.

For the Founding Fathers' belief in perfectibility had been wholly compatible with a pessimistic appraisal of the present state of mankind. Progress, in the view of John Adams or James Madison, resulted from the planned operation of mechanical checks within the framework of government which balanced conflicting selfish interests and neutralized private passions. Thus a properly constructed governmental machine might achieve by artifact what men, left to their own devices, could not—gradual improvement of social institutions and a measure of progress. Perfectionism, on the contrary, as an optative mood demanded total commitment and immediate action. A latent revolutionary force lay in its demand for immediate reform and its promise to release the new American from the restraints of institutions and precedent. In appealing to the liberated individual, perfectionism reinforced the Jacksonian attack on institutions, whether a "Monster Bank" or a secret Masonic order, entrenched monopolies or the Catholic Church. But in emphasizing the unfettered will as the proper vehicle for reform it provided a millenarian alternative to Jacksonian politics. Since social evils were simply individual acts of selfishness compounded, and since Americans could attempt the perfect society any time they were so inclined, it followed that the duty of the true reformer consisted in educating them and making them models of good behavior. As the sum of individual sins social wrong would disappear when enough people had been converted and rededicated to right conduct. Deep and lasting reform, therefore, meant an educational crusade based on the assumption that when a sufficient number of individual Americans had seen the light, they would automatically solve the country's social problems. Thus formulated, perfectionist reform offered a program of mass conversion achieved through educational rather than political means. In the opinion of the romantic reformers the regeneration of American society began, not in legislative enactments or political manipulation, but in a calculated appeal to the American urge for individual self-improvement.

Perfectionism radically altered the moral reform movement by shattering the benevolent societies themselves. Typical of these organizations was the American Peace Society founded in 1828 as a forum for clerical discussions of the gospel of peace. Its founders, hoping to turn American attention from the pursuit of wealth to the prevention of war, debated the question of defensive war, constructed hypothetical leagues of amity, and in a general way sought to direct American foreign policy into pacific channels. Perfectionism, however, soon split the Peace Society into warring factions as radical nonresistants, led by the Christian prefectionist Henry C. Wright, denounced all use of force and demanded the instant creation of an American society modeled on the precepts of Jesus. Not only war but all governmental coercion fell under the ban of the nonresistants who refused military service and political office along with the right to vote. After a series of skirmishes the nonresistants seceded in 1838 to form their own New England Non-Resistant Society; and by 1840 the institutional strength of the peace movement had been completely broken.

The same power of perfectionism disrupted the temperance movement.

The founders of the temperance crusade had considered their reform an integral part of the program of moral stewardship and had directed their campaign against "ardent spirits" which could be banished "by a correct and efficient public sentiment." Until 1833 there was no general agreement on a pledge of total abstinence: some local societies required it, others did not. At the first national convention held in that year, however, the radical advocates of temperance, following their perfectionist proclivities, demanded a pledge of total abstinence and hurried on to denounce the liquor traffic as "morally wrong." Soon both the national society and local and state auxiliaries were split between moderates content to preach to the consumer and radicals bent on extending moral suasion to public pressure on the seller. After 1836 the national movement disintegrated into scattered local societies which attempted with no uniform program and no permanent success to establish a cold-water America.

By far the most profound change wrought by perfectionism was the sudden emergence of abolition. The American Colonization Society, founded in 1817 as another key agency in the moral reform complex, aimed at strengthening republican institutions by deporting an inferior and therefore undesirable Negro population. The cooperation of Southerners hoping to strengthen the institution of slavery gave Northern colonizationists pause, but they succeeded in repressing their doubts until a perfectionist ethic totally discredited their program. The abolitionist pioneers were former colonizationists who took sin and redemption seriously and insisted that slavery constituted a flat denial of perfectibility to both Negroes and whites. They found in immediate emancipation a perfectionist formula for casting off the guilt of slavery and bringing the Negro to Christian freedom. Destroying slavery, the abolitionists argued, depended first of all on recognizing it as sin; and to this recognition they bent their efforts. Their method was direct and intensely personal. Slaveholding they considered a deliberate flouting of the divine will for which there was no remedy but repentance. Since slavery was sustained by a system of interlocking personal sins, their task was to teach Americans to stop sinning. "We shall send forth agents to lift up the voice of remonstrance, of warning, of entreaty, and of rebuke," the Declaration of Sentiments of the American Anti-Slavery Society announced. Agents, tracts, petitions and conventions—all the techniques of the moral reformers— were brought to bear on the consciences of Americans to convince them of their sin.

From the beginning, then, the abolitionists mounted a moral crusade rather than an engine of limited reform. For seven years, from 1833 to 1840, their society functioned as a loosely coordinated enterprise—a national directory of antislavery opinion. Perfectionist individualism made effective organization difficult and often impossible. Antislavery delegates from state and local societies gathered at annual conventions to frame denunciatory resolutions, listen to endless rounds of speeches and go through the motions of electing officers. Nominal leadership but very little power was vested in a self-perpetuating executive committee. Until its disruption in 1840 the national society was riddled with controversy as moderates, disillusioned by the failure of moral suasion, gradually turned to politics, and ultras, equally disenchanted by public hostility, abandoned American institutions altogether. Faced with the resistance of Northern churches and state legislatures, the perfectionists, led by William Lloyd Garrison, deserted politics for the principle of secession. The come-outer abolitionists, who eventually took for their motto "No Union with Slaveholders," sought an alternative to politics in the command to cast off church and state for a holy fraternity which would convert the nation by the power of example. The American Anti-Slavery Society quickly succumbed to the strain of conflicting philosophies and warring personalities. In 1840 the Garrisonians seized control of the society and drove their moderate opponents out. Thereafter neither ultras nor moderates were able to maintain an effective national organization.

Thus romantic perfectionism altered the course of the reform enterprise by appealing directly to the individual conscience. Its power stemmed from a millennial expectation which proved too powerful a moral explosive for the reform agencies. In one way or another almost all of the benevolent societies felt the force of perfectionism. Moderates, attempting political solutions, scored temporary gains only to receive sharp setbacks. Local option laws passed one year were repealed the next. Despite repeated attempts the Sunday School Union failed to secure permanent adoption of its texts in the public schools. The Liberty Party succeeded only in electing a Democratic president in 1844. Generally, direct political action failed to furnish reformers with the moral leverage they believed necessary to perfect American society. The conviction spread accordingly that politicians and legislators, as Albert Brisbane put it, were engaged in "superficial controversies and quarrels, which lead to no practical results."[4] Political results, a growing number of social reformers were convinced, would be forthcoming only when the reformation of society at large had been accomplished through education and example.

The immediate effects of perfectionism, therefore, were felt outside politics in humanitarian reforms. With its confidence in the liberated individual perfectionism tended to be anti-institutional and exclusivist;

[4] Arthur Brisbane, *Social Destiny of Man: or, Association and Reorganization of Industry* (Philadelphia, 1840), introduction, p. vi.

but at the same time it posited an ideal society in which this same individual could discover his power for good and exploit it. Such a society would tolerate neither poverty nor suffering; it would contain no condemned classes or deprived citizens, no criminals or forgotten men. Impressed with the necessity for saving these neglected elements of American society, the humanitarian reformers in the years after 1830 undertook a huge rescue operation.

Almost to a man the humanitarians came from moral reform backgrounds. Samuel Gridley Howe was a product of Old Colony religious zeal and a Baptist education at Brown; Thomas Gallaudet a graduate of Andover and an ordained minister; Dorothea Dix a daughter of an itinerant Methodist minister, school mistress and Sunday school teacher-turned-reformer; E. M. P. Wells, founder of the reform school, a pastor of a Congregational church in Boston. Louis Dwight, the prison reformer, had been trained for the ministry at Yale and began his reform career as a traveling agent for the American Tract Society. Robert Hartley, for thirty years the secretary of the New York Association for Improving the Condition of the Poor, started as a tract distributor and temperance lecturer. Charles Loring Brace served as a missionary on Blackwell's Island before founding the Children's Aid Society.

In each of these cases of conversion to humanitarian reform there was a dramatic disclosure of deprivation and suffering which did not tally with preconceived notions of perfectibility—Dorothea Dix's discovery of the conditions in the Charlestown reformatory, Robert Hartley's inspection of contaminated milk in New York slums, Samuel Gridley Howe's chance conversation with Dr. Fisher in Boston. Something very much like a conversion experience seems to have forged the decisions of the humanitarians to take up their causes, a kind of revelation which furnished them with a ready-made role outside politics and opened a new career with which they could become completely identified. With the sudden transference of a vague perfectionist faith in self-improvement to urgent social problems there emerged a new type of professional reformer whose whole life became identified with the reform process.

Such, for example, was the conversion of Dorothea Dix from a lonely and afflicted schoolteacher who composed meditational studies of the life of Jesus into "D. L. Dix," the militant advocate of the helpless and forgotten. In a very real sense Miss Dix's crusade for better treatment of the insane and the criminal was one long self-imposed subjection to suffering. Her reports, which recorded cases of unbelievable mistreatment, completed a kind of purgative rite in which she assumed the burden of innocent suffering and passed it on as guilt to the American people. The source of her extraordinary energy lay in just this repeated submission of herselt to human misery until she felt qualified to speak out against it. Both an exhausting schedule and the almost daily renewal of scenes of suffering seemed to give her new energies for playing her romantic reform role in an effective and intensely personal way. Intense but not flexible: there was little room for exchange and growth in the mood of atonement with which she approached her work. Nor was her peculiarly personal identification with the victims of American indifference easily matched in reform circles. Where other reformers like the abolitionists often made abstract pleas for "bleeding humanity" and "suffering millions," hers was the real thing—a perfectionist fervor which strengthened her will at the cost of psychological isolation. Throughout her career she preferred to work alone, deploring the tendency to multiply reform agencies and ignoring those that existed either because she disagreed with their principles, as in the case of Louis Dwight's Boston Prison Discipline Society, or because she chose the more direct method of personal appeal. In all her work, even the unhappy and frustrating last years as superintendent of nurses in the Union Army, she saw herself as a solitary spokesman for the deprived and personal healer of the suffering.

Another reform role supplied by perfectionism was Bronson Alcott's educator-prophet, the "true reformer" who "studied man as he is from the hand of the Creator, and not as he is made by the errors of the world." Convinced that the self sprang from divine origins in nature, Alcott naturally concluded that children were more susceptible to good than people imagined and set out to develop a method for uncovering that goodness. With the power to shape personality the teacher, Alcott was sure, held the key to illimitable progress and the eventual regeneration of the world. The teacher might literally make society over by teaching men as children to discover their own divine natures. Thus true education for Alcott consisted of the process of self-discovery guided by the educator-prophet. He sharply criticized his contemporaries for their fatal mistake of imposing partial and therefore false standards on their charges. Shades of the prison house obscured the child's search for perfection, and character was lost forever. "Instead of following it in the path pointed out by its Maker, instead of learning by observation, and guiding it in that path; we unthinkingly attempt to shape its course to our particular wishes. . . ."[5]

To help children avoid the traps set by their elders Alcott based his whole system on the cultivation of self-awareness through self-examination. His pupils kept journals in which they scrutinized their behavior

[5] For a careful analysis of Alcott's educational theories see Dorothy McCuskey, *Bronson Alcott, Teacher* (New York, 1940), particularly pp. 25–40 from which these quotations are taken.

and analyzed their motives. Ethical problems were the subject of frequent and earnest debate at the Temple School as the children were urged to discover the hidden springs of perfectibility in themselves. No mechanical methods of rote learning could bring on the moment of revelation; each child was unique and would find himself in his own way. The real meaning of education as reform, Alcott realized, came with an increased social sense that resulted from individual self-discovery. As the creator of social personality Alcott's teacher was bound by no external rules of pedagogy: as the primary social reformer he had to cast off "the shackles of form, of mode, and ceremony" in order to play the required roles in the educational process.

Alcott's modernity lay principally in his concept of the interchangeability of roles—both teacher and pupils acquired self-knowledge in an exciting give-and-take. Thus defined, education became a way of life, a continuing process through which individuals learned to obey the laws of their own natures and in so doing to discover the laws of the good society. This identification of individual development with true social unity was crucial for Alcott, as for the other perfectionist communitarians, because it provided the bridge over which they passed from self to society. The keystone in Alcott's construction was supplied by the individual conscience which connected with the "common conscience" of mankind. This fundamental identity, he was convinced, could be demonstrated by the learning process itself which he defined as "sympathy and imitation, the moral action of the teacher upon the children, of the children upon him, and each other." He saw in the school, therefore, a model of the good community where self-discovery led to a social exchange culminating in the recognition of universal dependency and brotherhood. The ideal society—the society he hoped to create—was one in which individuals could be totally free to follow their own natures because such pursuit would inevitably end in social harmony. For Alcott the community was the product rather than the creator of the good life.

Fruitlands, Alcott's attempt to apply the lessons of the Temple School on a larger scale, was designed to prove that perfectionist educational reform affected the "economies of life." In this realization lay the real import of Alcott's reform ideas; for education, seen as a way of life, meant the communitarian experiment as an educative model. Pushed to its limits, the perfectionist assault on institutions logically ended in the attempt to make new and better societies as examples for Americans to follow. Communitarianism, as Alcott envisioned it, was the social extension of his perfectionist belief in education as an alternative to politics.

In the case of other humanitarian reformers like Samuel Gridley Howe perfectionism determined even more precisely both the role and intellectual content of their proposals. Howe's ideal of the good society seems to have derived from his experiences in Greece where, during his last year, he promoted a communitarian plan for resettling exiles on the Gulf of Corinth. With government support he established his colony, "Washingtonia," on two thousand acres of arable land, selected the colonists himself, bought cattle and tools, managed its business affairs, and supervised a Lancastrian school. By his own admission these were the happiest days of his life: "I laboured here day & night in season & out; & was governor, legislator, clerk, constable, & everything but patriarch."[6] When the government withdrew its support and brigands overran the colony, Howe was forced to abandon the project and return home. Still, the idea of an entire community under the care of a "patriarch" shouldering its collective burden and absorbing all its dependents in a cooperative life continued to dominate the "Doctor's" reform thinking and to determine his methods.

The ethical imperatives in Howe's philosophy of reform remained constant. "Humanity demands that every creature in human shape should command our respect; we should recognise as a brother every being upon whom God has stamped the human impress." Progress he likened to the American road. Christian individualism required that each man walk separately and at his own pace, but "the rear should not be left too far behind . . . none should be allowed to perish in their helplessness . . . the strong should help the weak, so that the whole should advance as a band of brethren." It was the duty of society itself to care for its disabled or mentally deficient members rather than to shut them up in asylums which were "offsprings of a low order of feeling." "The more I reflect upon the subject the more I see objections in principle and practice to asylums," he once wrote to a fellow-reformer. "What right have we to pack off the poor, the old, the blind into asylums? They are of us, our brothers, our sisters—they belong in families. . . ."[7]

In Howe's ideal society, then, the handicapped, criminals and defectives would not be walled off but accepted as part of the community and perfected by constant contact with it. Two years of experimenting with education for the feeble-minded convinced him that even "idiots" could be redeemed from what he called spiritual death. "How far they can be elevated, and to what extent they may be educated, can only be shown by the experience of the future," he admitted in his report to the Massachusetts legislature but predicted confidently that "each succeed-

[6] Letter from Howe to Horace Mann, 1857, quoted in Harold Schwartz, *Samuel Gridley Howe* (Cambridge, 1956), p. 37.

[7] Letter from Howe to William Chapin, 1857, quoted in Laura E. Richards, *Letters and Journals of Samuel Gridley Howe* (2 vols.; New York, 1909), II, 48.

ing year will show even more progress than any preceding one."[8] He always acted on his conviction that "we shall avail ourselves of special institutions less and the common schools more" and never stopped hoping that eventually all blind children after proper training might be returned to families and public schools for their real education. He also opposed the establishment of reformatories with the argument that they only collected the refractory and vicious and made them worse. Nature mingled the defective in common families, he insisted, and any departure from her standards stunted moral growth. He took as his model for reform the Belgian town of Geel where mentally ill patients were boarded at public expense with private families and allowed maximum freedom. As soon as the building funds were available he introduced the cottage system at Perkins, a plan he also wanted to apply to reformatories. No artificial and unnatural institution could replace the family which Howe considered the primary agency in the perfection of the individual.

Howe shared his bias against institutions and a preference for the family unit with other humanitarian reformers like Robert Hartley and Charles Loring Brace. Hartley's "friendly visitors" were dispatched to New York's poor with instructions to bring the gospel of self-help home to every member of the family. Agents of the AICP dispensed advice and improving literature along with the coal and groceries. Only gradually did the organization incorporate "incidental labors"—legislative programs for housing reform, health regulations and child labor—into its system of reform. Hartley's real hope for the new urban poor lay in their removal to the country where a bootstrap operation might lift them to sufficiency and selfhood. "Escape then from the city," he told them, "—for escape is your only recourse against the terrible ills of beggary; and the further you go, the better."[9] In Hartley's formula the perfectionist doctrine of the salvation of the individual combined with the conservative appeal of the safety-valve.

A pronounced hostility to cities also marked the program of Charles Loring Brace's Children's Aid Society, the central feature of which was the plan for relocating children of the "squalid poor" on upstate New York farms for "moral disinfection." The Society's placement service resettled thousands of slum children in the years before the Civil War in the belief that a proper family environment and a rural setting would release the naturally good tendencies in young people so that under the

[8] Second Report of the Commissioners on Idiocy to the Massachusetts Legislature (1849), quoted in Richards, *Howe,* II, 214.

[9] New York A.I.C.P., *The Mistake* (New York, 1850), p. 4, quoted in Robert H. Bremner, *From the Depths: the Discovery of Poverty in the United States* (New York, 1956), p. 38.

supervision of independent and hard-working farmers they would save themselves.[10]

There was thus a high nostalgic content in the plans of humanitarians who emphasized pastoral virtues and the perfectionist values inherent in country living. Their celebration of the restorative powers of nature followed logically from their assumption that the perfected individual— the truly free American—could be created only by the reunification of mental and physical labor. The rural life, it was assumed, could revive and sustain the unified sensibility threatened by the city. A second assumption concerned the importance of the family as the primary unit in the reconstruction of society. As the great debate among social re- formers proceeded it centered on the question of the limits to which the natural family could be extended. Could an entire society, as the more radical communitarians argued, be reorganized as one huge family? Or were there natural boundaries necessary for preserving order and moral- ity? On the whole, the more conservative humanitarians agreed with Howe in rejecting those communal plans which, like Fourier's, stemmed from too high an estimate of "the capacity of mankind for family affections."[11]

That intensive education held the key to illimitable progress, however, few humanitarian reformers denied. They were strengthened in their certainty by the absolutes inherited from moral reform. Thus Howe, for example, considered his work a "new field" of "practical religion." The mental defective, he was convinced, was the product of sin—both the sin of the parents and the sin of society in allowing the offspring to languish in mental and moral darkness. Yet the social evils incident to sin were not inevitable; they were not "inherent in the very constitution of man" but the "chastisements sent by a loving Father to bring his children to obedience to his beneficent laws."[12] These laws—infinite perfectibility and social responsibility—reinforced each other in the truly progressive society. The present condition of the dependent classes in America was proof of "the immense space through which society has yet to advance before it even approaches the perfection of civilization which is attainable."[13] Education, both the thorough training of the

[10] Brace's views are set forth in his *The Dangerous Classes of New York and Twenty Years Among Them* (New York, 1872). For a brief treatment of his relation to the moral reform movement see Bremner, *From the Depths,* chap. iii.

[11] Letter from Howe to Charles Sumner, Apr. 8, 1847, quoted in Richards, *Howe,* II, 255–56.

[12] First Report of the Commissioners on Idiocy (1848), quoted in Richards, *Howe,* II, 210–11.

[13] *Ibid.,* pp. 210–11.

deprived and the larger education of American society to its obligations, would meet the moral challenge.

The perfectionist uses of education as an alternative to political reform were most thoroughly explored by Horace Mann. Mann's initial investment in public school education was dictated by his fear that American democracy, lacking institutional checks and restraints, was fast degenerating into "the spectacle of gladiatorial contests" conducted at the expense of the people. Could laws save American society? Mann thought not.

> With us, the very idea of legislation is reversed. Once, the law prescribed the actions and shaped the wills of the multitude; here the wills of the multitude prescribe and shape the law . . . now when the law is weak, the passions of the multitude have gathered irresistible strength, it is fallacious and insane to look for security in the moral force of law. Government and law . . . will here be moulded into the similitude of the public mind. . . .[14]

In offering public school education as the only effective countervailing force in a democracy Mann seemingly was giving vent to a conservative dread of unregulated change in a society where, as he admitted, the momentum of hereditary opinion was spent. Where there was no "surgical code of laws" reason, conscience and benevolence would have to be provided by education. "The whole mass of mind must be instructed in regard to its comprehensive and enduring interests." In a republican government, however, compulsion was theoretically undesirable and practically unavailable. People could not be driven up a "dark avenue" even though it were the right one. Mann, like his evangelical predecessors, found his solution in an educational crusade.

> Let the intelligent visit the ignorant, day by day, as the oculist visits the blind mind, and detaches the scales from his eyes, until the living sense leaps to light. . . . Let the love of beautiful reason, the admonitions of conscience, the sense of religious responsibility, be plied, in mingled tenderness and earnestness, until the obdurate and dark mass of avarice and ignorance and prejudice shall be dissipated by their blended light and heat.[15]

Here in Mann's rhetorical recasting was what appeared to be the old evangelical prescription for tempering democratic excess. The chief problem admittedly was avoiding the "disturbing forces of party and sect and faction and clan." To make sure that education remained nonpartisan the common schools should teach on the *"exhibitory"* method, "by an actual exhibition of the principle we would inculcate."

[14] Horace Mann, "The Necessity of Education in a Republican Government," *Lectures on Education* (Boston, 1845), pp. 152, 158.

[15] "An Historical View of Education; Showing Its Dignity and Its Degradation," *Lectures on Education*, pp. 260, 262.

Insofar as the exhibitory method operated to regulate or direct public opinion, it was conservative. But implicit in Mann's theory was a commitment to perfectionism which gradually altered his aims until in the twelfth and final report education emerges as a near-utopian device for making American politics simple, clean and, eventually, superfluous. In the Twelfth Report Mann noted that although a public school system might someday guarantee "sufficiency, comfort, competence" to every American, as yet "imperfect practice" had not matched "perfect theory." Then in an extended analysis of social trends which foreshadowed Henry George's classification he singled out "poverty" and "profusion" as the two most disturbing facts in American development. "With every generation, fortunes increase on the one hand, and some new privation is added to poverty on the other. We are verging toward those extremes of opulence and penury, each of which unhumanizes the mind."[16] A new feudalism threatened; and unless a drastic remedy was discovered, the "hideous evils" of unequal distribution of wealth would cause class war.

Mann's alternative to class conflict proved to be nothing less than universal education based on the exhibitory model of the common school. Diffusion of education, he pointed out, meant wiping out class lines and with them the possibility of conflict. As the great equalizer of condition it would supply the balance-wheel in the society of the future. Lest his readers confuse his suggestions with the fantasies of communitarians Mann hastened to point out that education would perfect society through the individual by creating new private resources. Given full play in a democracy, education gave each man the "independence and the means by which he can resist the selfishness of other men."

Once Mann had established education as an alternative to political action, it remained to uncover its utopian possibilities. By enlarging the "cultivated class" it would widen the area of social feelings—"if this education should be universal and complete, it would do more than all things else to obliterate factitious distinctions in society." Political reformers and revolutionaries based their schemes on the false assumption that the amount of wealth in America was fixed by fraud and force, and that the few were rich because the many were poor. By demanding a redistribution of wealth by legislative fiat they overlooked the power of education to obviate political action through the creation of new and immense sources of wealth.

[16] This quotation and the ones from Mann that follow are taken from the central section of the *Twelfth Report* entitled "Intellectual Education as a Means of Removing Poverty, and Securing Abundance," Mary Peabody Mann, *Life of Horace Mann* (4 vols.; Boston, 1891), IV, 245–68. See also the perceptive comments on Mann in Rush Welter, *Popular Education and Democratic Thought in America* (New York, 1962), pp. 97–102, from which I have drawn.

Thus in Mann's theory as in the programs of the other humanitarians the perfection of the individual through education guaranteed illimitable progress. The constantly expanding powers of the free individual ensured the steady improvement of society until the educative process finally achieved a harmonious, self-regulating community. "And will not the community that gains its wealth in this way . . . be a model and a pattern for nations, a type of excellence to be admired and followed by the world?" The fate of free society, Mann concluded, depended upon the conversion of individuals from puppets and automatons to thinking men who were aware of the strength of the irreducible self and determined to foster it in others.

As romantic perfectionism spread across Jacksonian society it acquired an unofficial and only partly acceptable philosophy in the "systematic subjectivism" of transcendental theory.[17] Transcendentalism, as its official historian noted, claimed for all men what a more restrictive Christian perfectionism extended only to the redeemed. Seen in this light, self-culture—Emerson's "perfect unfolding of our individual nature"—appeared as a secular amplification of the doctrine of personal holiness. In the transcendentalist definition, true reform proceeded from the individual and worked outward through the family, the neighborhood and ultimately into the social and political life of the community. The transcendentalist, Frothingham noted in retrospect, "was less a reformer of human circumstances than a regenerator of the human spirit. . . . With movements that did not start from this primary assumption of individual dignity, and come back to that as their goal, he had nothing to do."[18] Emerson's followers, like the moral reformers and the humanitarians, looked to individuals rather than to institutions, to "high heroic example" rather than to political programs. The Brook-Farmer John Sullivan Dwight summed up their position when he protested that "men are anterior to systems. Great doctrines are not the origins, but the product of great lives."[19]

Accordingly the transcendentalists considered institutions—parties, churches, organizations—so many arbitrarily constructed barriers on the road to self-culture. They were lonely men, Emerson admitted, who repelled influences. "They are not good citizens; not good members of society. . . ."[20] A longing for solitude led them out of society, Emerson

17 The phrase is Santayana's in "The Genteel Tradition in American Philosophy." For an analysis of the anti-institutional aspects of transcendentalism and reform see Stanley Elkins, *Slavery* (Chicago, 1959), chap. iii.

18 Octavius Brooks Frothingham, *Transcendentalism in New England* (Harper Torchbooks ed.: New York, 1959), p. 155.

19 John Sullivan Dwight as quoted in Frothingham, *Transcendentalism*, p. 147.

20 "The Transcendentalist," *Works*, I, 347–48.

to the woods where he found no Jacksonian placards on the trees, Thoreau to his reclusive leadership of a majority of one. Accepting for the most part Emerson's dictum that one man was a counterpoise to a city, the transcendentalists turned inward to examine the divine self and find there the material with which to rebuild society. They wanted to avoid at all costs the mistake of their Jacksonian contemporaries who in order to be useful accommodated themselves to institutions without realizing the resultant loss of power and integrity.

The most immediate effect of perfectionism on the transcendentalists, as on the humanitarians, was the development of a set of concepts which, in stressing reform by example, opened up new roles for the alienated intellectual. In the first place, self-culture accounted for their ambivalence toward reform politics. It was not simply Emerson's reluctance to raise the siege on his hencoop that kept him apart, but a genuine confusion as to the proper role for the reformer. If government was simply a "job" and American society the senseless competition of the marketplace, how could the transcendentalist accept either as working premises? The transcendentalist difficulty in coming to terms with democratic politics could be read in Emerson's confused remark that of the two parties contending for the presidency in 1840 one had the better principles, the other the better men. Driven by their profound distaste for manipulation and chicanery, many of Emerson's followers took on the role of a prophet standing aloof from elections, campaigns and party caucuses and dispensing wisdom (often in oblique Emersonian terminology) out of the vast private resources of the self. In this sense transcendentalism, like Christian perfectionism, represented a distinct break with the prevailing Jacksonian views of democratic leadership and the politics of compromise and adjustment.

One of the more appealing versions of the transcendental role was the hero or genius to whom everything was permitted, as Emerson said, because "genius is the character of illimitable freedom." The heroes of the world, Margaret Fuller announced, were the true theocratic kings: "The hearts of men make music at their approach; the mind of the age is like the historian of their passing; and only men of destiny like themselves shall be permitted to write their eulogies, or fill their vacancies."[21] Margaret Fuller herself spent her transcendentalist years stalking the American hero, which she somehow confused with Emerson, before she joined the Roman Revolution in 1849 and discovered the authentic article in the mystic nationalist Mazzini.

Carlyle complained to Emerson of the "perilous altitudes" to which the transcendentalists' search for the hero led them. Despite his own pen-

[21] Such was her description of Lamennais and Beranger as quoted in Mason Wade, *Margaret Fuller* (New York, 1940), 195.

chant for hero-worship he came away from reading the *Dial* "with a kind of shudder." In their pursuit of the self-contained hero they seemed to separate themselves from "this same cotton-spinning, dollar-hunting, canting and shrieking, very wretched generation of ours."[22] The transcendentalists, however, were not trying to escape the Jacksonian world of fact, only to find a foothold for their perfectionist individualism in it. They sought a way of implementing their ideas of self-culture without corrupting them with the false values of materialism. They saw a day coming when parties and politicians would be obsolescent. By the 1850s Walt Whitman thought that day had already arrived and that America had outgrown parties.

What right has any one political party, no matter which, to wield the American government? No right at all . . . and every American young man must have sense enough to comprehend this. I have said the old parties are defunct; but there remains of them empty flesh, putrid mouths, mumbling and speaking the tones of these conventions, the politicians standing back in shadow, telling lies, trying to delude and frighten the people. . . .[23]

Whitman's romantic alternative was a "love of comrades" cementing an American brotherhood and upholding a redeemer president.

A somewhat similar faith in the mystical fraternity informed Theodore Parker's plan for spiritual revolution. Like the other perfectionists, Parker began by reducing society to its basic components—individuals, the "monads" or "primitive atoms" of the social order—and judged it by its tendency to promote or inhibit individualism. "Destroy the individuality of those atoms, . . . all is gone. To mar the atoms is to mar the mass. To preserve itself, therefore, society is to preserve the individuality of the individual."[24] In Parker's theology perfectionist Christianity and transcendental method merged to form a loving brotherhood united by the capacity to apprehend primary truths directly. A shared sense of the divinity of individual man held society together; without it no true community was possible. Looking around him at ante-bellum America, Parker found only the wrong kind of individualism, the kind that said, "I am as good as you, so get out of my way." The right kind, the individualism whose motto was "You are as good as I, and let us help one another,"[25] was to be the work of Parker's spiritual revolution. He explained the

[22] Quoted in Wade, *Margaret Fuller,* pp. 88–89.

[23] Walt Whitman, "The Eighteenth Presidency," an essay unpublished in Whitman's lifetime, in *Walt Whitman's Workshop,* ed. Clifton Joseph Furness (Cambridge, 1928), pp. 104–5.

[24] Quoted in Daniel Aaron, *Men of Good Hope* (Oxford paperback ed.: New York, 1961), p. 35.

[25] Theodore Parker, "The Political Destination of America and the Signs of the Times" (1848) excerpted in *The Transcendentalists,* ed. Perry Miller (Anchor ed.: Garden City, N. Y., 1957), p. 357.

method of revolution as one of *"intellectual, moral* and *religious* educa-tion—everywhere and for all men." Until universal education had done its work Parker had little hope for political stability in the United States. He called instead for a new "party" to be formed in society at large, a party built on the idea that "God still inspires men as much as ever; that he is immanent in spirit as in space." Such a party required no church, tradition or scripture. "It believes God is near the soul as mat-ter to the sense. . . . It calls God father and mother, not king; Jesus, brother, not redeemer, heaven home, religion nature."[26]

Parker believed that this "philosophical party in politics," as he called it, was already at work in the 1850s on a code of universal laws from which to deduce specific legislation "so that each statute in the code shall represent a fact in the universe, a point of thought in God; so . . . that legislation shall be divine in the same sense that a true system of astron-omy be divine." Parker's holy band represented the full fruition of the perfectionist idea of a "Christian party" in America, a party of no strict political or sectarian definition, but a true reform movement, apostolic in its beginnings but growing with the truths it preached until it encom-passed all Americans in a huge brotherhood of divine average men. Party members, unlike time-serving Whigs and Democrats, followed ideas and intuitions rather than prejudice and precedent, and these ideas led them to question authority, oppose legal injustice and tear down rotten institu-tions. The philosophical party was not to be bound by accepted notions of political conduct or traditional attitudes toward law. When unjust laws interpose barriers to progress, reformers must demolish them.

So Parker himself reasoned when he organized the Vigilance Committee in Boston to defeat the Fugitive Slave Law. His reasoning epitomized perfectionist logic: every man may safely trust his conscience, properly informed, because it is the repository for divine truth. When men learn to trust their consciences and act on them, they naturally encourage others to do the same with the certainty that they will reach the same con-clusions. Individual conscience thus creates a social conscience and a collective will to right action. Concerted right action means moral revolu-tion. The fact that moral revolution, in its turn, might mean political revolt was a risk Parker and his perfectionist followers were willing to take.

Both transcendentalism and perfectionist moral reform, then, were marked by an individualist fervor that was disruptive of American insti-tutions. Both made heavy moral demands on church and state; and when neither proved equal to the task of supporting their intensely per-sonal demands, the transcendentalists and the moral reformers became

[26] Quoted in R. W. B. Lewis, *The American Adam* (Chicago, 1955), p. 182.

increasingly alienated. The perfectionist temperament bred a come-outer spirit. An insistence on individual moral accountability and direct appeal to the irreducible self, the faith in self-reliance and distrust of compromise, and a substitution of universal education for partial reform measures, all meant that normal political and institutional reform channels were closed to the perfectionists. Alternate routes to the millennium had to be found. One of these was discovered by a new leadership which made reform a branch of prophecy. Another was opened by the idea of a universal reawakening of the great god self. But there was a third possibility, also deeply involved with the educational process, an attempt to build the experimental community as a reform model. With an increasing number of reformers after 1840 perfectionist anti-institutionalism led to heavy investments in the communitarian movement.

The attraction that drew the perfectionists to communitarianism came from their conviction that the good society should be simple. Since American society was both complicated and corrupt, it was necessary to come out from it; but at the same time the challenge of the simple life had to be met. Once the true principles of social life had been discovered they had to be applied, some way found to harness individual perfectibility to a social engine. This urge to form the good community, as John Humphrey Noyes experienced it himself and perceived it in other reformers, provided the connection between perfectionism and communitarianism, or, as Noyes put it, between "Revivalism" and "Socialism." Perfectionist energies directed initially against institutions were diverted to the creation of small self-contained communities as educational models. In New England two come-outer abolitionists, Adin Ballou and George Benson, founded cooperative societies at Hopedale and Northampton, while a third Garrisonian lieutenant, John Collins, settled his followers on a farm in Skaneateles, New York. Brook Farm, Fruitlands and the North American Phalanx at Redbank acquired notoriety in their own day; but equally significant, both in terms of origins and personnel, were the experiments at Raritan Bay under the guidance of Marcus Spring, the Marlboro Association in Ohio, the Prairie Home Community of former Hicksite Quakers, and the Swedenborgian Brocton Community. In these and other experimental communities could be seen the various guises of perfectionism.

Communitarianism promised drastic social reform without violence. Artificiality and corruption could not be wiped out by partial improvements and piecemeal measures but demanded a total change which, as Robert Owen once explained, "could make an immediate, and almost instantaneous, revolution in the minds and manners of society in which it shall be introduced." Communitarians agreed in rejecting class struggle which set interest against interest instead of uniting them through association. "Whoever will examine the question of social ameliorations," Albert Brisbane argued in support of Fourier, "must be convinced that *the gradual perfecting of Civilization* is useless as a remedy for present social evils, and that the only effectual means of doing away with indigence, idleness and the dislike for labor is to do away with civilization itself, and organize Association . . . in its place."[27] Like the redemptive moment in conversion or the experience of self-discovery in transcendentalist thought, the communitarian ideal pointed to a sharp break with existing society and a commitment to root-and-branch reform. On the other hand, the community was seen as a controlled experiment in which profound but peaceful change might be effected without disturbing the larger social order. Massive change, according to communitarian theory, could also be gradual and harmonious if determined by the model.

Perfectionist religious and moral reform shaded into communitarianism, in the case of a number of social reformers, with the recognition that the conversion of the individual was a necessary preparation for and logically required communal experimentation. Such was John Humphrey Noyes' observation that in the years after 1815 "the line of socialistic excitement lies parallel with the line of religious Revivals. . . . The Revivalists had for their one great idea the regeneration of the soul. The great idea of the Socialists was the regeneration of society, which is the soul's environment. These ideas belong together and are the complements of each other."[28] So it seemed to Noyes' colleagues in the communitarian movement. The course from extreme individualism to communitarianism can be traced in George Ripley's decision to found Brook Farm. Trying to win Emerson to his new cause, he explained that his own personal tastes and habits would have led him away from plans and projects. "I have a passion for being independent of the world, and of every man in it. This I could do easily on the estate which is now offered. . . . I should have a city of God, on a small scale of my own. . . . But I feel bound to sacrifice this private feeling, in the hope of the great social good." That good Ripley had no difficulty in defining in perfectionist terms:

to insure a more natural union between intellectual and manual labor than now exists; to combine the thinker and the worker, as far as possible, in the same individual; to guarantee the highest mental freedom, by providing all with labor, adapted to their tastes and talents, and securing to them the fruits of their industry; to do away with the necessity of menial

[27] Albert Brisbane, *Social Destiny of Man,* p. 286, quoted in Arthur Eugene Bestor, *Backwoods Utopias: The Sectarian and Owenite Phases of Communitarian Socialism in America: 1663–1829* (Philadelphia, 1950), p. 9.

[28] John Humphrey Noyes, *History of American Socialisms* (Philadelphia, 1870), p. 26.

services, by opening the benefits of education and the profits of labor to all; and thus to prepare a society of liberal, intelligent, and cultivated persons, whose relations with each other would permit a more simple and wholesome life, than can be led amidst the pressure of our competitive institutions.[29]

However varied their actual experiences with social planning, all the communitarians echoed Ripley's call for translating perfectionism into concerted action and adapting the ethics of individualism to larger social units. Just as the moral reformers appealed to right conduct and conscience in individuals the communitarians sought to erect models of a collective conscience to educate Americans. Seen in this light, the communitarian faith in the model was simply an extension of the belief in individual perfectibility. Even the sense of urgency characterizing moral reform was carried over into the communities where a millennial expectation flourished. The time to launch their projects, the social planners believed, was the immediate present when habits and attitudes were still fluid, before entrenched institutions had hardened the American heart and closed the American mind. To wait for a full quota of useful members or an adequate supply of funds might be to miss the single chance to make the country perfect. The whole future of America seemed to them to hinge on the fate of their enterprises.

Some of the projects were joint-stock corporations betraying a middle-class origin; others were strictly communistic. Some, like the Shaker communities, were pietistic and rigid; others, like Oneida and Hopedale, open and frankly experimental. Communitarians took a lively interest in each others' projects and often joined one or another of them for a season before moving on to try utopia on their own. The division between religious and secular attempts was by no means absolute: both types of communities advertised an essentially religious brand of perfectionism. Nor was economic organization always an accurate means of distinguishing the various experiments, most of which were subjected to periodic constitutional overhauling and frequent readjustment, now in the direction of social controls and now toward relaxation of those controls in favor of individual initiative.

The most striking characteristic of the communitarian movement was not its apparent diversity but the fundamental similarity of educational purpose. The common denominator or "main idea" Noyes correctly identified as *"the enlargement of home—the extension of family union beyond the little man-and-wife circle to large corporations."*[30] Communities as

---

[29] Letter from Ripley to Ralph Waldo Emerson, Nov. 9, 1840, in *Autobiography of Brook Farm,* ed. Henry W. Sams (Englewood Cliffs, N. J., 1958), pp. 5–8.

[30] Noyes, *American Socialisms,* p. 23.

different as Fruitlands and Hopedale, Brook Farm and Northampton, Owenite villages and Fourier phalanstaeries were all, in one way or another, attempting to expand and apply self-culture to groups. Thus the problem for radical communitarians was to solve the conflict between the family and society. In commenting on the failure of the Brook Farmers to achieve a real community, Charles Lane, Alcott's associate at Fruitlands, identified what he considered the basic social question of the day— "whether the existence of the marital family is compatible with that of the universal family, which the term 'Community' signifies."[31] A few of the communitarians, recognizing this conflict, attempted to solve it by changing or destroying the institution of marriage. For the most part, the perfectionist communitarians shied away from any such radical alteration of the family structure and instead sought a law of association by which the apparently antagonistic claims of private and universal love could be harmonized. Once this law was known and explained, they believed, then the perfect society was possible—a self-adjusting mechanism constructed in accordance with their recently discovered law of human nature.

Inevitably communitarianism developed a "science of society," either the elaborate social mathematics of Fourier or the constitutional mechanics of native American perfectionists. The appeal of the blueprint grew overwhelming: in one way or another almost all the communitarians succumbed to the myth of the mathematically precise arrangement, searching for the perfect number or the exact size, plotting the precise disposition of working forces and living space, and combining these estimates in a formula which would ensure perfect concord. The appeal of Fourierism stemmed from its promise to reconcile productive industry with "passional attractions." "Could this be done," John Sullivan Dwight announced, "the word 'necessity' would acquire an altogether new and pleasanter meaning; the outward necessity and the inward prompting for every human being would be one and identical, and his life a living harmony."[32] Association fostered true individuality which, in turn, guaranteed collective accord. In an intricate calculation involving ascending and descending wings and a central point of social balance where attractions equalled destinies the converts to Fourierism contrived a utopian alternative to politics. The phalanx represented a self-perpetuating system for neutralizing conflict and ensuring perfection. The power factor—politics—had been dropped out; attraction alone provided the stimulants necessary to production and progress. Here

<hr />

[31] Charles Lane, "Brook Farm," *Dial,* IV (Jan. 1844), 351–57, reprinted in Sams, *Brook Farm,* pp. 87–92.

[32] John Sullivan Dwight, "Association in its Connection with Education," a lecture delivered before the New England Fourier Society, in Boston, Feb. 29, 1844. Excerpted in Sams, *Brook Farm,* pp. 104–5.

in the mathematical model was the culmination of the "peaceful revolution" which was to transform America.

The communitarian experiments in effect were anti-institutional institutions. In abandoning political and religious institutions the communitarians were driven to create perfect societies of their own which conformed to their perfectionist definition of the free individual. Their communities veered erratically between the poles of anarchism and collectivism as they hunted feverishly for a way of eliminating friction without employing coercion, sure that once they had found it, they could apply it in a federation of model societies throughout the country. In a limited sense, perhaps, their plans constituted an escape from urban complexity and the loneliness of alienation. But beneath the nostalgia there lay a vital reform impulse and a driving determination to make American society over through the power of education.

The immediate causes of the collapse of the communities ranged from loss of funds and mismanagement to declining interest and disillusionment with imperfect human material. Behind these apparent reasons, however, stood the real cause in the person of the perfectionist self, Margaret Fuller's "mountainous me," that proved too powerful a disruptive force for even the anti-institutional institutions it had created. It was the perfectionist ego which allowed the communitarian reformers to be almost wholly nonselective in recruiting their membership and to put their trust in the operation of an atomistic general will. Constitution-making and paper bonds, as it turned out, were not enough to unite divine egoists in a satisfactory system for the free expression of the personality. Perfectionist individualism did not make the consociate family. The result by the 1850s was a profound disillusionment with the principle of association which, significantly, coincided with the political crisis over slavery. Adin Ballou, his experiment at Hopedale in shambles, summarized the perfectionist mood of despair when he added that "few people are near enough right in heart, head and habits to live in close social intimacy."[33] Another way would have to be found to carry divine principles into social arrangements, one that took proper account of the individual.

The collapse of the communitarian movement in the 1850s left a vacuum in social reform which was filled by the slavery crisis. At first their failure to consolidate alternative social and educational institutions threw the reformers back on their old perfectionist individualism for support. It was hardly fortuitous that Garrison, Mann, Thoreau, Howe, Parker, Channing, Ripley and Emerson himself responded to John Brown's

[33] Letter from Ballou to Theodore Weld, Dec. 23, 1856, quoted in Benjamin P. Thomas, *Theodore Weld: Crusader for Freedom* (New Brunswick, N. J., 1950), p. 229.

raid with a defense of the liberated conscience. But slavery, as a denial of freedom and individual responsibility, had to be destroyed by institutional forces which could be made to sustain these values. The antislavery cause during the secession crisis and throughout the Civil War offered reformers an escape from alienation by providing a new identity with the very political institutions which they had so vigorously assailed.

The effects of the Civil War as an intellectual counterrevolution were felt both in a revival of institutions and a renewal of an organic theory of society. The war brought with it a widespread reaction against the seeming sentimentality and illusions of perfectionism. It saw the establishment of new organizations like the Sanitary and the Christian Commissions run on principles of efficiency and professionalism totally alien to perfectionist methods. Accompanying the wartime revival of institutions was a theological reorientation directed by Horace Bushnell and other conservative churchmen whose longstanding opposition to perfectionism seemed justified by the war. The extreme individualism of the ante-bellum reformers was swallowed up in a Northern war effort that made private conscience less important than saving the Union. Some of the abolitionists actually substituted national unity for freedom for the slave as the primary war aim. Those reformers who contributed to the war effort through the Sanitary Commission or the Christian Commission found a new sense of order and efficiency indispensable. Older perfectionists, like Dorothea Dix, unable to adjust to new demands, found their usefulness drastically confined. Young Emersonians returned from combat convinced that professionalism, discipline and subordination, dubious virtues by perfectionist standards, were essential in a healthy society. A new emphasis on leadership and performance was replacing the benevolent amateurism of the perfectionists.

Popular education and ethical agitation continued to hold the post-war stage, but the setting for them had changed. The three principal theorists of social reform in post-war industrial America—Henry George, Henry Demarest Lloyd and Edward Bellamy—denounced class conflict, minimized the importance of purely political reform, and, like their perfectionist precursors, called for moral revolution. The moral revolution which they demanded, however, was not the work of individuals in whom social responsibility developed as a by-product of self-discovery but the ethical revival of an entire society made possible by the natural development of social forces. Their organic view of society required new theories of personality and new concepts of role-playing, definitions which appeared variously in George's law of integration, Lloyd's religion of love, and Bellamy's economy of happiness. And whereas Nemesis in the perfectionist imagination had assumed the shape of personal guilt and estrangement from a pre-established divine order, for the post-war reformers it took on the social dimensions of a terrifying relapse into barbarism. Finally, the attitudes of the reformers toward individualism itself began to change as Darwinism with the aid of a false analogy twisted the prewar doctrine of self-reliance into a weapon against reform. It was to protest against a Darwinian psychology of individual isolation that Lloyd wrote his final chapter of *Wealth Against Commonwealth*, declaring that the regeneration of the individual was only a half-truth and that "the reorganization of the society which he makes and which makes him is the other half."

We can become individual only by submitting to be bound to others. We extend our freedom only by finding new laws to obey. . . . The isolated man is a mere rudiment of an individual. But he who has become citizen, neighbor, friend, brother, son, husband, father, fellow-member, in one is just so many times individualized.[34]

Lloyd's plea for a new individualism could also be read as an obituary for perfectionist romantic reform.

34 Henry Demarest Lloyd, *Wealth Against Commonwealth* (Spectrum paperback ed.: Englewood Cliffs, N. J., 1963), pp. 174, 178.

The Plantation Novel
and the Sentimental Tradition

WILLIAM R. TAYLOR

Ever since Henry Nash Smith in *Virgin Land* (1950) analyzed the American West as symbol and myth of an agrarian utopia, American historians have learned to exploit the possibilities of examining the social meaning of images found in popular literature. In ante-bellum America the plantation novel offers an instructive source of insight into the cultural conflict that developed over the meaning of slavery.

Uncle Tom's Cabin was the best seller of the century and a contribution to the Northern literature of abolitionism. Harriet Beecher Stowe, linked to New England theology by birth and marriage, created in Uncle Tom a contemporary symbol of "One whose suffering changed an instrument of torture, degradation and shame, into a symbol of glory, honor, and immortal life." While Negroes, as an injured race, deserved to have *"more* than the rights of common men," she believed that they could only "break their chains" by establishing a Christian republic in Liberia, where "the latest called of nations" would "reign with Christ when his kingdom shall come on earth." The novel captured the legacy of New England millennialistic religion as well as the moral indignation against the Fugitive Slave Law of 1850. But *Uncle Tom's Cabin* was also a plantation novel, and William R. Taylor shows how it can be related to popular literary and social tradition.

> How this book must cut a true-hearted Southerner to the
> quick!—cut us all, for we verily are all guilty together.
> WILLIAM HENRY CHANNING on *Uncle Tom's Cabin*[1]

William R. Taylor, *Cavalier and Yankee: The Old South and American National Character,* 1961, chapter IX, pp. 299–313. Reprinted by permission of George Braziller, Inc. Copyright 1961 by George Braziller.
[1] Octavius Brooks Frothingham, *Memoir of William Henry Channing* (Boston, 1886) p. 259.

THE HISTORICAL ISOLATIONISM OF THE ANTEBELLUM SOUTHERNER, THE fact that he felt increasingly cut off and isolated from the historical forces which were reshaping the society of the Western world left him more and more defensive and touchy about his place within the South. The social order which he had imposed on his household and the surrounding county—an order which required the subordination of woman, Negro slave and nonslaveholding white—was submitted to careful and uneasy scrutiny by the novelists, who often stumbled upon social tensions and expressed reservations of a very worrying sort. It was impossible to live in nineteenth-century America without sharing some of its new concerns and obsessions—its sentimental preoccupation with the family, its evangelical benevolence, its endorsement of democratic change and social mobility. And yet it was impossible to share these new civic values without discovering grave inconsistencies in the planter's social code. The novels written by Southerners reflect better than any other source this attempt of the South to wrestle with the nineteenth century and with itself.

SLAVERY AND THE SENTIMENTAL REVOLUTION

No aspect of the plantation setting finally assumed greater significance than the relationship between master and slave. Southerners were quick to discover that the strongest weapon which they possessed for justifying their peculiar institution to themselves and to others was the argument of plantation paternalism. The image of sunshine and happiness around the old plantation home could, it was felt, win the sympathies of many, especially women, whom the abstract justifiers—Biblical, Constitutional and historical—were unable to touch. This image worked its magic across the nation for close to twenty years, helping to allay the feelings of those who had grown uneasy over slavery. Then, in 1852, a "female scribbler" from the North named Harriet Beecher Stowe demonstrated that paternalism was a sword that cut two ways. *Uncle Tom's Cabin,* it must have seemed to many, exploded like a bombshell in the sentimental fiction of the fifties and left Southerners stunned and enraged by the use to which their favorite literary conventions had been put—and by a Yankee outsider and, to cap it all, a woman.

Most of the literary techniques for representing the slave were developed by the novelists of the thirties. The first crude efforts to render Negro speech—the talk of "laffing" and "luving," "Massa" and "Missus"—were made at this time, and most of the stock characters of the Uncle Tom fiction—the kind but crotchety old mammies, the wise old "aunts" and "uncles," and what Cash has called the "banjo-picking, heel-flinging, hi-yi-ing happy jacks"[2] of minstrelsy—all make their first appearance in this earlier writing. For a time, however, the significance which later attached to these characters remained muted, and the slave was kept in the plantation background as a kind of conversation piece which, sooner or later, most of these writers felt an obligation to take up.

It is scarcely surprising that they did. Everything for a few years had contributed to highlighting the slavery issue. On January 1, 1831, William Lloyd Garrison fired the opening shot in his holy war against slavery in the first issue of the *Liberator*. His stridency and his irreverent attacks on the Constitution startled not only Southerners but moderate and law-abiding men everywhere. Then on August 22 came the chain of events which began when a Negro Baptist exhorter named Nat Turner led a bloody insurrection in Southampton County, Virginia. The rebellion ended forty-eight hours after it began, but not before sixty whites had been brutally butchered in their beds, in many cases by their own slaves. The repercussions of this event—the periodic panics which swept other parts of the South—continued to be felt for close to thirty years. No important uprising ever again occurred in the South, yet the awful nightmare of the Santo Domingo massacres of the seventeen nineties now seemed an American reality, and from this time on the slightest rumor or anecdote of slave intransigeance was often sufficient to kick off a wave of hysteria and repression.[3]

Virginia itself tried to come to terms with these sobering events before the year was out. In the House of Delegates in Richmond, the slavery question was debated over a period of weeks as it was never again to be debated anywhere in the South. With the events in Southampton fresh in mind, Virginians weighed the ills of domestic slavery with candor and precision.[4] The most penetrating and severe criticisms came this time not from Northerners and outsiders but from Virginians, and they were not the criticisms, furthermore, of sentimentalists who pitied the slave but rather of those who feared and despised him. The most articulate of these critics, Charles J. Faulkner from Berkeley County in the Shenandoah Valley, spoke of the "slothful and degraded African" and, at one point, challenged the eastern delegates:

[2] Wilbur J. Cash, *The Mind of the South* (New York, 1954), p. 95.

[3] Kenneth M. Stampp, *The Peculiar Institution* (New York, 1956), pp. 132–140. The story of the Turner insurrection has been told a number of times. See Thomas R. Gray, *The Confessions of Nat Turner* (Baltimore, 1831); William S. Drewry, *The Southampton Insurrection* (Washington, D.C., 1900).

[4] William Summer Jenkins, *Pro-Slavery Thought in the Old South* (Chapel Hill, 1935), pp. 81–89.

Sir, tax our lands, vilify our country—carry the sword of extermination through our now defenseless villages; but spare us, I implore you, spare us the curse of slavery—that bitterest drop from the chalice of the destroying angel.[5]

Still other delegates went to the length of proposing that a separate western "free" state be established if Virginia refused to act on slavery.[6] The moment was in many ways opportune for some form of emancipation. The effects of the long agricultural depression were still being felt. The price of slaves, furthermore, had been depressed to one of the lowest levels it was to reach before the war. Even in the eastern counties no one arose as an avowed advocate of slavery.[7] In the western counties, meanwhile, resentment was still running high against the east and the memory of the failure to win relief from the odious three-fifths rule two years before was still fresh in the minds of some of the delegates. In a series of votes taken on January 25, the House proved to be almost evenly divided between those who wanted action on slavery and those who did not. The "abolitionists" successfully opposed an initial measure of indefinite postponement by a margin of 71 to 60. The slavery group, however, succeeded in blocking by a vote of 73 to 58 an amendment calling for immediate action on abolition.[8] Virginia thus began 1832 with its ranks divided and many of its individuals deeply troubled over the issue of slavery.

The fiction of the thirties, as much by its reticence as by its declarations, reflects this general uncertainty and uneasiness about slavery. The surprising thing is not that the novelists discussed the question but rather, in view of the publicity which it had been receiving, that they did not concern themselves with it more than they did. There is very little in any of these novels to suggest that any fresh thinking had taken place since the debate on Missouri twelve years before. The pattern for the literary handling of the slave, as a matter of fact, had been partly unfolded as early as 1824 in George Tucker's *The Valley of Shenandoah,* where the stereotype of the childish and dependent slave makes its first important appearance. Tucker's slaves, at the two or three points where they are discussed, are lighthearted, happy in their work, joyous in their play, fond of music and loyal to their master's interest. Their dependence on their

[5] *Ibid.,* p. 83.

[6] Joseph C. Robert, "The Road from Monticello. A Study of the Virginia Slavery Debate of 1832," *Historical Papers of the Trinity College Historical Society,* Series XXIV (Durham, N.C., 1941), p. 28.

[7] Jenkins, *Pro-Slavery Thought,* p. 87 n. This fact was noted by Faulkner in a speech January 31, 1832.

[8] Robert, "The Road from Monticello," pp. 29–35.

master is further emphasized in a scene where young Edward Grayson is forced to tell a grief-stricken family servant, old "Uncle Bristow," that he may have to be sold. Nonetheless, there is the familiar conflict between the subservience of the slave and the horrors which he threatens. When a visiting New Yorker brings up the question of emancipation, Grayson tells him that although slavery is a moral and political "evil," all the remedies which have been proposed promise worse problems still. Until some practical means have been found for transporting former slaves out of the country, he remarks, it seemed dangerous to discuss the question, since there could be no thought of permitting them to remain where they had once been held in bondage. To do so would risk "renewing the scenes which had made Santo Domingo one general scene of waste and butchery."[9]

Throughout these early novels, no point is more emphasized than the dependence and helplessness of the slave—except perhaps his unquenchable happiness. From the very start he was portrayed as the victim of the gentleman's improvidence, even by those most anxious to argue the merits of plantation paternalism. Colonel Grayson's extravagance has forced the sale of his slaves. In *Westward Ho!* Colonel Dangerfield's gambling has necessitated the sale of his plantation, and Paulding includes a brief scene in which Dangerfield is surrounded by his sorrowing Negroes, who clamor to be taken along to "Old Kentuck." When the local minstrel begins to pluck his banjo, however, the sorrow is immediately replaced by joy. These "light-hearted slaves," Paulding comments, are "the very prototypes of children in their joys, their sorrows, their forgetfulness of the past, their indifference to the future. . . ." But to this assurance he appended the very doubt which such portrayals of the slave were meant to allay:

They seemed to be happy, and we hope they were; for it is little consolation to know, or to believe, that a mode of existence of which millions of beings partake is inevitably a state of wretchedness.[10]

Not far beneath the surface of most of these fleeting portrayals of Negro life lurks the uneasy sense that slavery is a wretched, insupportable, human condition. This becomes evident in the quite contrary tendency of these writers to play down the humanity of the Negro and place him in some special category of livestock. Two conflicting impulses seem to be simultaneously at work. The first is concerned with portraying the Negro

[9] George Tucker, *The Valley of Shenandoah* (New York, 1828), Vol. I, pp. 61–62.

[10] James Kirke Paulding, *Westward Ho! A Tale* (New York, 1832), Vol. I, pp. 57–58.

as a child-dependent, while the other, which has almost exactly the reverse effect, is directed at dehumanizing the Negro by dwelling on his physical characteristics and stressing his animality. The slave most discussed in *Westward Ho!*, for example, is known as "Pompey Ducklegs," and Kennedy, too, for all his Happy Jacks, is inclined to dwell on the peculiarities of Negroes. He points out that they have faces that are chiefly made up of "protuberant lips," "noses that seemed to have run all to nostril" and "feet of the configuration of a mattock." They are "essentially parasitical" and "extravagantly imitative" and they are characterized by "intellectual feebleness."[11]

There is an important confusion at the root of this conflict between the Negro as child and the Negro as animal which was fast setting a trap for plantation novelists. For the purposes of argument, certainly, it would have been much simpler to hold, as some of the theorists did, that the slave was immune to most normal human emotions and hence did not require or deserve—or, indeed, even want—the things which other human beings needed and aspired to. At the same time, because of the fears which the slave inspired, it became necessary to prove to oneself and demonstrate to others that the slave was not after all so different, that he was something other than a monstrous and unpredictable being who could rise up and lay waste a whole county. It was therefore necessary to allow the slave certain "safe" emotions about the condition of servitude. As soon as the justification for slavery became the paternalism of the planter, furthermore, it was important to portray slaves as susceptible to passive feelings, at least—responsive to kindness, loyal, affectionate and co-operative. It became necessary, in other words, to take them into the family and assign them human feelings, however childlike. Once this had occurred—once the camel got his nose properly into the tent—the whole purpose of this kind of portrayal was subject to inversion and it became possible to argue that the planter, not the slave, was the beneficiary of familial love and affection. To attribute to someone the simplicity of a child, furthermore, especially in the middle of the nineteenth century, was a compliment of the first order, and dangerous, too, if the child were to be mistreated and sympathy was not the response sought for.

The rapid growth of sentimental modes of expression, particularly those having to do with the home and family, created an immense temptation for those who chose to write about Negro life, whatever their intentions with respect to slavery. Often the sentimental pull proved stronger than ideological convictions, and writers like Kennedy, for example, were betrayed into expressing attitudes toward slavery which run counter to

11 John Pendleton Kennedy, *Swallow Barn,* ed. with introd. by Jay B. Hubbell (New York, 1929), pp. 18, 375, 377–378.

their pronounced views, or at least seriously qualify them. This is notably true of *Swallow Barn*, nine tenths of which is devoted to a whimsical and somewhat patronizing portrayal of country life in Virginia. Toward the end of the book, however, Kennedy included a long chapter which recounts the pathetic efforts of an old slave, Mammy Lucy, to prevent her master from selling her wayward son, and dwells on her stubborn belief in his essential goodness, a belief which is ultimately justified by the child's reform.

In allowing himself to write sentimentally about a Negro's attachment to her children (the chapter is entitled "A Negro Mother"), Kennedy was unknowingly preparing the way for writers like Mrs. Stowe who were bent on showing the inhumanity and injustice of slavery through exploring the Negro consciousness. "My purpose," he announced, "is to bring to the view of my reader an exhibition of the natural forms in which the passions are displayed in those lowest and humblest of the departments of human society, and to represent truly a class of people to whom justice has seldom been done," people who have previously been thought outside the "pale of human sympathy, from mistaken opinions of their quality, no less than from the unpretending lowliness of their position." Even the muted irony which Kennedy employs in this instance suggests the possibilities which later writers exploited. Mammy Lucy's reluctance to grant the necessity of selling her son provokes Kennedy to comment that "it is very hard to convince the mind of a mother, of the justice of the sentence that deprives her of her child."[12] The irony of this whole incident is further complicated by the fact that the son Abe is given Caucasian features and some of the enterprise and intelligence of a white man.

Beverley Tucker was one of the first Virginians to argue that slavery was a "positive good,"[13] and yet even he, curiously enough, was unable to restrain himself from occasionally wringing pathos from the sale of a slave. When the narrator of *George Balcombe* returns to his ancestral plantation in the Tidewater, he hears the sad plaint of "Old Charles" at the misfortune of being sold away from "old Massa." Although Tucker denied the Christian doctrine of the unity of the human race and argued that the slave was a separate species, he was forced in his fiction to treat the slave as a nominal member of the planter's family and to attribute to him human feelings and family loyalties which are scarcely distinguishable from anyone else's. While his object was clearly to locate the basis of the planter's paternalism in his long and intimate contact with the slave, the result was to make the slave virtually the affectional equal of the

12 *Ibid.*, pp. 392–393.
13 Nathaniel Beverley Tucker, "Note to Blackstone's Commentaries," *SLM*, Vol. I, p. 230.

white man. The Southern family, as Tucker describes it, binds its members, Negro and white, with so many ties of affection and loyalty and commits them so deeply that it is almost impossible to conceive of anyone ever wishing to elude its bonds. The members of such a family are not disciplined or restrained by any form of external coercion; only the natural bonds of love and respect for superiority are needed to keep the plantation household—and, by implication, Southern society—in order. The Negroes "are one integral part of the great black family, which, in all its branches, is united by similar ligaments to the great white family." The Southern gentleman begins his life at the breast of a Negro mammy, takes as his first playmates the children of plantation slaves and, in later life views the pickaninnies about the place with affectionate regard, asks their names and inquires after their parents. "These are the filaments which the heart puts out to lay hold on what it clings to. Great interests, like large branches, are too stiff to twine. These are the fibres from which the ties that bind man to man are spun. The finer the staple, the stronger the cord." When a visitor asks one of Tucker's planters if he fears that his slaves "taken as a body," might someday rise up against him, the planter calmly replies, "I have not the least apprehension that they would."[14]

Uncle Tom's Cabin; or Life Among the Lowly was clearly a kind of watershed in this early fiction about the plantation. It was both the summation and the destruction of a literary tradition which had begun some twenty years before. It probably did more than any book ever published to alter the American image of the South, and, once it had appeared, no one could hope to write about the plantation and ignore or slight the Negro. On the contrary, the slave rather than the planter tended to become the center of the legend, especially in the rash of fictional answers to *Uncle Tom* written by Southerners. In quick succession books appeared bearing such titles as *Aunt Phillis's Cabin; Uncle Robin in His Cabin in Virginia and Tom Without One in Boston; The Cabin and Parlor; or, Slaves and Masters,* all of which gave the slave fictional equity with the planter. Some of these books do not profit technically from this sudden shift of the Negro from bit parts to starring roles, but the shift in emphasis was evident and sufficiently widespread to affect the stage and music hall as well as the novel. Its implications, furthermore, were still being felt some twenty years later when Joel Chandler Harris, Thomas Nelson Page and Samuel Langhorne Clemens began to write about the South.

All the internal evidence supports Harriet Stowe's claim that she wrote *Uncle Tom* not to incite the North but to persuade the South that slavery

[14] Nathaniel Beverley Tucker, *The Partisan Leader; A Tale of the Future* (Washington, 1856), Vol. II, pp. 6–7.

was unjust.[15] In February, 1852, when the Southern attack on her was most severe, she wrote to a friend in North Carolina a brief resumé of her attitude toward the South:

> It has seemed to me that many who have attacked the system [of slavery] have not understood the Southern character, nor appreciated what is really good in it. I think *I* have; at least I have tried, during this whole investigation, to balance my mind by keeping before it the most agreeable patterns of Southern life and character.[16]

To accomplish this purpose she adopted in *Uncle Tom* and in *Dred* many of the conventions of the plantation novel as it had developed, and even her innovations seem to be mainly extrapolations from practices already scouted out by these novelists. Certainly, she made use of the plantation setting in its classical form. Decayed old houses, kind masters and mistresses, docile and affectionate household "servants" are placed center stage in both of these stories. While her image of Southern society was in some ways less complex and less detailed than that drawn by Southerners like Kennedy and the two Tuckers, the principal features are still there. For the most part, for example, she adopts the familial pattern for portraying the institution of slavery just as she accepts many of the Southern arguments concerning the intellectual and cultural limitations of the slave. Her exceptional slaves like Uncle Tom (whom she calls "a moral miracle") and some of her mulattoes are clearly meant to be regarded as exceptions. In no sense, moreover, is it possible to argue that either of her books is an indictment of the South to the exclusion of the North. Some of her sharpest invective is aimed at the temporizing and hypocrisy of churchmen and politicians in the North, and, as a reviewer in the *Southern Literary Messenger* noted with surprise, almost all of her villains and monsters are of Northern birth.[17] It would be difficult, in fact, anywhere in Southern writing to assemble a stable of degraded Yankee types to match hers. There is, of course, Simon Legree from Vermont, who represents the culmination of half a century of anti-Northern rhetoric, and there is his less sensational blood brother Abijah Skinflint in *Dred* ("For money he would do anything; for money he would have sold his wife, his children, even his own soul. . . ."),[18] but there are many others who strike off such legendary Yankee traits as acquisitiveness, hypocrisy, emotional frigidity,

[15] Forrest Wilson, *Crusader in Crinoline. The Life of Harriet Beecher Stowe* (Philadelphia, 1941), p. 276.

[16] *Ibid.*, p. 336. The letter, dated February 9, is addressed to Daniel Reeves Goodloe.

[17] *SLM*, Vol. XVIII (October, 1852), pp. 635–636.

[18] Harriet Beecher Stowe, *Dred: A Tale of the Great Dismal Swamp* (Boston 1856), Vol. I, p. 282.

prudishness and Philistinism. She leaves no doubt that she accepts, furthermore, some of the sentimental clichés about the plantation home. When that charming and doomed little child, Eva, is asked to compare family life with her cousins in Vermont with plantation life in the South, this exchange takes place:

"Oh, of course, our way is the pleasantest," said Eva.
"Why so?" said St. Clare, stroking her head.
"Why, it makes so many more round you to love, you know," said Eva, looking up earnestly.[19]

One other consideration about *Uncle Tom's Cabin* places it even more firmly in the center of the plantation tradition, in tenor as well as in form. Harriet Stowe's sharpest barbs are not, finally, aimed at either Northerners or Southerners as such, but at the ruthless masculine world of business enterprise. Plantation fiction from the beginning had celebrated the virtues of country life over city life, agriculture over commerce and business, impracticality over prudence and providence, and, perhaps most important of all, the primacy of home and family over all other values. Most of the villainous figures who penetrate this pastoral world, like the New York merchant's son James Gildon in *The Valley of Shenandoah,* issue from the world of business and finance, but none of these earlier villains was as profitably employed as the "businessmen" in *Uncle Tom's Cabin,* where commerce in slaves is represented as the ultimate in human exploitation. For in the slave trade, as in no other, all human values are converted into pecuniary values, and human beings are quite literally being turned into dollars and cents. Harriet Stowe's most impressive tactical feat was to connect the kindly, impractical master with the brutalities of the slave trade by showing that his boasted immunity from Yankee acquisitiveness—his carelessness concerning money and his high sense of honor—were often purchased at the expense of the slave's security and welfare, that the Legrees, in other words, battened on the failures and weaknesses of the St. Clares. The sentimental image of the Southern family is again and again projected against the heartless image of business life, never more effectively than in the scenes set at Legree's plantation on the Red River, where Legree as an anti-planter presides over what can only be thought of as an anti-home. Harriet Stowe employs for these scenes the traditional ruined plantation house and all of its appurtenances, but the house is a hollow shell, not a home. Instead of the harmonious family group there is Legree and his mulatto mistresses, and instead of love there is brutal sexual subjection. The building itself has become defiled. Litter is strewn about and the very altar of domesticity, the hearth, is used only to

19 Harriet Beecher Stowe, *Uncle Tom's Cabin* (Boston, 1887), p. 205.

heat water for Legree's toddies and provide embers to light his cigars. Even the bare plaster walls where the paper has fallen away are covered with the arithmetic scribblings of Legree's accounts. The plantation itself is an inversion of the plantation as sketched by the paternalists. The only discipline is fear and brutality; the slaves are made to beat one another, and nothing is done unless it "pays." What we are given in a few pages is an evocative vision of the home become factory, where everything, finally, is weighed in the balance scale at Legree's cotton house. Southerners, who almost universally objected to these scenes, never fully understood that Harriet Stowe had simply imported into the South the factory scenes which Southerners were fond of invoking as a contrast to the paternalism of the plantation.

In most of what she did, Harriet Stowe had only taken the Southerner at his word. Her method, if it can be called this, had not been to deny the Southern defense of slavery but to suggest that it was inadequate, even if its claims were allowed. In instance after instance she had underlined the fact that, so long as the slave was regarded as property, kindness, generosity and affection provided no assurance against cruelty and brutality. She also attempted to show that a slave could love his master and mistress and still wish to be free. Most subversively of all, she intimated in *Dred,* parts of which were based on the Nat Turner insurrection, that the slave under some circumstances could be goaded into open rebellion against his master. At every opportunity, furthermore, she blurred the color line both by projecting her readers into the feelings of slaves and by employing mulatto slaves without Negro characteristics. In particular, she directed her largest generalizations at the plight of the American family, and for this purpose she chose her examples indiscriminately from the family life of the Negro and the white. "If it were *your* Harry, mother, or your Willie, that were going to be torn from you by a brutal slave trader, tomorrow morning," she asked, what would you do?[20] In touching upon the separation of families, as she constantly did, she was making the strongest possible appeal to Southern women. Similarly, there seems little question that the human qualities attributed to Tom were, many of them, precisely those which had the greatest attraction for women. Tom is sensitive, tender, pious, trusting and totally passive in his response to brutality and oppression. Indeed, he is so completely without aggressive male traits that there may be some truth in Helen Papashvily's startling assertion that he was a kind of cryptofemale who represented the real image of the American woman as she saw herself.[21]

[20] *Ibid.,* p. 56.
[21] Helen Waite Papashvily, *All the Happy Endings* (New York, 1956), pp. 73–74.

In retrospect, it seems evident that Harriet Stowe employed the plantation setting because she herself believed in it as a meaningful evocation of
American family life and not out of any shrewd and vindictive intent, as
Southerners tended to think. What she feared for the plantation was
simply a heightened version of the anxiety she felt for modern family life
in general. As Charles Foster has shown, many of the incidents in *Uncle
Tom,* such as the death of Eva, were drawn from Harriet's own family
life[22] and reflect the spiritual crisis she was undergoing. The extraordinary
and unexampled appeal of the novel throughout the Western world,
furthermore, suggests its capacity to touch upon and illuminate wider
themes. Nonetheless, the novel, as it was interpreted, had quite a special
meaning for the South and it is hardly surprising that Southerners did
not contribute to the general enthusiasm. The novel's sympathetic portrayal of plantation life and its indictment of the North when coupled
with its obvious attack on slavery made for a more complicated response.
Confusion, consternation, blanket denials and personal attacks on Mrs.
Stowe followed its publication as a book—and in just that order. No
one, of course, can say with any assurance what Southerners felt as they
read this compelling fantasy, but there is evidence to suggest that many
were deeply troubled. Everywhere it was discussed, analyzed and criticized.
The *Southern Literary Messenger* reviewed it twice in the same three-
month period,[23] and Mrs. Chesnut's diary, written almost ten years later,
is studded with references both to *Uncle Tom* and to Mrs. Stowe, not
one of which is altogether favorable or altogether hostile. Fictional re-
buttals appeared in a matter of months, all of them by moderate and well-
meaning people, mostly self-declared Southern Whigs—one book is dedi-
cated to Henry Clay—who looked upon *Uncle Tom* as exaggerated and
inflammatory and sought to correct the unfair picture of slavery which they
felt Harriet Stowe had drawn. They, too, were caught within the sentimental logic of plantation paternalism, however, and the stories which
they wrote, with their harmonious patriarchal plantations and their gullible
Northern visitors, were often simply crude imitations of the book they
set out to answer, with slave-snatching Yankee abolitionists substituted for
Harriet's ruthless Yankee slave traders.[24] Since she had made it clear

[22] Charles H. Foster, *The Rungless Ladder; Harriet Beecher Stowe and New
England Puritanism* (Durham, N.C., 1954), pp. 13–63.
[23] *SLM,* Vol. XVIII (October, 1852), pp. 630–638; (December, 1852), pp.
721–731.
[24] John W. Page, *Uncle Robin in his Cabin in Virginia and Tom Without One
in Boston* (Richmond, 1853); Robert Criswell, *"Uncle Tom's Cabin" Contrasted
with Buckingham Hall, The Planter's Home; or A Fair View of Both Sides of
the Slavery Question* (New York, 1852); Mrs. Mary H. Eastman, *Aunt Phillis's
Cabin; or, Southern Life as It Is* (Philadelphia, 1852); Charles Jacobs Peterson

from the beginning that she was examining the moral logic of slavery rather than its sociology, there really was no answer to what she had written, as Southerners began to discover to their intense frustration. As Mrs. Chestnut seemed to say: she was right but *she had no right!*

Here and there bits of evidence turn up which suggest what the pattern of response to this discovery may have been. A young Williams graduate from New England who was living as a tutor on a plantation in Rockingham County, North Carolina, recorded this interesting sequence of events. On October 1, 1852, a Mr. Glenn arrived from New York bringing with him a copy of *Uncle Tom*. The tutor, whose name was Charles Holbrook, began reading it the same night and had finished it three days later. "I believe it to be the most interesting book I ever read," he wrote in his diary. Almost at once he began reading it to the Galloway children, who easily provided him with incidents of cruelty similar to those described in the book. On October 9 the planter, Mr. Galloway, who had finished the book, suddenly changed his mind about selling a slave named Henderson away from his wife and children. A few days later Galloway bitterly reported to Holbrook that he had met a slave trader transporting a "drove" of Negroes which had included some twenty children. The same day Holbrook noted: "Mr. G. likes *Uncle Tom's Cabin* but Mrs. G. is bitter against it." On October 15 the book was the talk of the household. "Mr. G. is honest—he says he admires 'Uncle Tom's Cabin' for its true characters." On the very next day, however, there was a surprising change. "Mr. Galloway says he will burn 'Uncle Tom's Cabin,' " Holbrook noted. "He has changed his mind on it. Mrs. G. thinks Mrs. Stowe is worse than Legree!" This entry of October 16 was the last mention of the book, which was apparently not further discussed.[25]

(pseud. J. Thornton Randolph), *The Cabin and Parlor; or, Slaves and Masters* (Philadelphia, c. 1852); Rev. Baynard Rush Hall, *Frank Freeman's Barber Shop: A Tale* (New York, 1852); Martha Haines Butt, *Anti-Fanaticism: A Tale of the South* (Philadelphia, 1853).

[25] D. D. Hall, "A Yankee Tutor in the Old South," *The New England Quarterly,* Vol. XXXIII (March, 1960), pp. 89–90.

A Conservative Prophet in the Romantic South

LOUIS HARTZ

While tending an amputation case in a Union Army hospital tent, Walt Whitman heard two soldiers discussing John C. Calhoun's monument in Charleston. One of the wounded veterans said: "I have seen Calhoun's monument. That you saw is not the real monument. But I have seen it. It is the desolated, ruined south. . . ." Calhoun was not only the practical defender of nullification and of slavery; he also aspired to be a political philosopher. He did not live to see published either his *A Disquisition on Government* or *A Discourse on the Constitution and Government of the United States,* but both works have the distinction of his effort to make a systematic critique of the theory of government derived from *The Federalist.* Modern scholars have sometimes seen in Calhoun a consistent prophet of the pluralistic interest-group politics of party government in America. Others have seen him as a theorist of reaction.

Louis Hartz finds a more complex and paradoxical Calhoun by examining the inner conflicts of Calhoun's thought. Hartz exposes the ambiguities of the political labels liberal vs. conservative or radical vs. reactionary when used as analytical terms for American political thought. He also relates Calhoun to the romantic conservatism which Southern apologists, like George Fitzhugh in *Sociology for the South* (1854), developed into a systematic defense of slavery as the cornerstone of society.

I

IN THE SUMMER OF 1832 A BITTERLY CONTESTED ELECTION WAS HELD in South Carolina. Voters were bribed and kidnapped, street violence was

Louis Hartz, "South Carolina vs. the United States," in Daniel Aaron, ed., *America in Crisis,* 1952, pp. 73–88. Reprinted by permission of Alfred A. Knopf, Inc.' Copyright 1952 by Alfred A. Knopf.

on the verge of breaking out, and both sides were secretly collecting arms in the event of civil war. The issue was whether the "sovereign" state of South Carolina should take it upon itself to nullify the tariff legislation of the federal government. Few South Carolinians supported the tariff, but the state had had a vigorous tradition of nationalism, and there were many who looked with horror on the "revolutionary" policy of nullification. The election went against them. Spurred on by the legal logic of Calhoun and the wild oratory of McDuffie, a strange but effective pair of influences, the Nullifiers swept the state and achieved an objective they had failed to achieve two years before: a legislative majority sufficiently large to call a constituent convention. After that there was no stopping the headlong rush toward nullification. Governor Hamilton called a special session of the legislature, the legislature immediately called a convention, and by November South Carolina's famous Ordinance of Nullification had been issued. The Tariff Acts of 1828 and 1832 were "null, void, and no law."

The Nullifiers, however, had rushed into a situation they did not quite foresee. If you had asked them before nullification what was going to happen afterward, you would not have received a very clear answer, except possibly from Calhoun. The reason was that they were relying on such overwhelming support from other Southern states and even from President Jackson himself that they did not believe that their action would seriously be challenged by the federal government. As it turned out, however, this was precisely the support they did not get. Every Southern state condemned the Ordinance of Nullification. Jackson denounced it as "treason." A force bill was introduced in Congress to put its provisions down. Wherever they turned the Nullifiers faced the bitter pill that passionate men again and again have to swallow in politics: the realization that even their friends are not as passionate as they. Instead of putting South Carolina at the head of a glorious movement against "consolidation," they had isolated it from the Union, and left it facing alone the imminent threat of civil war.

It has been said of a certain French politician of the nineteenth century that he followed the formula of Danton except for one variation: he believed in audacity, audacity, and then *no* more audacity. One might say the same thing, if it were not a bit too cruel, about the South Carolina Nullifiers. Of course, when they saw the drift of events, they began to drill a volunteer army, and to set up arsenals throughout the state, but in the process they silently searched their souls. Eleven days before the Ordinance of Nullification was supposed to go into effect, on the very day that the Force Bill was reported in the Senate, that search came to a spectacular end. A large meeting of Nullifiers gathered at the Circus in

Charleston and, saying that reform of the tariff was imminent, they virtually suspended the Nullification Ordinance. Nothing could hide the panic that went into this assembly. It was composed of private citizens, not of legislators or members of a constituent convention. The setting aside of the action of a sovereign state by such a body must surely be ranked as one of the hastiest forms of "nullification" that has ever been devised.

But the Nullifiers were right in one thing: action was being taken to reform the tariff. Jackson and Clay, while determined that the Force Bill should make no concession to nullification, were ready to compromise on the tariff itself. Clay introduced a measure, later replaced by one originating in the House, that modified the Act of 1832. Both this bill and the Force Bill were signed by Jackson on the same day, with the result that, as William Graham Sumner once put it, "the olive branch and the rod were bound up together." The Nullifiers hailed the reduction in the tariff as a victory they had won, and though the episode ended in a complete defeat for the legal principles they put forth, they had a chance of saving face. Jonathan Trumbull said: "We have driven the enemy from his moorings, and compelled him to slip his cables and put to sea."[1] The nullification crisis, on the surface at least, had ended in a draw.

II

This essay will concern itself with the theory of nullification, and after the events just described, the point I intend to make about it is bound to seem perverse. I intend to agree with Calhoun that the theory was a "conservative" theory. It is a tribute to Calhoun's gloomy genius as a political prophet that it is possible to stress his view again today. For it is, of course, in light of the Civil War that came after Calhoun died that the nullification idea takes on conservative significance. In the perspective of the Civil War the Harpers and McDuffies of 1832 cease to be "revolutionaries," cease to be "jacobins." They become men of peace, trying to solve by legal means the only problem in American history that has shattered completely the framework of our legal institutions.

In that perspective, too, our traditional approach to the theory of nullification has to be turned around a bit. What becomes even more important than the way the Nullifiers tried to limit the national government is the way they tried to limit themselves. It is easy to overlook this second matter. The Nullifiers could have chosen the path of secession, and indeed some of their opponents in South Carolina, like William Drayton and

---

[1] Quoted in Frederic Bancroft: *Calhoun and the South Carolina Nullification Movement* (Johns Hopkins Press; 1928), p. 167.

Langdon Cheves, would have gone along with them if they had. They could have appealed to a Jeffersonian right of revolution, as the violent McDuffie came close to doing on many occasions. But they did not want to secede and they did not want to revolt. The whole purpose of their philosophy was to construct a legal framework within which the battle between North and South could be contained, a peaceful "preservative," as Calhoun put it, of the American federal system. If their action symbolizes a trigger-happy impulse on the part of Americans to resist oppression, it symbolizes also something else that has been its curious counterpart: perhaps the most sensitive legal conscience in the world.

Here, indeed, was the root of their philosophic troubles. They would not have had to agonize themselves to justify secession or revolution. The premise of state "sovereignty" from which they began led directly to the most radical conclusions. What actually bothered them was how to bring a state conceived as supreme and uncontrollable into any sort of binding relationship with other states that, of course, were as supreme and uncontrollable as it was. It was this question that inspired the elaborate apologetics in which they engaged, the labyrinthine subtleties that few men outside of Calhoun and Chancellor Harper, even in South Carolina, were able to follow. If South Carolina was sovereign, why bother with the tariff at all? Why trouble yourself over the opinion of other states? The Nullifiers were astride the wild horse of Bodin and Hobbes, and it was not their radicalism that was illogical but their conservatism.

The North, however, was not quite in a position to make the most of this embarrassment. The Nullifiers argued that in 1787 South Carolina had entered into a "compact" with other "sovereign" American states for the purpose of creating a federal government that was the "joint agent" of them all. Now the real problem in this argument is that when you impose a binding compact on sovereign states you have bound them *too much:* technically they cannot be bound at all. But what troubled Daniel Webster was that South Carolina had not been bound *enough,* and so instead of pointing out that the conclusions of the Nullifiers did not match their premises, he assailed both as empirically false. This reduced the argument to a historical plane where, because the evidence was sufficiently vague, an endless stream of charge and countercharge became the order of the day. Webster denied that the Constitution was a "compact"; they asserted it. He asserted that a compact could create a vital American nation; they denied it. He insisted that the nation had acted in 1787; they insisted that the states had acted. The central logical flaw of nullification, its attempt to limit at all an illimitable sovereign, was removed from the spotlight of controversy.

Calhoun saved his logic, but in the process he virtually lost his constitutional "preservative." It has been said of Calhoun that he is the most rigorous thinker in American political thought; but his rigor, I suggest, was the rigor of John Stuart Mill: he tried to unite antitheses as logically as any man could. In a letter to Governor Hamilton, in which he insisted on the "total dissimilarity" between secession and nullification, he outlined the course a sovereign state should take after it had nullified an act of the "joint agent." Solemnly obeying legal process, it would wait for the issue to be submitted to the other sovereign states, but three quarters of them would be required for a decision against it, since that is the number needed for amending the Constitution. It is shocking to think what would happen to the federal government under such a procedure, but it is puzzling to see why a sovereign state should bother to embark upon it. What if three quarters of the states actually do go against it? Is it any less sovereign then? Calhoun is too honest to evade this question. And so he tells Governor Hamilton, quite by the way: "Nullification may, indeed, be succeeded by secession."[2] In other words, two things that are "totally dissimilar" on one page blend into another on the next as if nothing at all has happened.

The truth is, nothing has happened. The state was sovereign to begin with and it was sovereign to end with. What is curious is the elaborate ritual of legalism that has intervened in the middle. But there is no use laboring this point further. It would be possible to follow the struggle with "sovereignty" out at length in the nullification literature, and to show how it finally mastered its verbal limitations in the claim for independence that came with the Civil War. But the Civil War was not brought about because the sixteenth century had fashioned a concept that the American Southerners insisted on using in the nineteenth. If we want to get at some of the deeper causes of the breakdown of Calhoun's constitutional conservatism, it would be well to turn to the social alignments of the age, and to Calhoun's attempt to deal with them.

III

It is a commonplace of American history that the theory of states' rights has followed the course of economic interest. What makes the process bizarre is that at the same time the theory has been developed with infinite logical labor, so that one gets the odd impression that Hegel is proving himself on the American scene while Marx is doing so too. If the pure metaphysical passion is to be found in American political thought at

[2] Calhoun: *Works* (Cralle, ed.), Vol. VI (D. Appleton & Co.; 1883), p. 169. *Cf.* A. C. McLaughlin: *A Constitutional History of the United States* (D. Appleton-Century Co.; 1936), p. 444.

all, where would we place it if not in the men who have struggled so heroically with the categories of state and nation? And yet everyone knows that Jefferson tended to forget his metaphysics at the time of the Louisiana Purchase and that the New England Federalists tended to discover theirs at the time of the Embargo. The same principle holds true of the South Carolina Nullifiers. Before Calhoun became concerned over the tariff and slavery, he had denounced the notion of strict constitutional construction, and McDuffie, who joined the nullification movement late, had said things that were even worse. He had said that politicians who exalted the states were inferior men who did so because they could not win a place on the national scene.

The fact that the Nullifiers misunderstood their economic ills does not alter the fact that we are dealing here with a genuine problem in the politics of economic interest. Basically the troubles of South Carolina did not come from the tariff: they came from concentration on the production of cotton at a time when the settlement of new lands in the Southwest was forcing the price of that commodity down. But whatever might be said about cotton, or the slave economy on which it rested, South Carolina was pretty well destined to be an agricultural state, and above all it would be absurd to insist on a classical pattern of perfect rationality in the behavior of economic interests. If such a pattern were the normal thing, the record of American history would read a good deal differently from the way it does. It would read a good deal differently on the score of the tariff itself, and not because of the kind of enlightenment South Carolina needed. It is reasonable to suspect that more economic mistakes have been made in the process of supporting the American tariff than have been made in the process of opposing it.

Calhoun's defense of the South as an economic interest represents the same failure of conservatism that we find in his defense of the South as a collection of states. In terms of theory, to be sure, this is not entirely true. When in his political speeches and in the *Disquisition on Government* Calhoun substitutes "minorities" and "interests" for "states" and gives them the power of nullifying national policy, he releases himself from the wild theoretical horse he is trying to ride on the legal plane. Minorities and interests can hardly be called "sovereign," and Calhoun does not call them that. But all that Calhoun really accomplishes by this is to remove his problem from the realm of logic and put it in the realm of social fact. In social fact the Southern minority that Calhoun starts with has been torn away from the rest of the American nation as effectively as the concept of sovereignty would ever tear it away. It is a grim and isolated group, engaged in a war it cannot win, whose secession he actually predicted before he died. Under such circumstances preserving the Union by the simple technique of the "concurrent majority," if not legally illogical, is at any rate practically impossible.

Calhoun's method was to shatter the fabric of American community and then to attempt to restore it by a purely mechanical device. But this was to overlook a very important truth: mechanical devices are only as strong as the sense of community that underlies them. And yet his error was not unprecedented in American thought. The Founding Fathers had made it too. In the minds of many of them, Adams and Hamilton and Morris for example, the American scheme of checks and balances was designed to control a destructive war between proletarians on the one hand and aristocrats on the other. This war, which in the case of Adams was deduced largely from the irrelevant experience of ancient Greece and the Renaissance city-states, would surely have shattered the American Constitution as quickly as the struggles of France after the Restoration shattered the Charter of 1814. Happily such war has not been a general characteristic of American life, which has been permeated by a sense of social agreement that has been the wonder of foreign critics since the time of Tocqueville, and so the wrongness of the premises of the Founding Fathers has been obscured by what seems to be the "rightness" of their conclusions. But the case of Calhoun, alas, was somewhat different. The desperate struggle that he was describing was actually becoming a fact. He was making the mistake of the Founding Fathers at the only time in our history when it could readily be exposed. Of course, the "concurrent majority" was not adopted, and neither was his scheme of a dual executive, which embodied it. But if it had been, is it fair to assume that the North would have found it tolerable?

Notice, however, that Calhoun does not merely accept the scheme of Adams: the "concurrent majority" goes beyond it and supplements political checks with economic-interest checks. A threefold division of the functions of government on the national plane is not enough, because a single party can gain control of them simultaneously. Calhoun, in other words, is busily piling up checks in face of the very situation that is going to explode them all. This seems strange but, given the premises of the eighteenth century, is it? Once you concede that mechanical devices can serve as a substitute for the spirit of community which permits them to function, are you not automatically embarked on such a course? There is logic here, even if of a rather inverted kind: the more conflict you have, the more checks you need, and the more certain it is that no checks will work. Calhoun, like some tragic hero, was fated to bring the tradition of Adams to a climax in American thought at the moment it collapsed completely.

This is just another version of the paradox that Mr. Peter Drucker should recently rediscover Calhoun as the chief philosopher of our free and easy system of pressure politics—Calhoun who wrote on the eve of the Civil War. It is possible, I think, to carry Mr. Drucker's point too far. Weak as party discipline is in America, single interests do not have a veto on public policy, as real estate knows in connection with rent control and labor in connection with the Taft-Hartley Act. But the relevance of the "concurrent majority" principle to the pulling and hauling of interests on the American political scene is striking enough, and it reveals again the strange tragedy of Calhoun's nullification conservatism. The system of American logrolling is a system of "checks and balances" that bears a curious resemblance to the one our Founding Fathers had in mind, but instead of being imposed on the fabric of the American community, it has largely risen out of it. It has had many causes, one of which is the constitutional scheme itself, but no one can doubt that the social unity of American life has been among the most important. Societies frozen by deep and permanent conflict have never inspired the easy barter of individual interests.

But what Calhoun was doing, if he is to be considered a philosopher of our interest-group system, was offering it as a substitute for the social unity on which it rests. Of course, if we were to agree with what he often implies, that the struggles between the North and South were simply the result of using the device of the "numerical majority," there would be nothing fantastic about this procedure. Legislating the log-rolling technique into existence would be a perfectly reasonable act. But the sectional struggle obviously came from deeper sources, as he himself practically admits when he declares the South to be a permanent and hopeless minority. Minorities cannot be permanent unless there is some profound division of interest to make them so. And under such circumstances not even legislation can produce the spirit of pressure-group adjustment. For that spirit is ordinarily possible precisely because the nation is not split into warring social camps, because majorities and minorities are *fluid* and the groups that make them up know that they can easily exchange places on another issue or at another time. Calhoun said that the "concurrent majority" produced the spirit of compromise. What was actually the case, however, was that the spirit of compromise produced the "concurrent majority."

Nothing shows up the anguish of the man more clearly than this perpetual putting of the cart before the horse. Looked at from one angle, his mood is the authentic mood of irrational desperation: not merely because he clings to the form of compromise while its substance is disappearing, but because he has convinced himself that an exaggeration of its form will somehow compensate for a loss of its substance. Mr. Drucker's point, as I have said, ought not to be taken too literally: we have never had the "concurrent majority" in American politics. The spirit of compromise Calhoun calls for outdoes in amiability even the spirit that pervades a Congressional cloakroom in a time of high profits and high wages. As he himself puts it, each interest will "promote its own prosperity by conciliating the good will, and promoting the prosperity of others." There will be a "rivalry to promote the interests of each other." There will be "patriotism, nationality, harmony, and a struggle only for supremacy in promoting the common good of the whole." All of this when the country is on the brink of civil war, and simply by extending a notch the logic of John Adams! One is tempted to wonder whether the keenest pathos of the compromise spirit before the Civil War lies in the speeches of Henry Clay, or whether it lies right here, in Calhoun, dreaming up out of the South's own bitterness a mirage of social peace the like of which even a peaceful nation has never experienced.

At the time in which Calhoun was writing, however, neither South Carolina nor the South as a whole was quite in the position he made it out to be. There is one problem that Calhoun and other Nullifiers were careful to avoid: the problem of the minority within the minority—the problem, in other words, of the Unionists in South Carolina. It is not strange, given the treatment the Unionists received, that they should blast the Ordinance of Nullification with the very language the Nullifiers used to defend it, that they should call it "the mad edict of a despotic majority." How were the Calhounians to meet this charge? It would have been suicidal for the Nullifiers to give their opponents a veto, but let us suppose, out of passion for logic that they did. There was also a minority within the Unionist minority, and a minority within that. Were these minorities to be gven a veto too? The point I am making is the fairly obvious one that if the minority principle is carried to its logical conclusion it unravels itself out into Locke's state of nature where separate individuals execute the law of nature for themselves. Locke's acceptance of majority rule was by no means ill considered.

But this is merely a logical victory over Calhoun, and it is likely to lead us away from rather than closer to the central problem to be faced. In politics most principles break down when carried to their "logical conclusion," and if a man is brave enough to match his mind against reality, provided he does not use concepts like "sovereignty," which make it impossible, he ought to be given the privilege of silently drawing a few lines. The real significance of the Unionist minority lies in another place. It lies not in the fact that it was a minority but in the fact that it was *Unionist*. And the reason why this is important is that it reveals an important mechanism by which groups are held together in a political community: the mechanism of crisscrossing allegiances. Had the South Carolinians been one hundred per cent in favor of Nullification, or had the Unionist minority simply been indifferent to the question, they would hardly have given up so quickly their challenge to the federal government. But Jackson was in direct negotiation with the Unionist minority— he had promised them all the aid they needed—and this was a very sobering piece of knowledge for the Nullifiers to have. In other words, the fact that South Carolina was not a monolithic entity, as the Calhounian terms of "state" or "interest" or "minority" might imply, had a lot to do with uniting it to the rest of the nation.

If Calhoun's concern with a national "preservative" had transcended everything else, he would have welcomed this empirical defect in his premises. And as a matter of fact, there is a certain amount of evidence, on the wider plane of the struggle between North and South, to suggest that he actually did. With a number of other Southerners, as the Civil War approached, he suggested an alliance between Northern capitalists and Southern planters to keep both the slaves and the free working-class down. This alliance presumably would have helped to save the Union by exploiting common tensions within the sectional interests he usually described in monolithic terms. But Calhoun was in general no philosopher of intrasectional conflict, for the obvious reason that he was too embittered a Southerner. Instead of welcoming this imperfection in his premises, he glossed it over. Which, of course, made it harder than ever for him to reach his conservative conclusions.

History, as usual, was on the side of his premises. The drift toward civil war was a drift toward the consolidation of North and South into increasingly monolithic interests. Intersectional allegiances, one by one, began to disappear. America approached what is probably the most dangerous moment in the political life of any community: the moment of the almost perfect *rationalization* of its internal conflict. This made Calhoun's simplistic antithesis of majority and minority a real one, but what it did for the mechanical approach to politics is a matter of the obvious record. Once again, as in the case of his states'-rights legalism, Calhoun had laid a foundation that exploded the structure he tried to build upon it.

IV

I have discussed nullification as a legal issue and as an issue of social interest. There was also a moral question in the crisis of 1832, the question of slavery, which already, at the hands of Harper and Senator

Smith, had begun to produce that massive defense of a stratified society which flowered in the South before the Civil War. As this argument evolved, fed by the attack of Northern abolitionism, it did as much as anything else to produce the sectional intransigence that shattered Calhoun's nullification conservatism, but it challenged nullification in another way as well: philosophically. For the doctrine of nullification was, as I have shown, an exaggerated version of the mechanical rationalism of the eighteenth century, while the theory of slavery was a romantic revolt against it. Even if they had not had Burke, Disraeli, and Carlyle to read, the logic of their attack on Jefferson would have impelled the Southerners to discover that the Social Contract was a myth, that governments were divinely inspired, and that coercion was a law of life. But if this was so, how could the Constitution be a "compact," and why should minorities be so diligently defended? The philosophy of slavery struck hammer-blows at the finespun rationalism of nullification, and because Calhoun contributed to it he found himself caught in the most painful contradiction of his strange career, more painful even than the conflict between "sovereignty" and "preservative" or, on the plane of practice, between the war of the sections and the "concurrent majority."

Interestingly enough, it is this devotion of Calhoun to the theory of slavery that has given him his familiar reputation as a "conservative." In terms of what I have been saying, it is precisely this devotion that is "radical," that challenges his clinging to the Union. One is tempted now to give up Calhoun's own Nullification Act terminology. For while a case can be made for abolishing the term "conservative" from the study of American thought as a whole, it is precisely in connection with the theory of slavery that it has its most legitimate use. That theory, with its predominantly feudal image, comes as close to the authentic mood of the Western reaction as anything America has ever turned up. But though it does not pay to quibble over terms, provided the substance of an issue is clear, a word can still be said for Calhoun's claim that the rationalist theory of nullification was "conservative," and not merely in the obvious political sense that it sought to preserve the Union, but in the philosophic sense as well. For the "reaction" that the defense of slavery inspired in Southern thought was strangely enough an Enlightenment, since the philosophy of Jefferson was the vested theoretical interest that men like Bledsoe and Harper were forced to assail. This miraculous inversion of the European pattern, which gave to the Southern disciples of Burke the spirit of iconoclastic discovery we might expect to find in Diderot, confounds the issue of terminology so badly that we can even call rationalism reactionary. We can say, at any rate, that it was an older thing than the "feudal conservatism" it confronted.

Mixing nullification with "feudal conservatism" was like mixing water with oil. Things could not have been worse. What is inevitably the *bete noire* of any reactionary attack is precisely what the Nullifiers had to advance: the idea of the manmade constitution. Fitzhugh branded it as "absurd." Calhoun, courageous to the end, drew a distinction between "constitution" and "government," as if by keeping Sieyes and Maistre in watertight compartments he might be able to enjoy them both. Governments were natural and divinely inspired, but constitutions, which controlled them, were not. It was a tenuous enough distinction. Can it reasonably be argued that what governs government is any less governmental than government itself?

The clash between the Enlightenment and the reaction became even more vivid when the question of "rights" came up. There is a happily unconscious paradox in a lot of Southern oratory: slavery is excellent, but Southerners will die rather than be "slaves" of the North. Of course, as long as the defense of slavery grounds itself in racial theory concerning the Negro, this is a paradox easily resolved. But Southern thought, as in the case of men like Hughes, Holmes, and Fitzhugh, refused to stop at the color line, insisting that slavery or something like it was the ideal system of life for whites as well as blacks. Even here, to be sure, the "slavery" of the South is not automatically justified, since slaves ought to be inferior men and Southern gentlemen are certainly not in that class. But once again the bottom falls out of the Southern position. The definition of justifiable slavery is the mysterious status quo ordained by a mysterious Providence, and only wild Jeffersonian "metaphysicians" would dare to overturn it. If this is true, the enslavement of the South by the tariff would seem to be just as valid as the enslavement of the slave by the lash. The Hegelian type of conservatism, which young Thomas Dew brought back to Virginia from Germany, has burnt many fingers in the history of social thought.

One of the reasons the Southerners would not stop their defense of slavery at the racial line was that they wanted to belabor the "wage-slavery" of the North and to insist that their own system of labor, suitably defined by Henry Hughes and others as a kind of feudal "warranteeism," was actually superior to it. There was a movement of thought, partially inspired by the Young England philosophy of Disraeli, in which iron laws of capitalist oppression and proletarian revolt were contrasted with sentimental laws of paternal care and social peace. Calhoun himself contributed something to this movement, which gave him a curious resemblance to the European "feudal socialists" whom Marx so bitterly derided. But the main point for us to grasp is the striking way in which this philosophy clashed with the rational mechanics of nullification. If the corporate ideal of the plantation is to be maintained, how can one also maintain a theory of minority rights which logically unravels itself out into Locke's state of nature? An anonymous critic of the "concurrent majority" in *DeBow's Review* assailed Calhoun for deserting the great slave truth that the best type of rule was the "natural" rule of the "despot."[3] He was, alas, on solid ground.

These contradictions were bad enough, but what was even worse, from the angle of Calhoun's nullification conservatism, was that the romantic theory of slavery itself threatened to resolve them. Men who have read Burke and Scott do not need to rely on constitutional apologetics in order to defend their sectional life. They are led automatically to another type of claim: the blood-and-soil claim of any ancient culture. This claim solved Calhoun's problem at a single stroke. It absorbed into the organicism of his defense of slavery the very sectional plea that had impelled him to repudiate it. It made Burke do the job of Adams as well. And as time passed, and the cult of "Southernism" defined itself in contrast to the commercialism of Yankeedom, it grew enormously in the Southern mind. Mr. Rollin Osterweiss has documented it brilliantly in a recent study.[4] But the question is, what did it do to Calhoun's "preservative" of the nation? Didn't it pack even more explosive power than the concept of "sovereignty" itself?

It is strange that this idea should begin to evolve in the South and not the North, for it was of course the basic idea of modern nationalism— in its liberal form, the passionate thesis of Rousseau and Mazzini. Webster could surely have used it. A charge of Burkian or Rousseauian romanticism would have lifted his concept of the American "people" to a high ground where the constitutional exegesis of the Nullifiers could not have undermined it. But Webster, the great philosopher of American "nationalism," remains as dry and legalistic as Marshall. The ironic fact was that the liberal romanticism of the North did not lead to the nationalism of Rousseau as the conservative romanticism of the South led to the nationalism of Burke or Scott. With the exception of a few men like Barlow and perhaps Emerson, it led in other directions: radical individualism, as in Thoreau, or radical cosmopolitanism, as in Garrison. The South, the home of "particularism," became in a curious sense the originator of romantic nationalism in American political theory.

It is not hard to see that the idea of blood-and-soil nationalism was more explosive than either the idea of "sovereignty" or the idea of "minority." Sovereignty was an uncontrollable concept, but it was at any rate a concept, a rational abstraction, something you could argue about.

[3] Vol. 23 (1857), p. 170.
[4] *Romanticism and Nationalism in the Old South* (Yale University Press; 1949).

So was "minority." But there was really no arguing with the spirit of Southern culture, for by definition its ethos was irrational and its claim divine. As the romantic philosophy of slavery swept forward it not only corroded the mechanical premises of nullification but it advanced in their place a sectional plea colored with the most frightening overtones. Fitzhugh, with his "organic nationality," with his bitter attack on the "Calhoun school," was the great philosopher of this movement. He is the man, I suggest, who ought to have the reputation for theoretical consistency which Calhoun has attained. Flamboyant, reckless, a Maistre without reading Maistre, he nevertheless sought in almost everything he wrote to unify the Southern mind around the authentic principles of the Western reaction. He had Maistre's love of violence, which came to him from his attack on the humanitarians, and he did not hesitate to fuse it with "organic nationality." When war came, he hailed it as a veritable boon to the Southern soul.

This was the end of Calhoun's constitutional conservatism, this swallowing up of the Southern argument into the romantic logic of reactionary thought. Of course, the South was never as logical as Fitzhugh wanted it to be. It continued to divide its time between the world of Burke and the world of Jefferson, as indeed it still does. Even in 1861, after all of Fitzhugh's lessons, it appealed to a Jeffersonian right of revolution. But there is no doubt that the rise of the naturalistic authoritarianism that Fitzhugh represented did as much as anything else in the South to discredit the reasoning of Calhoun. And the irony of it, as usual, was that Calhoun himself had helped its rise along.

A Bibliographical Note
on American Intellectual History

Although there is a steadily expanding literature on specific areas of American intellectual history, there is no major synthesis that has imposed itself by the power of its persuasion, insight, and research. For studies of American historians who have played an important part in the development of intellectual history in America see Robert A. Skotheim and Kermit Vanderbilt, "Vernon Louis Parrington: The Mind and Art of a Historian of Ideas," *Pacific Northwest Quarterly,* 53 (July, 1962), 100–13; Robert A. Skotheim, "The Writing of American Histories of Ideas: Two Traditions in the XXth Century," *Journal of the History of Ideas,* 25 (April-June, 1964), 257–78; "Perry Miller and the American Mind," a memorial issue of *The Harvard Review,* 2 (Winter-Spring, 1964); Cushing Strout, *The Pragmatic Revolt in American History: Carl L. Becker and Charles A. Beard* (New Haven, Yale University Press, 1953); Burleigh Taylor Wilkins, *Carl Becker* (Cambridge, Mass., Harvard University Press, 1961). For historical studies of American intellectual history as a discipline, see John Higham, "American Intellectual History: A Critical Appraisal," *American Quarterly,* 13 (Supplement, Summer, 1961). 219–33; "The Rise of American Intellectual History," *American Historical Review,* 56 (April, 1951), 453–71. For a recent anthology of articles surveying the whole span of American intellectual history and aimed at the general reader as well as the student, see Arthur M. Schlesinger, Jr. and Morton White, eds., *Paths of American Thought* (Boston, Houghton Mifflin, 1963).

Index

0477